The Shakespearean Inside

The Shakespearean Inside

A Study of the Complete Soliloquies and Solo Asides

Marcus Nordlund

EDINBURGH
University Press

Edinburgh University Press is one of the leading university presses in the UK. We publish academic books and journals in our selected subject areas across the humanities and social sciences, combining cutting-edge scholarship with high editorial and production values to produce academic works of lasting importance. For more information visit our website: edinburghuniversitypress.com

Edinburgh University Press Ltd
The Tun – Holyrood Road
12(2f) Jackson's Entry
Edinburgh EH8 8PJ

Typeset in Sabon and Futura by
Servis Filmsetting Ltd, Stockport, Cheshire,
and printed and bound in Great Britain by
CPI Group (UK) Ltd, Croydon CR0 4YY

A CIP record for this book is available from the British Library

ISBN 978 1 4744 1897 3 (hardback)
ISBN 978 1 4744 1898 0 (webready PDF)
ISBN 978 1 4744 1899 7 (epub)

Contents

List of Tables and Figures

Acknowledgements

Though this is a study of soliloquies and solo asides, it must be said that dialogue is so much more rewarding. I have benefited from literature tips and advice on aspects large and small from, among others, Anna Hellén, the late Gunilla Florby, Jim Hirsh, Ben Crystal, Brett Hirsch, Will Sutton, Farah Karim-Cooper, Ewan Fernie, John Jowett, Mats Malm, Anders Cullhed, Carin Franzén, Per Sivefors, and Roland Heiel. Needless to say, I lay full claim to any errors and oversights in this book.

I am grateful to the anonymous readers at Edinburgh University Press for their helpful suggestions, many of which were taken on board to the betterment of my book. Warm thanks to commissioning editor Michelle Houston at EUP for believing in my project and to Adela Rauchova, Rebecca Mackenzie, James Dale and Ian Davidson for seeing it through. Special thanks to Fiona Sewell for brilliant copy-editing that saved me from a number of embarrassing errors.

I would also like to thank my students in the EN1C01 and EZ1C16 Shakespeare courses for useful feedback on the *Richard II* section. I want to thank my current and former doctoral students – especially Emelie, Evelyn, Gaby, and Houman – for being such excellent human beings, and for keeping me abreast of all things pop-cultural. Thanks are also due to the English work-in-progress seminar at the Department of Languages and Literatures for intermittently constructive and helpful feedback.

I want to acknowledge the generous support of the Swedish Research Council (2010–2012, dnr. 421–2009–1481) and the Department of Languages and Literatures at the University of Gothenburg. This book would not have been possible without their financial support.

A section of the Introduction and Appendix 1 has been published previously as 'Shakespeare's Insides: A Systematic Study of a Dramatic Device', in *The Shakespearean International Yearbook* 14, guest edited by Brett D. Hirsch and Hugh Craig (Farnham: Ashgate, 2014, 37–56). Published with the permission of Taylor & Francis Group. A section on *Richard II* from Chapter 2 has been published previously as 'The King's Speech: Rhetorical Boundary Issues in *Richard II*', in *Mellan makt och vanmakt: Romateaterns Shakespearesymposium 2015*, edited by Julia Hackman (Gothenburg: Makadam förlag, 2016, 67–74). Published with the permission of Makadam förlag. The readings of *The Two Noble Kinsmen* in Chapters 3 and 4 have been culled from the book chapter 'Divisive Desires in *The Two Noble Kinsmen*', in *Pangs of Love and Longing: Configurations of Desire in Premodern Literature*, edited by Anders Cullhed, Carin Franzén, Anders Hallengren, and Mats Malm (Newcastle upon Tyne: Cambridge Scholars Publishing, 2013, 130–43). Published with the permission of Cambridge Scholars Publishing.

This book is dedicated to my father, Hans Nordlund, who introduced me at an early age to many lifelong joys, from drawing and painting to football and classical music: 'I had it from my father' (*Henry VIII*, 1.4.27).

Introduction

What if we could produce new data of real literary interest about Shakespeare's complete plays? What if such data could uncover overriding patterns, and interesting exceptions from these patterns, that are not easily perceived by a single reader, or even by their author when he was still among the living? And what if we could combine these findings with traditional forms of scholarship that attend to finer nuances and place the works in a larger context? This could throw new light on Shakespeare's authorial habits and help us perceive the special nature of individual plays, characters, and scenes.

This book is the outcome of a project which applies a combination of computer-assisted quantitative analysis and traditional literary scholarship to all soliloquies and solo asides (excluding choruses and epilogues) in Shakespeare's complete plays. These two types of speech are brought together under the rubric 'inside' because their most important characteristic is shared: the speech forms part of the action but is not intended to be heard by any other character on the stage.[1] Among other things, this communication of inside information to the audience makes these speeches central to the construction of fictional minds and individual point of view.

Over the years, many excellent books and articles have been devoted to Shakespeare's soliloquies and his construction of literary interiority, privacy, or selfhood.[2] The chief novelty of *The Shakespearean Inside* lies in the employment of computer-assisted analysis as a complement to traditional interpretive practices. This fusion of traditional literary scholarship and 'meso-level analysis'[3] – the systematic scrutiny of a limited collection of texts – stems from the recognition that literary particulars can only be understood as such in relation to a larger totality. It is only when we can generalise defensibly about broader tendencies in Shakespeare's dramatic practice that we can convincingly establish the unusual or even singular nature of individual plays, scenes, characters, or speeches.

The ideal, therefore, has been a marriage between modern information technology and traditional literary scholarship where the computational component is understood as a technological prosthetic that extends the processing power of the scholarly brain. This was accomplished by (1) defining a set of textual attributes that can be subjected to quantitative analysis; (2) manually coding all soliloquies and asides in the complete plays with the help of said attributes; (3) subjecting these individual codes to quantitative analysis; and finally (4) using the patterns derived from this quantitative investigation as reference points for the interpretation of complex particulars (with access to traditional tools of literary analysis, such as close reading and psychological or historical modes of interpretation).

The database covers many different kinds of data, including the distribution of soliloquies and asides according to *locus* (the location of the speech: play, act, and subgenre); *genus* (the speaker's gender and class); and finally *modus* (the nature of the speech). Among other things, the last category covers more complex speech acts (such as characters reporting past events, planning future ones, describing other characters, or engaging in thematic reflection) and selected rhetorical figures. The computer software employed, NVivo, can turn these variables into rich descriptive data by means of search strings of varying complexity. The resulting *Shakespearean Inside Database* ('SID' for short) will be made freely available online to anyone with access to the software in question. A description of the theoretical and methodological framework, including a coding sheet, definitions of all codes, and various principles of selection, can be found in Appendices 1 to 3.

In its double pursuit of Shakespeare's habitual practices and unusual choices, my study bridges the gap between what Manfred Pfister calls the internal and the external levels of dramatic communication.[4] As soon as actors speak, two things happen. On the *internal* level of the dramatic fiction, the characters speak on their own behalf – analysing their social position in the fictional play-world, expressing their point of view, or trying to solve their own problems. As James Hirsh has demonstrated convincingly, this point of view probably never took the form of interior monologue in Shakespeare's plays, and the most frequent mode of delivery for soliloquies was probably self-address rather than direct address to the audience.[5] Hence a Shakespearean soliloquy need not be more truthful or dependable than ordinary dialogue or self-talk; the character may be self-deluded, testing out ideas, cheering himself up, or perhaps even manipulating himself, as Iago appears to do at times in *Othello*.

Even if soliloquies or solo asides need not be more truthful than dialogue, they still transmit privileged inside information to the audience. When a Shakespearean character speaks in solitude, the audience listens with special attention because the words have not been accommodated to the interests or expectations of other characters. In this restricted sense, we are being let in on a secret or made privy to inside information on the *external* level, on the audience's behalf. It follows that a study of Shakespeare's insides feeds directly into the ongoing debate about Shakespearean stage conventions and techniques, especially concerning the actor's mode of delivery on the original stage and the relationship between the stage fiction and the audience's reality.[6] These questions will be tackled primarily in Chapter 1, but my book will return again and again to the interplay between the internal and the external levels of dramatic communication.

There is yet another sense in which this is a study of the Shakespearean inside. If a combination of qualitative and quantitative analysis can uncover patterns that a human interpreter could not easily detect by just reading or watching the plays, then there is some chance that even Shakespeare himself might not have been aware of them. In this tentative and limited sense, the present study aims to get *inside Shakespeare*, to get under his skin, to trace meaningful patterns in his works that are so complex that he himself might not have been aware of them. Such an approach is not offered as a solution to the vexing problem of authorial intention but seeks to circumvent it by focusing on the author's habitual practices.

Why 'Insides'?

In recent decades – especially in the 1990s, when the subject became particularly *en vogue* – there have been many studies of literary interiority, privacy, or selfhood in Shakespeare and his contemporaries. None of these have been fully systematic or computational in nature, and surprisingly few have tried to define more closely what a soliloquy or aside really is.[7] For example, when Richard Hillman set out to study something he called 'self-speaking' in medieval and early modern literature – that is, different dramatic techniques for producing fictional interiority – he focused not just on soliloquies but also on 'various kinds of monologues, asides, and even silences'.[8] In other words, the criterion for something to count as 'self-speaking' was that a character was either speaking or not speaking and that this had something to do with someone's self. Such an inclusive approach brings considerable interpretive freedom, and Hillman went on to say some interesting things about the plays under consideration, especially in relation to the religious problem of self-knowledge. But such freedom is dearly bought since it naturally limits the kind of generalised observations and explanations that might be strung into a systematic argument about an identifiable object of study. For a project like the present, where it is vital to define the object of study with maximum precision, such explorations in the spirit of the late Wittgenstein will be of little use.

Terms like 'soliloquy' and 'aside' may be highly familiar to literary scholars, but this hardly makes them unproblematic. As Alan Dessen notes, we know very little about Elizabethan and Jacobean stage practices, and '[a]ny attempt to deal with the original staging or stage conventions must ... build almost exclusively upon the evidence within the texts themselves'.[9] Since early modern playbooks and manuscripts were not particularly forthcoming with explanatory stage directions, we cannot even say if Shakespeare really thought of himself as writing 'soliloquies' – there is, as Nevill Coghill points out, 'no indication that Shakespeare knew the word'.[10]

Along similar lines, Alan Dessen notes that

> [r]eaders today know (or think they know) what an *aside* is, just as they know (or think they know) what a morality play is ... But the actual use of the term by Elizabethan playwrights and playhouse annotators sometimes does not conform to such expectations, a disparity that can generate interpretive problems, especially with Shakespeare.[11]

This historiographic problem is compounded by modern-day terminological confusion about even the most natural-sounding words in the dramatic vocabulary. Take 'monologue', for example: is it the opposite of dialogue, speech which is not addressed to another character, or is it an extended, uninterrupted speech by a single character, which may well be dialogical in nature?

In this area, as in so many others, we must try to reap the benefits of historical hindsight and conceptual clarity while respecting the integrity of the research object; we must seek to read *with* Shakespeare but not necessarily *like* Shakespeare. To use Plato's famous analogy with the butcher, we must try and 'carve his plays at the joints' without recourse to early modern anatomy charts. Luckily, James Hirsh has already done an important service to the Shakespeare community in this precise area. In *Shakespeare and the History of Soliloquies* (2003) he puts forward the following definition:

> In this study the term *soliloquy* refers to any dramatic passage with the following characteristics: (1) it is spoken by a single actor and (2) the character

portrayed by that actor does not intend the words to be heard by any other character.[12]

Hirsh calls this 'soliloquy', Alan Richardson calls lengthy versions of the same thing 'monologue',[13] and for the purposes of this study I will call it an 'inside' (with some additional restrictions and a suggested stress on the second syllable). This neologism is not primarily motivated by a sense that the academic world needs more controversy based on terminological separatism. My adoption of the term 'inside' stems partly from the need for a convenient shorthand and umbrella term, and partly from a desire to preserve the traditional distinction between soliloquies and solo asides, as will be explained further below. It is also an outcome of my decision to exclude formal choruses and choral epilogues – both of which are included in Hirsh's concept of 'soliloquy' – from my corpus, on the grounds that they constitute very different types of speech and would have been perceived as such on the early modern stage.

The Shakespearean chorus, first of all, is not so much a representation of individual point of view as a narrative function. Even in those plays where Choruses are given proper names, the little individuality they have is subsumed by the task of guiding the audience through the play, commenting on and explaining the action, filling in offstage events, and so forth. Most importantly, the Chorus always stands outside the fictional world it describes; as Hirsh points out, 'no Shakespeare Chorus ever interacts with the characters who are engaged in the fictional action'.[14] An inside, by contrast, is always the representation of an individual subjectivity or point of view on the internal level of the dramatic fiction. This is the case even when the character performs speech acts that closely resemble those of the formal chorus, such as the reporting of offstage events.

Hirsh also notes that Shakespeare's plays contain six choral epilogues addressed directly to the audience by characters who were previously engaged in the action, five of which count as soliloquies.[15] Although the actors delivering these speeches remain in character (Prospero is still Prospero, and Pandarus is still Pandarus), the characters they play have clearly been transported from their fictional world and thrust into an actual world where they stand before the audience and hope that their little entertainment has not offended.

Given the sharp line that separates Shakespeare's choruses and epilogues from the internal level of the dramatic fiction, it might seem feasible to follow Hirsh and classify all remaining speeches that are not intended to be heard by another character as 'soliloquies'. I have not done so, however, because this would jar too much with the common scholarly idiom and make an established term unnecessarily imprecise.

According to Hirsh's inclusive definition, there are more than thirty soliloquies in *Hamlet*, of which Hamlet the character speaks twelve, and no distinction is made between the long, anguish-ridden 'O what a rogue' and Hamlet's super-brief aside 'So be it' (1.5.116). It seems wrong to call the latter snippet a 'soliloquy' when most Shakespeare scholars and ordinary mortals think of soliloquies as longish speeches uttered in solitude. In fact, the shortest speech of this kind in Shakespeare's plays is not even a complete word:

> FABIAN Very brief, and to exceeding good sense
> [aside] -less.
>
> (*Twelfth Night*, 3.4.158)

To call this single syllable a 'soliloquy' is, admittedly, a bit of a mouthful. Replacing Hirsh's superordinate term 'soliloquy' with the term 'inside' is my attempt to reconcile the digital coder's need for conceptual stringency with the scholar's desire for effective dialogue. It is not a perfect accommodation of the critical terminology to the common scholarly idiom, but it does allow us to retain both *soliloquy* and *solo aside* as subordinate terms that are consistent with standard usage.

A *soliloquy* is spoken (*locutus*, from *loquor*) when the speaker thinks he or she is alone (*solus*), and therefore it tends to be longish except during exits, entrances, or other scenic shifts. (The speaker's belief that he or she is alone must be the central criterion here, rather than actual solitude, since some soliloquies are overheard by other characters.)[16] A *solo aside* is, to combine Bernard Beckerman's classic term with Hirsh's precise parlance, spoken in the presence of other characters but *guarded from their hearing*, and therefore tends to be fairly short.[17] This terminology preserves the conventional distinction between a long speech delivered in solitude and a rapid quip uttered under one's breath.

As I have defined it here, an 'inside' can thus be spoken either as a 'soliloquy' or as a 'solo aside'. Of course, the conceptual neatness of this regime will not always translate into methodological plain sailing, based as it is on the putative intentions of fictional characters. There will always be instances of ambiguous speech, of lines that can be spoken either as dialogue or as asides, of speech mumbled when other characters are half offstage, and so forth. Such ambiguities must not be swept under the carpet in a project of this kind: on the contrary, they will often constitute worthwhile objects of study in themselves, as we will see extensively in Chapter 2. Nor should we overstate their significance, since those ambiguous speeches that can be spoken either as dialogue or as asides tend to be short and thus have little impact on overriding quantitative patterns.

Chapter Outline

This book resembles many other scholarly works on Shakespeare in that it combines close attention to his text with an eclectic range of interdisciplinary perspectives (from sociohistorical and philosophical explanation to recent developments in cognitive science). It seeks to uncover general principles in Shakespeare's dramatic practice; it grapples with the meaning of individual plays, and passages; it explores character motivation; and it connects textual patterns to overriding themes.

The chief difference is that my book combines these approaches with a new type of descriptive statistics whose variables have been tailor-made for literary analysis. The idea is that computer-assisted analysis can help uncover overriding patterns, and exceptions from these patterns, that are hard to detect by just reading the plays.[18] As I suggested above, some of these patterns may have escaped not just modern interpreters but even Shakespeare himself. It is of course very hard to determine what Shakespeare did or did not do consciously, but we can determine the nature of his literary *habits* with a much higher degree of objectivity. Such a focus on Shakespeare's habits can circumvent the hairy problem of authorial intention while retaining the author's usual practices as adjudicating principles in matters of interpretation. Once we have established what his habitual practice looked like we can also identify significant departures from it.

The argument is structured cumulatively so that the quantitative component becomes increasingly pronounced from Chapter 1 to Chapter 4. The first two chapters (especially the first) make slender use of statistical patterns, devoting more attention to questions about Shakespeare's stagecraft. Under what conditions do his soliloquists employ self-addressed speech, and when do they address the audience? At what points does the dividing line between inside and ordinary dialogue become blurred, and what are the consequences? The last two chapters, in contrast, exhibit a fairly intensive interplay between traditional interpretative practices and the analysis of larger quantitative patterns. Readers who are mainly interested in the new digital methodology will therefore be most interested in the final two chapters, together with the appendices where the theoretical and methodological principles are spelled out.

All four chapters, however, combine the discussion of general aspects of Shakespeare's stagecraft with the analysis of specific literary examples. They all end with an extended literary analysis of one or more individual plays: *The Two Gentlemen of Verona* (Chapter 1), *The Tempest* and *Richard II* (Chapter 2), *Hamlet* (Chapter 3), and *The Taming of the Shrew*, *The Two Noble Kinsmen*, and *All's Well that Ends Well* (Chapter 4).

Chapter 1 is entitled 'Direction', with a pun on the theatrical and the spatial senses of the word 'direction'. What dramatic conventions appear to have governed the physical direction in which Shakespeare's actors delivered their insides on the stage? Did Shakespeare assume that his actors would mix different styles, or did he keep them separate? The main purpose of the chapter is to mediate between, on the one hand, James Hirsh's extended argument that Shakespeare's soliloquies and asides were almost exclusively self-addressed, and, on the other, the modern tendency of scholars, actors, and directors to return Shakespeare to his medieval, audience-addressed roots. I accept Hirsh's general claim for the dominance of self-address but also suggest a number of principled variations in the dramatist's practice involving audience address. The key factor behind direct address to the audience, I argue, may be the degree of *detachment* exhibited by the character on the internal level of the dramatic fiction. This detachment can be either *structural* (affected by the placing of the speech within the larger scene); *mental* (resulting from the character's psychological detachment from his or her play-world); or *conventional* (since some Shakespearean characters can transcend the confines of their own play-world).

The chapter then turns to an extended reading of Launce's soliloquies in *The Two Gentlemen of Verona* which explores how their satirical counterpoint to the main plot interrogates the underlying conditions of Shakespeare's dramatic art. I show that his comic employment of audience address in these soliloquies consistently targets the intrinsic absurdity of an art form – and, more specifically, a particular type of speech – where people who are not who they are (actors, characters) communicate directly with others who are not really there (the audience) or who cannot understand what is being said (such as dogs). While Hirsh argues that Shakespeare thought of audience address as a ridiculous medieval relic, I argue that Shakespeare's use of audience address in *Verona* is not deflationary or distancing but allows him to interrogate the deeper conditions of his theatrical medium in a benign and inclusive manner. In Launce's second soliloquy especially, audience address is used to extract rich metaleptic effects from the absurd idea that a fictional clown in Verona might talk directly to a crowd of actual people in London. We are invited to laugh *with* Launce – not *at* him, as Robert Weimann contends – and at our own complicity in this game of adult make-believe.

Chapter 2, entitled 'Divergence', explores a number of situations in Shakespeare's plays where the sharp boundary between inside and dialogue becomes muddled. The chapter begins with a survey of different situations where this line is difficult to draw, often because it is hard to gauge the speaker's fictional intentions on the basis of the printed page. In some cases this uncertainty may have direct consequences for how the audience understands a character or scene in performance, so that the text more or less forces the actor or director into a binary choice between different interpretations. In other situations the ambiguity is better described as a dramatically productive transgression of the conventional boundary between inside and dialogue. Characters may, for example, speak dialogue as if they were really talking to themselves, or there may be some other complicating factor that undermines the distinction between talking to oneself and talking to others, producing rich dramatic effects.

The chapter then gives extended attention to two examples of such dramatically productive divergence from Shakespeare's standard practice. The conventions governing insides are transformed in significant ways by the intrusion of magic in *The Tempest* and by the early modern discourse of royalty in *Richard II*. In both plays we find a powerful protagonist with rhetorical boundary issues that either transcend (Prospero) or dismantle (Richard II) the ordinary distinction between private and interpersonal speech.

Prospero, first of all, is endowed with magic powers that allow him to transcend the normal conventions of Shakespearean drama: he can overhear guarded asides and address his spellbound enemies face to face without being seen or heard. In *Richard II*, the protagonist does not soliloquise until the very last act when he is forcibly removed from human intercourse, but he frequently speaks as if he were alone when in the company of other people. This inability to adapt his speech to the situation is firmly rooted in the sociohistorical and political tensions that have preoccupied so much criticism on Shakespeare's play, from Kantorowicz onwards. Richard speaks the way he does because he simply conflates his greedy body natural with his role as head of the body politic and therefore knows no genuine outside. In both *The Tempest* and *Richard II*, I argue, the protagonist's divergent speech makes a central contribution to the play's total meaning and effect. The reading of *Richard II* also makes a subtle transition to the more quantitatively oriented mode of analysis in Chapters 3 and 4 through its emphasis on the play's unusually lopsided distribution of insides.

If – as I argue with the help of James Hirsh in Chapter 1 – the Elizabethans and Jacobeans were quite sparing in their use of audience address in non-comic contexts, preferring a more self-contained mode of stage delivery that distanced itself from the practices of the medieval stage, then long soliloquies would have been quite risky when it came to holding the audience's attention. One way for Shakespeare to counter this problem was to infuse his insides with various elements that mimicked dialogical discourse. Another reason for this inveterate dialogism, I argue with reference to cognitive, neuroscientific, and sociological theory, is that real human beings are deeply dialogical creatures, and that some of this tendency persists even we find ourselves alone. Chapter 3, entitled 'Dialogue', explores these dialogical tendencies in Shakespeare's insides.

The chapter begins with a systematic overview of selected figures of speech and related techniques that imbue the Shakespearean inside with some of its dialogical qualities: **apostrophe** (addressing absent or abstract entities), **reported words, prosopopoeia** (personating an external speaker), **erotema** (the rhetorical question), **illeism** (speaking of oneself in the third person), and **tuism** (addressing oneself in the second person). Among other things, I show that descriptive statistics can be just as useful for ubiquitous aspects of Shakespeare's art (such as **apostrophe**) as for other traits that he used less frequently than his co-authors (such as **illeism** and **tuism**).

Chapter 3 ends with a reading of *Hamlet*, demonstrating how the new research methodology can both produce fresh insights into one of the most closely studied works in world literature and place some aspects of received opinion about the play on a firmer footing. My reading begins by noting the play's unusually low score for Shakespeare's favourite dialogical speech element, **apostrophe**, indicating a depression of the dialogical impulse in private speech. It is of course tempting to connect this lack of internal dialogue with the protagonist's depression and social isolation, and a more detailed scrutiny of the play's apostrophes adds more fuel to this fire. *Hamlet* may be low on **apostrophe** in general, but it is also extraordinarily *rich* in a particular *type* of **apostrophe**, the kind that is addressed reflexively to one's own bodily or mental faculties. I also show that these opposing tendencies – the *general* dearth of apostrophes and the wealth of *introverted*, self-addressed apostrophes – can be traced back convincingly to the protagonist's verbal dominance of the play's insides.

Building on Matthew Arnold's classic description of Hamlet's soliloquies as 'the mind's dialogue with itself', as well as prior work by Alex Newell and John Lee, I argue that the aforementioned aspects of Hamlet's inward language reflect his depressive oscillation between self-absorbed weariness and objectifying hatred, both of which involve a radical estrangement of the self from the surrounding world. I also demonstrate that the loss of social dialogue in *Hamlet* forms part of a larger trend in Shakespeare's dramatic practice in the first years of the seventeenth century. This trend stands in powerful contrast to a massive spike of apostrophes in the plays produced between 1605 and 1609, where tragic protagonists like King Lear and Timon of Athens almost cannot open their mouths without producing a volley of apostrophes. The chapter ends with an investigation of another dialogical element, the **question**. I present evidence confirming *Hamlet*'s unusually question-ridden nature and perform a detailed exploration of the tense interplay between genuine questions and rhetorical questions in the speeches of Hamlet and Claudius.

Chapter 4, entitled 'Distribution', explores some tonal and interpretative consequences of the large-scale distribution of insides within and between Shakespeare's plays. Particular attention is paid to how Shakespeare guides audience sympathy for his characters through the selective distribution of insides: that is, how some characters are given copious private speech while others are denied it altogether, or how insides are distributed differently according to variables like gender or class. The chapter begins with a conceptual analysis of the concepts of sympathy, empathy, and perspective taking, grounding these in a discussion of the antagonist in Shakespeare's *Othello*. Once these concepts are in place, I turn to an extended account of three plays where the selective distribution of sympathy and insides becomes particularly salient. I show how Shakespeare's distribution of sympathy and his distribution of insides are closely intertwined and inflected according to gender and class in three plays from three different phases in his career: *The Taming of the Shrew*, *All's Well that Ends Well*, and *The Two Noble Kinsmen*.

The Taming of the Shrew, first of all, is one of eleven Shakespeare plays that have zero female insides, with the result that the audience never receives any direct insight into Katherina's point of view during her brutal wooing by Petruchio. Drawing primarily on Robert Heilman's account of *Shrew*'s farcical qualities, I demonstrate how the play more or less empties its soliloquies and insides of any content that might inspire moral or thematic reflection in the audience. Instead, its male characters devote more than 60 per cent of their insides – an extraordinary figure by Shakespearean standards – to the instrumental **planning** of future actions. This is a major difference from *The Two Noble Kinsmen*, where the women characters speak an exceptional 75 per cent of the insides, and where human sympathy is actively foregrounded rather than excised.

The tonal dissonance of *All's Well that Ends Well*, finally, can be attributed partly to its combination of central traits found in the other two plays. While *Shrew*'s morally problematic nature is reinforced by inveterately action-oriented insides that leave little room for evaluation of Petruchio's brutal reformation of his spouse, *All's Well* grafts a richly elaborated moral and thematic framework onto a similar plot.[19] Where *Shrew* systematically empties its insides of sympathy, *All's Well* goes in the opposite direction, in the direction of *Kinsmen*, by heightening the sympathetic attitudes that Shakespeare removes so surgically from *Shrew*, and by placing more than half of its insides in the mouths of the female characters. But since Bertram, like Katherina, never gets a single inside, he comes to share only indirectly in the play's soliloquised expressions of sympathy for human imperfection.

As a result, the play never reconciles its forced marriage and its farcical plot device with a private language oriented towards sympathy and forgiveness. I end this reading, the fourth chapter, and the entire monograph by relating the chafingly uncomic ending of *All's Well* to larger patterns in Shakespeare's distribution of insides according to act and subgenre. More specifically, I show how Shakespeare's insides follow a distinct M-shaped pattern in three out of four subgenres, and how the unresolved tension *All's Well* persists partly because of its distinctively comic form (its complete lack of insides in the fifth act).

Notes

1. The full definition, partly derived from the work of James Hirsh, will be given below. Compare Maurice Charney's remark that '[f]or all practical purposes, soliloquy and aside have the same dramatic function in relation to the audience'. 'Asides, Soliloquies, and Offstage Speech in *Hamlet*: Implications for Staging', in *Shakespeare and the Sense of Performance*, ed. Marvin and Ruth Thompson (Newark and London: University of Delaware Press, 1989), 116–31, 122.
2. Two modern studies of Shakespeare's soliloquies that I have found particularly valuable are Wolfgang Clemen, *Shakespeare's Soliloquies*, trans. Charity Scott Stokes (London: Methuen, 1987) and James Hirsh, *Shakespeare and the History of Soliloquies* (Cranbury, NJ: Fairleigh Dickinson University Press, 2003). Particularly important things have been said about Shakespearean interiority in Anne Ferry, *The Inward*

Language (Chicago: University of Chicago Press, 1983); Katherine Eisaman Maus, *Inwardness and Theater in the English Renaissance* (Chicago: University of Chicago Press, 1995); and John Lee, *Shakespeare's Hamlet and the Controversies of Self* (Oxford: Oxford University Press, 2000). Early attempts to describe different types and functions of Shakespearean soliloquies and asides systematically were made by Morris LeRoy Arnold, *The Soliloquies of Shakespeare: A Study in Technic* (New York: Columbia University Press, 1911); Wolfgang Riehle, *Das Beiseitesprechen bei Shakespeare; ein Beitrag zur Dramaturgie des elisabethanischen Dramas* (Munich: Ludwig-Maximilians-Universität, 1964); A. C. Sprague, *Shakespeare and the Audience: A Study in the Technique of Exposition* (Cambridge, MA: Harvard University Press, 1935); Warren Smith, 'The Third Type of Aside in Shakespeare', *Modern Language Notes* 64:8 (1949): 510–13; M. C. Bradbrook, *Themes and Conventions of Elizabethan Tragedy*, 2nd edn (Cambridge: Cambridge University Press, 1980), ch. 5, 'Conventions of Speech'; and Raymond Williams, 'On Dramatic Dialogue and Monologue', in *Writing in Society* (London: Verso, 1983).

3. In the terminology of Matthew Jockers, *micro-level* analysis explores (part of) an individual text; *meso-level* analysis is based on a limited collection of texts that would take a long time to read (in this case, Shakespeare's complete plays); and *macro-level* analysis trawls through vast quantities of data (in the most extreme case, millions of Google books, or corpuses containing hundreds or thousands of open source texts). See Matthew L. Jockers, *Macroanalysis: Digital Methods and Literary History* (Champaign: University of Illinois Press, 2013).

4. See Manfred Pfister, *The Theory and Analysis of Drama*, trans. John Halliday (Cambridge: Cambridge University Press, 1991).

5. Hirsh, *History of Soliloquies*. My own position, which will be spelled out in Chapter 1, is that Hirsh's argument seems correct in its broad outlines but becomes too rigid. It underestimates Shakespeare's tendency to capitalise on the *flexibility* and *complexity* of the relation between the fictional world and the actual world, and it may also blind us to Shakespeare's principled employment of audience address in specific contexts.

6. For a fine account of the overlap between ordinary social cognition and theatrical experience, see Bruce McConachie, *Engaging Audiences: A Cognitive Approach to Spectating in the Theatre* (New York: Palgrave Macmillan, 2008), esp. ch. 2. Some metatheatrical implications of the blending of actual and theatrical space are explored usefully by Jenn Stephenson in 'Spatial Ambiguity and the Early Modern/Postmodern in *King Lear*', in *Drama and the Postmodern: Assessing the Limits of Metatheatre*, ed. Daniel K. Jernigan (Amherst, NY: Cambria, 2008), 23–44.

7. See note 2 above.

8. Richard Hillman, *Self-Speaking in Medieval and Early Modern English Drama: Subjectivity, Discourse and the Stage* (Basingstoke: Macmillan; New York: St. Martin's Press, 1997), 1.

9. Alan C. Dessen, *Elizabethan Stage Conventions and Modern Interpreters* (Cambridge: Cambridge University Press, 1984), 19.

10. Nevill Coghill, *Shakespeare's Professional Skills* (Cambridge: Cambridge University Press, 1965), ch. 6: 'Soliloquy', 130.
11. Alan C. Dessen, *Recovering Shakespeare's Theatrical Vocabulary* (Cambridge: Cambridge University Press, 1995), 48. See also E. A. J. Honigmann, 'Re-Enter the Stage Direction: Shakespeare and Some Contemporaries', *Shakespeare Survey* 29 (1976): 117–25.
12. Hirsh, *Shakespeare and the History of Soliloquies*, 13.
13. Alan Richardson defines *monologue* as 'any lengthy speech by a figure on stage that is not intended to be heard by a character. It may be an extended soliloquy, a declamatory set piece, the verbal account of a character's thoughts, scene-setting *protasis* or description, metadramatic commentary, direct address to the audience, or feigned dialogue with a real or imaginary character off-stage' ('Point of View in Drama', 200).
14. Hirsh, *History of Soliloquies*, 199.
15. Hirsh, *History of Soliloquies*, 200.
16. Alan Richardson rightly submits that Seymour Chatman's two criteria for soliloquy – that 'it is spoken by a character, and that "either he is alone on stage, or if there are others they show by their demeanor and actions that they do not hear him"' – are insufficient since they fail to account for overheard soliloquies (the balcony scene in *Romeo and Juliet* being a notable example). See Seymour Chatman, *Story and Discourse: Narrative Structure in Fiction and Film* (Ithaca: Cornell University Press, 1978), 179; Richardson, 'Point of View in Drama', 199.
17. Bernard Beckerman distinguishes the 'solo aside' from the 'conversational aside' spoken to another character; see *Shakespeare at the Globe, 1599–1609* (London: Macmillan, 1962).
18. Hugh Craig's 'Shakespeare's Vocabulary: Myth and Reality' (*Shakespeare Quarterly* 62:1 (2011): 53–74) is a lucid example of how basic quantitative methodology can clarify traditional literary problems that lie beyond the grasp of more intuitively based scholarly approaches.
19. Katherina and Bertram are both married off after declaring that the marriage is entirely against their wishes; neither character ever delivers a single inside where they might comment privately on their difficult experience; they are both reined in by means of a cruel prank; and Shakespeare ends both plays by having Katherina and Bertram deliver unexpected speeches about how happy they are to have been brought into the marital fold.

Chapter 1

Direction

The Shakespearean inside, as I define it here, is a speech spoken by a character who forms part of the action and whose words are not intended to be heard by any other character on the stage. This makes it possible to isolate insides conceptually from other types of speech and to study them systematically. The chapters that follow will become progressively more empirical and quantitative in nature, weaving together the detailed textual analysis of individual plays and passages with accounts of larger patterns in Shakespeare's dramatic practice. But before we bring out the graphs and tables in Chapters 3 and 4 we must look more closely at the nature of the Shakespearean inside, since the definition leaves two questions unanswered:

1. If Shakespeare's insides are not addressed to another character, then who is being addressed? Do the speakers address themselves or the audience?
2. Can we always know if a Shakespearean actor or character intends to address another character? Will there not be hybrids and border-line cases?

This chapter will concern itself with the first question, about self-addressed versus audience-addressed speech, and the title is meant as a pun on the *theatrical* and the *spatial* senses of the word 'direction'. What dramatic conventions appear to have governed the physical direc-tion in which Shakespeare's actors delivered their insides – did they normally address them to themselves, or to the audience? How strict were these conventions? Did Shakespeare write his plays with the idea that his actors would mix different styles, or did he keep them sepa-rate? Did he prefer one over another? Chapter 2, entitled 'Divergence', will then explore the second question about hybrids and borderline cases between insides and ordinary dialogue, with a particular eye to how Shakespeare seems to have worried the line between dialogue and soliloquy for dramatic purposes.

If we were simply in the business of classifying and counting insides, the question of their direction could be left open. An inside is an inside irrespective of how it is addressed, as long as it is not addressed to another character. As I explained in the Introduction, however, the present study is more than an exercise in literary quantification; it seeks to combine the opportunities offered by modern digital scholarship with more traditional interpretative practices like historical analysis and close reading. As soon as we consider the finer nuances of Shakespearean drama – such as tonal qualities, interpretative cruces, thematic functions, or other kinds of dramatic complexities – it becomes obvious that a speech can be understood and experienced quite differently depending on its mode of delivery. The direction in which Shakespeare's asides and soliloquies are spoken can sometimes have a direct bearing on the borderline cases to be discussed in Chapter 2 (because some ambiguities may be resolved by the actor's choice of addressee) and the dialogical dimensions explored in Chapter 3 (because self-addressed speech is by nature less dialogical than direct address).

My argument in this chapter will strike a middle path between Hirsh's strong claim for the centrality of self-addressed soliloquies and the modern emphasis among scholars, actors, and directors on direct address to the audience. To this end, I will explore a number of areas that suggest principled variations in the dramatist's practice, with the key factor being the degree of *detachment* exhibited by the *character* (and not, as Robert Weimann would have it, the *actor*). This detachment can be either *structural* (as in exit and entrance speeches or speeches that begin and end a scene); *mental* (as in the moral and psychological detachment of the Vice figure); or *conventional* (as when the clown or fool transgresses the boundary that separates his play-world from the actual world of the audience).

Self-Address versus Audience Address

There is a strong consensus among Shakespeare specialists about two major influences on Shakespeare's use of soliloquies and asides. The first and most general is that the Elizabethan soliloquy can be traced back to the audience-addressed speeches of the medieval drama, which gradually developed into the early modern convention of 'thinking aloud'.[1] There is also widespread agreement that Shakespeare's soliloquists think aloud in ways that betray a more local debt to the plays of Christopher Marlowe.[2] But what does it really mean to say that Shakespeare's characters think aloud? Should the actor's speech be understood as a symbolic externalisation of the character's inner thoughts, so that Hamlet or Petruchio or Cloten cannot be said to be 'really' talking at all? Or should we take 'think aloud' to mean 'speak out loud' because Shakespeare's characters (and not just the actors) are meant to be *speaking* the words in a literal sense? In that case, to whom will these words normally be directed: to the characters themselves or to the audience?

The most ambitious attempt to conceptualise Shakespeare's soliloquies and asides was made in 2003 by the very same scholar who also supplied us with part of the definition above (though he prefers 'soliloquy' as his umbrella term). James Hirsh's *Shakespeare and the History of Soliloquies* is worthy of extended consideration in this chapter because it constitutes the first modern attempt to give a systematic account of this aspect of Shakespeare's soliloquies and asides. Hirsh's approach is both synchronic (situating Shakespeare in a larger historical process from Greek drama to the modern age) and anachronic (comparing him to selected contemporaries), without ever losing the attention to smaller details that the subject demands.

Hirsh begins his history of soliloquies by noting that these speeches have traditionally been delivered in one of three ways: as audience address, as self-address, or as interior monologue. His survey of drama from the ancient Greeks to Shakespeare and beyond traces a historical pendulum effect between audience address and self-address:

> Soliloquies occur sporadically in ancient Greek tragedy and Old Comedy; many plays begin with an expository soliloquy but contain few other soliloquies. The dominant kind of soliloquy was audience address. In Greek New Comedy and Roman comedy, soliloquies occur with great frequency; many are guarded in asides; many occur in intricate eavesdropping episodes; and the dominant form was self-address. In medieval drama, audience-addressed soliloquies occurred frequently, and self-address infrequently.[3]

Hirsh omits interior monologue from the pre-modern periods on the grounds that it was not practised until the late seventeenth century:

> Before the late seventeenth century the frustrating inaccessibility of the minds of others and of parts of one's own mind was accepted as a fundamental and inescapable feature of the human condition, but various efforts since the late seventeenth century have been made to deny or to overcome that inaccessibility. In the Age of Reason it was widely hoped that reason would eventually ferret out and tame irrational impulses. In the Romantic era, those impulses were romanticized; they did not need to be hidden or suppressed. In the age of Freud it was widely hoped that psychoanalysis would unlock the secrets of the mind. In the context of these developments,

it no longer seemed an arrogation of divine authority to provide readers and playgoers with the fantasy experience of reading minds.[4]

He also claims not to have 'encountered any interior monologues in any dramatic work written before the middle of the seventeenth century'.[5] A cautious philosopher may object here that absence of evidence is not evidence of absence. It is not obvious that one can draw such far-reaching ontological conclusions from the epistemological problems faced by the modern interpreter, especially since the dumbshows of the early modern English theatre sometimes look suspiciously like the theatrical staging of mental events.[6] Nor is it obvious what incontro-vertible evidence of interior monologue could be expected to look like in a Shakespeare play.

So what happened to the audience-addressed speeches that were so dominant in the Middle Ages? Hirsh puts forward plentiful evidence that the fashion shifted again, so that self-address, not audience address, became the dominant approach in Shakespeare's theatre. Except for a few isolated exceptions, he contends, audience address never occurs in the midst of the action. It is restricted to twenty-four choruses, six 'choral epilogues' spoken by characters previously engaged in the action, and three speeches in early comedies where it is actively ridiculed as an old-fashioned and amateurish activity (*The Two Gentlemen of Verona*, 2.3.14, *The Taming of the Shrew*, 4.1.210–11, and *The Merchant of Venice*, 2.2.49). Since Hirsh finds so very few examples of audience-addressed soliloquies he comes to regard self-address as a Shakespearean default mode that can be assumed to be in operation 'unless overridden by an explicit and unambiguous signal of audience address'.[7]

As a consequence of the almost total dominance of self-addressed soliloquies, Hirsh continues, Shakespeare's soliloquies typically give voice to *privacy* but not *interiority*. The audience or reader is eaves-dropping on the characters, not listening in on their private thoughts, with the result that their fictional minds remain almost as inscrutable as those of real people. Even when they engage in deeply soul-searching activities, the audience is confronted not so much with their *inner* nature as with the verbal processes by which they come to terms with their own experience:

> In many cases a character who speaks to himself is bursting with emotion and finds *relief* only in giving voice to the emotion. In many episodes a char-acter uses the act of speaking to herself as a tool in an attempt to *discover* her own motives because she is unsure of her own motives or uncertain about her own intellectual or emotional capacities. Everyone has had the experience of not knowing what one thinks about an issue until one actually

hears what one says about it … Speaking to oneself can also be used to change what one thinks. In many episodes, a character tries to *talk* herself into doing something that some unvoiced part of herself resists.[8]

Hirsh complements and complicates the picture further by adding *overheard*, *guarded*, and *feigned* soliloquies. The standard Shakespearean convention is that soliloquies will be *overheard* by other characters as a matter of course unless the speaker is aware of the interlocutor's presence and therefore *guards* his speech (so that it isn't picked up by others) by means of an aside or by 'standing aside'. Such awareness of being spied upon can also be used to *feign* a soliloquy for strategic purposes: characters may simply pretend to speak to themselves in order to trick their interlocutors into believing that they are expressing their private point of view. Most notably, Hirsh devotes the entire eighth chapter of his book to proving that Hamlet's most famous soliloquy about the relative merits of being and non-being is not so much a heart-felt philosophical argument as a feigned soliloquy, a ruse designed to send the eavesdropping elders down the wrong path. Hirsh has since revisited this argument in a separate research article that adduces additional evidence for this case.[9] A second article from 2015 repeats the claim for the dominance of self-address and traces its roots in the works of Kyd, Marlowe, and Shakespeare.[10]

The most striking and controversial aspect of Hirsh's argument is surely his claim that addressing Shakespeare's soliloquies directly to the audience is largely a modern tendency – and a somewhat anachronistic one at that, since it would have struck Shakespeare himself as painfully, even ludicrously, medieval.[11] The modern acting profession seems squarely rooted in a consensus that the recent collapse of the dramatic 'fourth wall' and the reintegration of the audience as an active participant in the drama has liberated Shakespeare from the shackles of modern realism, returning him to his post-medieval roots.

This holds particularly true for some theatres, like Shakespeare's Globe, that often seek to approximate the original performances of Shakespeare's plays. The performance vision of the Baltimore Shakespeare Factory, likewise, is 'to imitate as closely as possible the theatre conditions that an audience in the Elizabethan and Jacobean Periods would have experienced if they attended the Globe Theatre, Blackfriars Theatre, or any other theatre of that time'. This means, among other things, that 'many speeches and comments in Shakespeare should be spoken directly to the audience in general or to specific audience members'.[12]

According to one of Hirsh's modern-day scholarly detractors, Bridget Escolme, direct audience address involves an acute degree of metatheatrical awareness on the part of Shakespeare's fictional characters. 'They want the audience to listen to them, notice them, approve their performance, ignore others on stage for their sake. The objectives of these figures are bound up with the fact that they know you're there.'[13] Though Escolme works primarily with the modern stage, her argument is rooted in Shakespeare's historical context:

> Whatever the debates around the authenticity of the Bankside Globe, however, the reconstructed Elizabethan playhouse with its visible audience – partly mobile and potentially restless, partly seated at eye-level with the actor – clearly demonstrates that talking to oneself is an improbable way of engaging and securing the attention of the spectator.[14]

So if Hirsh is right, we have a major irony on our hands. Modern actors and directors who claim to liberate Shakespeare from the shackles of modern realism may in fact be forcing him into a medieval straitjacket that he himself refused to wear because he deemed it old-fashioned.

In chapter 6 of *Shakespeare and the History of Soliloquies*, Hirsh puts forward ten types of evidence for the ubiquity of self-address in Shakespeare's plays. Most strikingly, a stage direction from the Folio version of *Richard III* declares that Richard '*[s]peakes to himselfe.*'. Some of Shakespeare's characters comment actively on how their fellow characters talk to themselves, as when Luciana in *The Comedy of Errors* reacts to Dromio of Syracuse's failure to guard his aside from her: 'Why prat'st thou to thyself' (2.2.193). The best example I have found in my own investigations is a passage in *Julius Caesar* where Portia see-saws between solo asides and dialogue, showing clearly that her asides are meant to represent actual speech that can be overheard by another character:

> PORTIA I must go in. Ay me, how weak a thing
> The heart of woman is! O Brutus,
> The heavens speed thee in thine enterprise!
> *[aside]* Sure, the boy heard me: Brutus hath a suit
> That Caesar will not grant.
>   *[aside]* O, I grow faint.
> Run, Lucius, and commend me to my lord;
> Say I am merry: come to me again,
> And bring me word what he doth say to thee.
>   *Exeunt severally.*

(2.4.39–46)

In this passage Shakespeare moves back and forth between three different conventions of speech. Portia's first three lines constitute a self-addressed soliloquy in the form of an apostrophe to the absent Brutus, but then she quickly realises that she may have spoken too loudly, at which point she switches rapidly to a solo aside ('Sure the boy heard me') and then to some obfuscating dialogue designed to cover up her *faux pas* ('Brutus hath a suit'). The last four lines constitute another aside followed by more dialogue. Shakespeare's characters could hardly be overheard (or suspect that they had been overheard) by other characters in this way if they did not literally *speak* their soliloquies and asides on the internal level of the dramatic fiction. Nor would passages of the following kind – where a character once again reworks a partly or completely overheard aside into more palatable dialogue, pretending that this interlocutor simply misheard – make much sense:

> RICHARD [*aside*]
> So wise so young, they say, do never live long.
> PRINCE What say you, uncle?
> RICHARD I say, without characters fame lives long.
> > (*Richard III*, 3.1.79–81)

Once again the character's revision of the initial line presupposes an act of overhearing that, in turn, presupposes actual speech.

Like real human beings, Shakespeare's characters often resort to self-talk as they grapple with their problems:

> CLOWN I cannot do 't without counters. Let me see; what am I to buy for our sheep-shearing feast?
> > (*The Winter's Tale*, 4.3.36–7)

True to the modern insistence on direct address to the audience, however, many modern scholars appear to assume automatically that speeches of this kind will be addressed to the audience, when self-address seems more natural and dramatically productive. Consider the following scene from *All's Well that Ends Well*, where the boastful Parolles chides himself for having written cheques that he is in no position to cash:

> PAROLLES Ten a'clock. Within these three hours 'twill be time enough to go home. What shall I say I have done? It must be a very plausive invention that carries it. They begin to smoke me, and disgraces have of late knock'd too often at my door. I find my tongue is too foolhardy, but my heart hath the fear of Mars before it and of his creatures, not daring the reports of my tongue.
> 1 LORD This is the first truth that e'er thine own tongue was guilty of.
> PAROLLES What the devil should move me to undertake the recovery of this drum, being not ignorant of the impossibility, and knowing I had no such purpose? I must give myself some hurts, and say I got them in exploit; yet slight ones will not carry it. They will say, 'Came you off with so little?' And great ones I dare not give; wherefore, what's the instance? Tongue, I must put you into a butter-woman's mouth, and buy myself another of Bajazeth's mule if you prattle me into these perils.

1 LORD Is't possible he should know what he is, and be that he is?
(4.1.24–44)

Erika Lin contends that '[u]pon entering the scene ... Parolles speaks directly to the audience in soliloquy',[15] but these lines are almost certainly meant to be self-addressed. They are lucid examples of Hirsh's principle that 'unguarded' soliloquies – that is, speeches where the character (and not just the actor) spoke actual words out loud, was not aware of being eavesdropped upon, and therefore did not take precautionary measures – would be overheard as a matter of course. It goes without saying that a speech cannot be overheard by another character unless it is formulated in actual words on the internal level of dramatic communication. It also seems clear from the general tenor of these speeches that Parolles is not combing the audience for helpful advice: he is fretting, wrapped up in himself, muttering to himself, berating himself, and struggling to find a solution to his predicament.

My own position is that Hirsh has made an important contribution to our knowledge of Shakespeare's original dramatic practice. Hirsh can rightly claim to have shifted the burden of evidence: unless new, powerful evidence is brought forward, we can postulate that self-address was a dominant convention for the delivery of soliloquies and solo asides in Shakespeare's theatre. This is, however, very different from saying that self-address was cordoned off neatly or completely from other techniques. The main limitation in Hirsh's argument, I will argue below, is that the dominance of self-address is emphasised so forcefully at the expense of other alternatives that it becomes a near-exclusive convention. As a result, modern readers may be blinded to subtle nuances, rich dramatic effects, and principled variations when Shakespeare departs from the self-addressed norm.

My purpose in the rest of this chapter, therefore, will be to strike a middle path between Hirsh's argument and other scholars who regard direct address to the audience as central to Shakespeare's dramatic practice. This will be done partly through a detailed scrutiny of Hirsh's arguments, and partly by exploring what the alternatives might look like. As Hirsh himself notes, Shakespeare 'employed the conventions governing soliloquies in the theater of his time more imaginatively, more diversely, more subtly, more elaborately, and more profoundly than did any other dramatist'.[16] He took a flexible view of artistic conventions and discarded those that did not appeal to him. So why is it so unthinkable that he might have experimented with alternatives to the convention of self-addressed speech or engaged in a mixed practice? A closer consideration of Hirsh's arguments raises some important questions.

Explicit Signals of Audience Address

Let us first consider the textual qualities that allow Hirsh to identify isolated instances of audience address in three early comedies. Can similar passages be found elsewhere in Shakespeare's plays, which would suggest that his argument is too restrictive? Hirsh singles out the following three passages as instances of direct audience address:

> Nay, I'll show you the manner of it.
> <div align="right">(<i>The Two Gentlemen of Verona</i>, 2.3.13–14)</div>

> He that knows better how to tame a shrew,
> Now let him speak: 'tis charity to show.
> <div align="right">(<i>The Taming of the Shrew</i>, 4.1.198–9)</div>

> [aside] Mark me now, now I will raise the waters;
> <div align="right">(<i>The Merchant of Venice</i>, 2.2.46)</div>

In each of these lines, the presence of an unnamed interlocutor is foregrounded by means of a personal pronoun or an imperative construction. Somebody is being promised something, is being urged to do something, or is told to observe something, and Hirsh is clearly right to identify this somebody as the audience (or, perhaps, individual members thereof).

Technically speaking, the key elements in these passages are what applied linguists call 'relational markers', that is, devices that 'that explicitly address readers, either by selectively focusing their attention or by including them as participants in the text situation'.[17] These devices are not abundant in Shakespeare's complete insides, but several plays do contain elements that that closely resemble the examples above. While Launce offers to *show* the audience in the soliloquy cited above, Falstaff's soliloquy from *Henry IV, part 2* promises that they will *see*:

> O, you shall see him laugh till his face be like a wet cloak ill laid up!
> <div align="right">(<i>Henry IV, part 2</i>, 5.1.83–5)</div>

Since Falstaff is alone on the stage, and since the speech is clearly not an **apostrophe**, it seems logical to interpret this relational marker in the same way that Hirsh interprets Launce's speech above: as an unambiguous signal of direct address. An identical relational marker is used in *Henry IV, part 1* when Hotspur derides the writer of a letter he is reading:

What a pagan rascal is this, an infidel! Ha! You shall see now in very sincerity of fear and cold heart will he to the King, and lay open all our proceedings!

(*Henry IV, part 1*, 2.3.28–31)

I will examine this interesting speech more closely in Chapter 3 because of its complex dialogical qualities, but the important thing for now is that Hotspur is alone on the stage and refers to the letter writer in the third person. What else could this be than an instance of direct address to the audience? The only alternative would be the rhetorical device **tuism**, so that Falstaff and Hotspur would address themselves in the second person, but we will see below that Shakespeare never uses tuistic formulations in this way.

The passages above are, in my view, lucid examples of direct address that appear to disprove Hirsh's restriction of this type of speech to selected early comedies. There are several other passages from different genres that contain similar imperatives to *see* a particular aspect of the stage action, even if these do not contain the same explicit reference to an interlocutor. This is a complete list of all imperatives to *see* or *look* in Shakespeare's complete insides where the addressee is left undefined:

See! they forsake me.

(*1 Henry VI* 5.3.24)

see, here he comes.

(*Comedy of Errors* 2.2.6)

see where my cousin comes!

(*Edward III*, 1.2.81)

See how my sword weeps for the poor King's death.

(*3 Henry VI*, 5.6.63)

See the hell of having a false woman:

(*Merry Wives of Windsor*, 2.2.281)

See how she leans her cheek upon her hand.

(*Romeo and Juliet*, 2.2.23)

see how I lay the dust with my tears.

(*The Two Gentlemen of Verona*, 2.3.31)

See where she comes.

(*The Two Gentlemen of Verona*, 5.1.7)

Look where she comes:

(*Othello*, 3.3.281)

Look where he comes.

(*Othello* 3.3.333)

Such passages are effective cues for actor and audience alike. They cement the connection between individual actors and characters for the audience, and they signal to the actor that another actor's entrance must be acknowledged. Since many of these passages can at least conceivably be self-addressed and do not require a direct appeal to the audience's attention, their evidential value as instances of direct address is naturally fairly low. In the case of Iago and Richard of Gloucester, especially, such exhortations to *see* or *look* seem very much in line with the sardonic detachment exhibited by the speaker.

It is still worth noting, however, that Shakespeare appears to have stopped writing such explicit exhortations to *see* or *look* in the latter half of his career,[18] as if there were no longer any need to tell his audience actively where to look or to explain that a particular character was now entering the stage. The tapering off of such relational markers seems more compatible with the view, taken by scholars such as Robert Weimann and Leah Marcus, that Shakespeare's theatre dissociated itself in the first years of the seventeenth century from its more populist and presentational dimensions (involving a high level of interaction with the audience) and embraced a more distinctively representational form (where the characters move about in an increasingly self-enclosed space).[19] There may also be a connection here with other changes in Shakespeare's practice over time. As we shall see in Chapter 4, the early Shakespeare was particularly keen to keep his audience abreast of the action by having his characters announce their impending actions by means of soliloquies and solo asides.

Telling Yourself What You Already Know

Hirsh's strict claim for self-address in soliloquies and solo asides intensifies the traditional problem of how conventional or naturalistic these speeches were intended to be. The main problem with *solo asides* from a naturalistic viewpoint is what I like to call *the argument from acoustics*: if there was no interior monologue on the Elizabethan stage, then how could a character really say these secretive things in the midst of a conversation without being overheard? A frequent problem with *soliloquies*, which is also shared by some solo asides, is when they convey information that the speakers themselves know only too well: we can call this the problem of *redundancy*. It is one thing for characters to try and talk themselves into a particular belief or emotional state, or to reason with themselves about the best course of action, but it is quite another to inform themselves at length about their own proper name, what they've been up to recently, where they come from, or basic trivia about other characters.

Consider the following speech from *Cymbeline*, where Belarius provides the audience with vital information:

BELARIUS How hard it is to hid the sparks of nature!
These boys know little they are sons to th' king,
Nor Cymbeline dreams that they are alive.
The think they are mine, and though train'd up thus meanly,
I'th cave wherein they bow, their thoughts do hit
The roofs of palaces, and Nature prompts them
In simple and low things to prince it, much
Beyond the tricks of others. This Polydore,
The heir of Cymbeline and Britain, who
The king his father call'd Guiderius, – Jove!
When on my three-foot stool I sit, and tell
The warlike feats I have done, his spirits fly out
Into my story: say 'Thus mine enemy fell,
And thus I set my foot on's neck', even then
The princely blood flows in his cheek, he sweats,
Strains his young nerves, and puts himself in posture
That acts my words. The younger brother, Cadwal,
Once Arviragus, in as like a figure
Strikes life into my speech, and shows much more
His own conceiving. Hark, the game is rous'd!
O Cymbeline, heaven and my conscience knows
Thou didst unjustly banish me: whereon,
At three and two years old, I stole these babes,
Thinking to bar thee of succession as
Thou refts me of my lands. Euriphile,
Thou wast their nurse, they took thee for their mother,
And every day do honour to her grave:
Myself, Belarius, that am Morgan call'd,
They take for natural father. The game is up.   *Exit.*

(3.3.79–107)

This speech has zero function on the internal level of dramatic communication because its sole purpose is to convey factual information that the character knows all too well. Since Belarius the character has no conceivable reason to deliver such a lengthy speech to himself, the speech is motivated exclusively on the external level of communication; it is spoken entirely for the audience's benefit. Something similar happens in the following speech by Autolycus in *The Winter's Tale:*

Enter AUTOLYCUS, singing.
        …
I have served Prince Florizel, and in my time wore three-pile, but now I am out of service.
        …

My traffic is sheets; when the kite builds, look to lesser linen. My father
named me Autolycus; who, being as I am, littered under Mercury,
was likewise a snapper-up of unconsidered trifles. With die and drab I
purchased this caparison, and my revenue is the silly cheat. Gallows and
knock are too powerful on the highway: beating and hanging are terrors
to me: for the life to come, I sleep out the thought of it. A prize! a prize!
                                                                 (4.3.13–14, 23–31)

The standard view among Shakespeare scholars is that expository or
explanatory soliloquies of this kind were retained in Shakespeare's
drama as a relic of medieval conventions,[20] even if the exact degree to
which they strained the boundaries of naturalistic performance must
have depended partly on the actor's delivery. It is not impossible, for
example, that Shakespeare's actors sometimes spoke such soliloquies
into thin air – that is, without addressing either themselves or the audience directly. Raymond Williams, for example, takes the view that
Shakespeare's theatre did not operate with a binary distinction between
direct address and the

> wholly enclosed and internal speech relations of the 'naturalist' convention.
> Between the explicitly direct and such indirect cases, there are intermediate
> cases, which we can properly call 'semi-direct', in which speech is given in
> full consciousness of the audience but without the marks of direct address.[21]

It does not seem obvious that speeches that were so drastically
and obviously redundant from the fictional character's own perspective could have been combined smoothly with a rigid adherence to
self-address (where, as we have seen, the audience is supposed to be
eavesdropping on characters who are talking to themselves). It would
no doubt have been much easier for Shakespeare's original audience
to accept the conventional function of such speeches if they clearly
grasped that the information was being divulged on their behalf in the
form of audience address. It seems hard to get around this objection
without constructing some sort of awkward ad hoc convention such as
'non-purposive self-addressed speech'.

The same problem surrounds several asides in *King Lear*, such as
when Kent explains that the letter he is about to read is from Cordelia
(2.2.167–9), or when Edgar explains somewhat awkwardly that
he is not really torturing his blind old father but trying to cure him
(4.6.33–34). If Shakespeare really was as contemptuous of medieval
practices as Hirsh suggests, then surely this sort of informational redundancy would have been the first thing to be rooted out of his plays?

In 1904, A. C. Bradley submitted that

> in listening to a soliloquy we ought never to feel that we are being addressed.
> And in this respect, many of the soliloquies are master-pieces. But certainly

in some the purpose of giving information lies bare, and in one or two the actor openly speaks to the audience.[22]

In *Shakespeare and the History of Soliloquies*, Hirsh argues along similar naturalistic lines that Shakespeare was dead against direct address because it constitutes 'an intrusion of the narrative mode of *telling* into the dramatic mode of *showing* and tends to be static, redundant, and hence undramatic – a "defect" indeed'.[23] Such an argument works both ways, however. As soon as we come across a particularly static, redundant, and undramatic speech of the kind spoken by Belarius and Autolycus above, we have reason to ask ourselves if Shakespeare did not intend it to be addressed directly to the audience. Bradley certainly did so, unwillingly, because it conflicted with his naturalistic leanings:

> Such faults are found chiefly in the early plays, though there is a glaring instance at the end of Belarius's speech in *Cymbeline* (III. Iii. 99 ff.), and even in the mature tragedies something of this kind may be traced.[24]

Where is the Midst of the Action?

One basic convention that Hirsh detects in Shakespeare's works, and which constitutes a necessary adjunct to his general argument for self-address, is that characters never address the audience directly in the midst of the action. As we have seen, he even suggests that 'Shakespeare regarded audience address in the midst of the action as a ridiculous device',[25] as evidenced by the aforementioned examples from early comedies.

An important problem here is what counts, and does not count, as 'in the midst of the action' in a Shakespeare play, and also what it means for a character to be 'engaged in the action'.[26] These are not necessarily either/or terms. We have already touched upon two speeches whose complete lack of motivation on the internal level squares badly with the claim for self-address. These speeches were taken from plays that were written towards the end of Shakespeare's career, and my main argument was on the level of content, that their informational redundancy rendered self-address unlikely. Now let us consider a very famous speech that looks very like a borderline case between a chorus and an ordinary soliloquy – the Porter scene in *Macbeth*, written around 1606:

> PORTER Here's a knocking, indeed! If a man were Porter of Hell Gate, he should have old turning the key. [*knocking*] Knock, knock, knock. Who's there, i'th' name of Belzebub? – Here's a farmer, that hang'd

himself on th' expectation of plenty: come in, time-pleaser; have napkins
enow about you; here you'll sweat for't. [*knocking*] Knock, knock!
Who's there, i'th' other devil's name? – Faith, here's an equivocator,
that could swear in both the scales against either scale; who committed
treason enough for God's sake, yet could not equivocate to heaven: O!
come in, equivocator. [*Knocking within*] Knock, knock, knock. Who's
there? – Faith, here's an English tailor come hither for stealing out of a
French hose: come in, tailor; here you may roast your goose. [*knocking*]
Knock, knock; never at quiet! What are you? – But this place is too cold
for Hell. I'll devil-porter it no further: I had thought to have let in some
of all professions that go the primrose way to th'everlasting bonfire.
[*knocking*] Anon, anon: I pray you, remember the Porter.

> [*Opens the gate.*]
> (2.3.1–20)

It is hard to imagine a more conspicuous signal of audience address –
short of a 'Dear Audience' – than the Porter's closing words. There is
no other character on the stage during the speech, which means that the
persons he addresses are imaginary, and he can hardly be asking himself
to remember himself. It is also possible that the Porter addresses parts
of this speech to individual spectators rather than to the audience as
a collective. According to David Wiles, the early Shakespearean fools
played by Will Kemp tend to address the audience as a collective while
the more sophisticated Robert Armin – who would almost certainly
have played the Porter – 'acknowledges the audience only as a collection of individuals. He occasionally incorporates individual spectators
into the action of the play – probably gentry sitting on stools on the
stage.'[27] Though this reading is inescapably speculative, Wiles suggests
that lines like 'Faith, here's an equivocator' could have been spoken in
this way.

Since the Porter's speech forms part of a tragedy written around
1606 it seems to belie both parts of Hirsh's argument against audience
address in later non-comic plays. It could of course be argued that the
Porter's speech may not be a Chorus in the usual sense but still serves
as a kind of comic interlude which is partly detached from the rest of
the play. There is, in other words, at least a vague possibility that the
speech has been omitted on the grounds that it is not delivered 'in the
midst of the action', which would make the argument consistent. But
then one would have expected the Porter to turn up in Hirsh's supposedly exhaustive list of choric speeches.[28]

The important point here is that the vagueness of the 'midst of the
action' criterion may blind us to principled variations in Shakespeare's
dramatic practice. There are two basic types of speech in Shakespeare
that differ markedly from choruses and epilogues and yet can be said

Table 1.1 Shakespeare's exit and entrance insides (% of total word count).

Category	%
A. Entrance insides	25
B. Exit insides	33
C. Insides that begin a scene	23
D. Insides that end a scene	27
Combinations of A and C	23
Combinations of B and D	20
Combinations of A, B, C, D	3

to place their speakers at one remove from the rest of the action. The first category is the *exit* or *entrance* inside, spoken by a character as he or she either enters or exits the stage. The second category, which over-laps significantly with the first, is the inside that either *begins* or *ends* a scene. A search in the SID reveals that these speeches make up no less than a fourth of all insides in the Shakespeare canon. In the majority of cases, a character's entrance or exit inside also begins or concludes an individual scene, effectively placing the character at a temporary remove from the rest of the action (Table 1.1.).

The figures show that Shakespeare rarely wrote self-contained scenes like that of the Porter, where a character enters, delivers a soliloquy, and then leaves the stage again. Such speeches make up only 3 per cent of Shakespeare's total insides, more than half of which are attributable to a formal experiment performed together with John Fletcher in *The Two Noble Kinsmen*. I will return to these unusual soliloquies, where a single character is isolated by formal means from the rest of the action, in Chapter 3.

Many of Shakespeare's entrance and exit insides sound suspiciously like something that might be addressed to the audience, as indeed they often are in modern dramatic practice. Few are formulated in a way that speaks directly against audience address, and some contain evidence that speaks strongly for it. We have already examined three entrance insides spoken by characters at the beginning of an individual scene, which means that that they are not spoken 'in the midst of the action' in any strict sense: Belarius, Autolycus, and the Porter. We have also touched briefly upon a speech spoken by Falstaff towards the end of act 5, scene 1, of *Henry IV, part 2*, whose relational marker strongly suggested audience address. As this latter scene draws to an end, the actor playing Falstaff effectively clears the stage for some quality time alone with the audience:

[FALSTAFF] I'll follow you, good Master Robert Shallow.

Exit Shallow.

Bardolph, look to our horses.
> *Exeunt Bardolph and Page.*

The stage directions are modern editorial clarifications, but they are not completely necessary since the important cues are already encoded in Falstaff's dialogue. He is meant to linger on the stage for a while as Shallow leaves, and then he also sends Bardolph on a small errand. Now that he is no longer 'in the midst of the action' he delivers a speech that gives the audience vital inside information about plot and character, ending with an unmistakable sign of audience address:

> If I were sawed into quantities, I should make four dozen of such bearded hermits' staves as Master Shallow. It is a wonderful thing to see the semblable coherence of his men's spirits and his. They, by observing of him, do bear themselves like foolish justices; he, by conversing with them, is turned into a justice-like serving-man. Their spirits are so married in conjunction, with the participation of society, that they flock together in consent, like so many wild-geese. If I had a suit to Master Shallow, I would humour his men with the imputation of being near their master: if to his men, I would curry with Master Shallow that no man could better command his servants. It is certain that either wise bearing or ignorant carriage is caught, as men take diseases, one of another; therefore let men take heed of their company. I will devise matter enough out of this Shallow to keep Prince Harry in continual laughter the wearing out of six fashions, which is four terms, or two actions, and a shall laugh without intervallums. O, it is much that a lie with a slight oath, and a jest with a sad brow, will do with a fellow that never had the ache in his shoulders! O, you shall see him laugh till his face be like a wet cloak ill laid up!
> SHALLOW [within] Sir John!
> FALSTAFF I come, Master Shallow, I come, Master Shallow.
> > *Exit.*
> > (5.1.60–87)

Falstaff's meditation is not a pure exit speech since he reverts ever so briefly to dialogue with Shallow before following him offstage. Hence it does not form part of the statistics for exit speeches listed above. The important thing, however, is that the actor/character Falstaff places himself at one remove from the action as the scene draws to a close and delivers inside information to the audience. As we saw above, the relational marker 'O, you shall see' is hardly an apostrophic address to absent characters but a clear signal of audience address. Exactly the same phrase is used in the (undeniably audience-addressed) performance of Pyramus and Thisbe in *A Midsummer Night's Dream*:

> THESEUS The wall, methinks, being sensible, should
>   curse again.

PYRAMUS No, in truth sir, he should not. 'Deceiving me' is Thisbe's cue: she is to enter now, and I am to spy her through the wall. You shall see it will fall pat as I told you: yonder she comes.

Enter THISBE.

(*A Midsummer Night's Dream*, 5.1.180–5)

The main difference between Bottom's botched performance and Falstaff's dramatically successful speech is that the former is not in control of his performance. He speaks out of character in response to a snide remark from Theseus, with the effect of interrupting an already inept performance and destroying what is left of the theatrical illusion. The actor/character Falstaff, by contrast, has ensured that this will not happen by engineering a smooth transition from self-address to audience address: he has cordoned off a private space from the rest of the action to deliver a speech that rounds off the previous action and prepares the audience for what is to come.

It is, I think, a strong hypothesis that Shakespeare thought of speakers of exit and entrance insides as *part* of the action but not in the *midst* of it, and that this partial detachment from their social context sometimes enabled them to communicate directly with the audience. In the case of Falstaff and the Porter we even have strong linguistic evidence in the form of interpersonal markers.

The next question is if other exit speeches should be regarded as self-addressed unless they exhibit unambiguous evidence to the contrary. Is Hirsh being impossibly harsh when he raises the evidential bar so high? Consider this famous speech from *Othello*:

IAGO And what's he then that says I play the villain?
When this advice is free I give and honest,
Probal to thinking and indeed the course
To win the Moor again? For 'tis most easy
Th'inclining Desdemona to subdue
In any honest suit. She's framed as fruitful
As the free elements: and then for her
To win the Moor, were't to renounce his baptism,
All seals and symbols of redeemed sin,
His soul is so enfettered to her love
That she may make, unmake, do what she list,
Even as her appetite shall play the god
With his weak function. How am I then a villain
To counsel Cassio to this parallel course
Directly to his good? Divinity of hell!
When devils will the blackest sins put on
They do suggest at first with heavenly shows
As I do now. For whiles this honest fool
Plies Desdemona to repair his fortune,

And she for him pleads strongly to the Moor,
I'll pour this pestilence into his ear:
That she repeals him for her body's lust.
And by how much she strives to do him good
She shall undo her credit with the Moor –
So will I turn her virtue into pitch,
And out of her own goodness make the net
That shall enmesh them all.

(2.3.325–51)

This exit speech is often audience-addressed on the modern stage, and for good effect; the actor may even confront the audience head-on, with a combination of rhetorical appeal and aggression, actively searching for someone who is groundling enough to call him a villain. Iago's speech is neither a chorus nor an interlude, but he has momentarily detached himself from the other characters to forge new plans (on the internal level) and reveal important things to the audience (on the external level) as the scene draws to a close.[29]

It is a scholarly commonplace that Iago draws upon the medieval Vice figure, who would frequently taunt the audience directly in the hope of inspiring titillating laughter. Direct audience address always brings with it a measure of actorial and spectatorial detachment from the internal level of the fiction, an overt blending of fictionality and actuality, and this aspect is naturally detrimental to the intensely absorptive mood associated with tragedy. Since few Shakespearean tragedies are free of comic relief we should not be surprised to find occasional intrusions of audience address even in dark and sombre plays like *Hamlet* and *Macbeth*, perhaps even in the midst of the action. We have seen that *Macbeth* has its semi-detached, audience-addressing Porter, but can we also find an audience-addressed speech uttered in the midst of the action in another Shakespearean tragedy?

Mental Detachment

In the previous section I considered how the *structural* detachment that characterises speeches delivered at the outskirts of Shakespeare's scenes might have paved the way for direct address to the audience. I would now like to consider how another type of detachment – the character's *mental* detachment from the rest of the action – might produce similar scenic effects. I will begin by paying scrupulous attention to the exact meaning of a single line from act 2, scene 2, of *Hamlet*, because I think it can be demonstrated beyond reasonable doubt that this line *has* to be audience-addressed.

To examine this line in its immediate dramatic context not only provides more ammunition against Hirsh's argument against audience address in later, non-comic plays, but can also throw some light on the conditions under which direct audience address can be expected to operate. As I hope to show, the line gives us a first reason to question Robert Weimann's influential argument that actors in the so-called *platea* position would partly detach themselves from the characters they played in order to address the audience. As Weimann puts it in *Author's Pen and Actor's Voice*, the *platea* was the intermediate down-stage space where '[p]layers, representing something and someone else, also (re)presented themselves'.[30] What really matters, I will argue, is not the *actor's* but the *character's* degree of mental detachment from his or her social world on the internal level of the dramatic fiction. It is this detachment that allows the character to step outside the boundaries of his fictional space momentarily and address the audience as if they were really there.

In act 2, scene 2, of *Hamlet*, the older generation is struggling to uncover the cause of the Prince's melancholy. The line I am interested in is spoken by Polonius, who has just wagered his head on the theory that Hamlet has been driven mad by Ophelia's rejection of his courtship. Polonius now smugly approaches the Prince in the hope of teasing out additional confirmation of what he already thinks he knows:

> POLONIUS [aside] How say you by that? Still harping on my daughter.
> Yet he knew me not at first; a said I was a fishmonger. A is far gone.
> And truly in my youth I suffered much extremity for love, very near
> this. I'll speak to him again.
>
> (2.2.186–91)

A search in the *Literature Online* full-text database for the slightly shorter phrase 'how say you by' reveals that Shakespeare and other contemporary playwrights used it consistently in the sense of 'what do you make of'.[31] We can thus more or less rule out the idea that Polonius first addresses Hamlet dialogically and then switches to an aside in the course of the same speech. Theoretically speaking, the line could still be addressed to four different interlocutors: to Hamlet (as a self-addressed **apostrophe**), to Polonius himself, to the audience, or to another character who is not Hamlet. It is evident from the text that no other characters are present, which leaves us with the first three sugges-tions: Hamlet, Polonius himself, or the audience.

The first (mere) possibility is that Polonius speaks the words rhetorically and under his breath to Hamlet. This does not seem very plausible since he would then be *pretending* to *ask* Hamlet to *answer* his own question, with the added complication that the actor would have no way to explain what he was doing to the audience ('Psst! I'm not *really* asking him this question, even if it looks that way!'). A second, less absurd interpretation might be that Polonius, who thinks he knows the source of Hamlet's melancholy, is asking himself a rhetorical question in the second person. This sounds a bit odd, but it is not entirely impossible, and it brings us back to a term I mentioned briefly above. **Tuism**, or self-address in the grammatical second person, will be explored systematically in relation to other 'dialogical' aspects of Shakespeare's insides in Chapter 3. A coding query in the SID reveals a few scattered cases where characters do ask themselves tuistic questions, half of which may have been written by Shakespeare's co-authors (*Troilus and Cressida*, 2.3.1–3; *Measure for Measure*, 2.2.173–7; *1 Henry VI*, 5.3.67–9; *Titus Andronicus*, 1.3.344–5).

The problem with the self-addressed tuistic reading, however, is that it jars so markedly with Shakespeare's normal usage. A systematic examination of all instances of **tuism** in Shakespeare's plays reveals that his characters simply do not use it to assert the truth of their own convictions. On the contrary, they typically employ **tuism** for the opposite purpose of creating a mental space where they might become what they are currently not – to confront themselves, or to rouse themselves into action.[32]

It would seem, then, that we need to find Polonius an external interlocutor, and that this interlocutor is the audience. This is the interpretation offered by Anne Thompson and Neil Taylor in the third Arden edition: 'Polonius in effect addresses the audience here.'[33] Such a reading does not sit well with Hirsh's restriction of audience address to selected early comedies, but the problem seems to lie with the inflexible rule rather than with the exception.

Let us now ask a more interesting question. What allows the actor playing Polonius to turn suddenly to the audience as he speaks this line? We saw above that according to Robert Weimann, direct address to the audience is associated with the non-localised and non-representational downstage space of *platea*, where the actors playing clowns and Vice figures would partly dissociate themselves from the characters they played and collude with the audience. Polonius is not a clown, of course, but he is something of a self-important buffoon, so it might be possible to see him as a comic cousin of Shakespeare's clowns. The problems arise, however, as soon as we try to picture the actor playing Polonius putting this scheme into practice. It is hard to see how such a brief aside could offer any actor the opportunity to detach himself

meaningfully from his character, or perhaps even to occupy the down-
stage position that would allow him to ingratiate himself with the audience at the expense of the character he is playing.

In the light of these problems, Erika Lin has sought to revise
Weimann's concept of *platea* in two related ways.[34] One of her moves
is to disconnect the *platea* position from specific character types such
as clowns or Vice figures as well as from the downstage location. Both
steps seem more or less necessary here. More problematically, however,
she also attempts to rescue Weimann's view of the *platea* position as a
privileged and authoritative space by associating it with characters who
enjoy superior knowledge and can manipulate their environment (thus
approximating the audience's perspective). The question is, however,
whether the *platea* position – either physical or metaphorical or both –
is necessarily a privileged or authoritative position. According to Nova
Myhill, at least, it 'does not necessarily carry with it the superior understanding and authority that Weimann's discussion implies'.[35]

This problem disappears as soon as we separate the character's
detachment from the question of *authority*, regarding only the former
as a necessary condition for audience address. The fictional character
called Polonius is in a position to address the audience because he has
mentally detached himself from his social situation and *believes* that he
occupies a privileged and authoritative position with respect to Hamlet.
As the audience well knows, however, there is nothing privileged or
authoritative about his perspective; it is, in fact, deeply ironic, since he
has no inkling of the real problems that Hamlet is facing. At least in
the case of Polonius, it is therefore the character's mental detachment
on the internal level of the dramatic fiction that creates an opportunity
for direct address. I will return to this central question of who actually
addresses the audience – the character or the actor? – towards the end
of this chapter when I examine Weimann's paradigmatic example of the
platea character: Launce in *The Two Gentlemen of Verona*.

Most of the potentially audience-addressed speeches I have considered in this chapter – Autolycus's autobiography, Falstaff's character
assassination of Shallow, Iago's sarcasm, the Porter's topical jokes, and
Polonius's pompous but misguided assessment of Hamlet's troubles
– have a strong comic element to them. This should not surprise us
given the intimate relationship that Larry S. Champion traces between
comedy and detachment:

> Shakespeare throughout the comedies demonstrably works to achieve for
> the spectator the detached view so vital to the comic experience –
> not a Jonsonian detachment which presumes an attitude of derisive
> hostility, but a detachment of tolerance resulting from a position of

knowledgeable security. The fullest enjoyment depends, not on the laughter arising from the shock of surprise or incongruity, but on this superior level of perception which permits the spectator to observe the plot without a total emotional commitment to it.[36]

Champion is interested in the spectator's rather than the character's perspective, obviously, but the same principle holds on the internal level of the dramatic fiction. Seeing *comic detachment* as a specific instance of the larger principle of *mental detachment* allows us to incorporate those deeply unpleasant scenes where Shakespeare's Vice-like villains delight in elaborate sarcasms. Richard of Gloucester's murder of the King in *3 Henry VI* is a case in point:

> RICHARD I'll hear no more: die, prophet, in thy speech.
>
> > [*Stabs him.*]
>
> For this, amongst the rest, was I ordain'd.
> KING HENRY Ay, and for much more slaughter after this.
>   O God, forgive my sins and pardon thee! [*Dies.*]
> RICHARD What, will the aspiring blood of Lancaster
>   Sink in the ground? I thought it would have mounted.
>   See how my sword weeps for the poor king's death.
>   O, may such purple tears be always shed
>   From those that wish the downfall of our house!
>   If any spark of life be yet remaining,
>   Down, down to hell; and say I sent thee thither –
>
> > [*Stabs him again.*]
>
> I, that have neither pity, love, nor fear.
>
> > (5.6.56–69)

The crucial line here is 'See how my sword weeps for the poor king's death.' Taken together, the relational marker 'See' and the reference to the King in the third person strongly suggest that Richard briefly looks up from Henry's body and addresses the first five lines of his second speech to the audience. He then turns back to Henry and wishes him to hell as he stabs him for the second time. Four lines further down, Richard injects another relational marker into a jocular reference to having been born with his feet first:

> Had I not reason, think ye, to make haste
> And seek their ruin that usurp'd our right?
>
> > (72–3)

Richard actively cultivates the emotional detachment that results from his discrepant awareness, his sense of being partly embroiled in a black comedy where cold-blooded murder is merely something to be smiled at. It is the character's mental distance on the internal level of the dramatic fiction that opens up for direct address on the external level. The emotional contagiousness of such speeches can be extremely unnerving for the audience, as we shall see more clearly in Chapter 4.

The Need for a Fixed Convention

Another cornerstone of James Hirsh's argument for the dominance of self-address is that Shakespeare's characters sometimes state explicitly that they are talking to themselves. While this evidence speaks strongly for the prevalence of self-address, it can hardly be enlisted as an argument against the parallel employment of audience-addressed speeches. This is because characters who comment on their own self-addressed speeches are making not any old statements but metalinguistic ones. When Cloten in *Cymbeline* says, 'I dare speak it to myself, for it is not vain-glory for a man and his glass to confer in his own chamber' (4.1.7–9), he is not simply talking to himself: *he is talking about talking to himself*, and the line itself does not specify the direction in which it should be delivered. Wouldn't it make more sense for the actor playing Cloten to look up and deliver this metacommentary to the audience, before returning to his self-addressed ruminations?

Hirsh's answer to such objections is emphatic: no, Shakespeare would have had very strong reasons to avoid confusing his audience by mixing different types of address. This dichotomous view – where audience address becomes the rival of self-address, rather than its complement – is grounded in a perceived need for a dominant convention that would silently relieve the dramatist of the onerous task of clarifying the direction of the actor's speech. Hirsh writes:

> If a dramatist merely omitted overt traces of self-addressed speech from a particular soliloquy, experienced playgoers would nevertheless assume that the soliloquy represented self-addressed speech … As long as an artist regards the dominant convention as a useful artistic tool, he or she will have strong reservations about overriding it.

Why is that? Hirsh submits that '[i]f there are too many exceptions, the rule disappears'; if Shakespeare had used too many audience addressed speeches then 'he might have begun to weaken the automatic operation of the convention whereby soliloquies were assumed to represent self-address'.[37]

This argument is open to an objection based on the nature of the dramatic medium. Let us assume, for the sake of argument, that it really was so vital for audiences always to distinguish sharply between self-address and audience address (a point which is at least arguable in the light of Raymond William's aforementioned argument for hybrid speeches). Such distinctions would not have been particularly difficult for actors to establish on a case-by-case basis. An important aspect of dramatic performance is the translation of the written word into flesh, of the written text into the limiting and constraining physicality of the actor's body. This process necessarily reduces much of the play's textual ambiguity: unlike the student of the play-text, the theatregoer has access to the actor-character's body language, and particularly the delimiting direction of the gaze. The actor's gaze is a subtle and highly effective tool for guiding audience response, and modern actors frequently use it to orchestrate intermediate effects between strict self-address and audience address.

Is it so unthinkable that early modern actors would have done the same? On Shakespeare's stage, the simplest of theatrical ground rules would have been quite sufficient, and they would not have required any special knowledge of theatrical conventions on the part of the audience: *if you want be perceived to be talking to yourself, avert your gaze from the audience and pretend they are not there. If you want to address the audience directly, look them right in the eye. For more ambiguous effects, cast your eyes absent-mindedly in their general direction.* With such rules in place, which would really only be a slightly ritualised version of what happens in everyday life, the distinction between self-address and audience would rarely have posed a serious practical problem for either the actor or the audience. This line of thinking also drives a minor wedge into Hirsh's claim that self-address must be in operation unless there are unequivocal signals to the contrary. If actors could guide audience response by such simple means then there would not be any need for unequivocal signs of this kind in the dramatic text.

This leaves us with a second reason why Shakespeare might have wanted to run a tight ship regarding self-address: that the problem was not so much for actors to communicate effectively with the audience as for Shakespeare to control his actors. Did he perhaps expect them to reproduce a predetermined authorial distinction between self-address and audience address in performance? Was he looking to convey certain things that could only be conveyed by means of self-address and that would change their import drastically if they were instead addressed to the audience?

It is not an implausible proposition that Shakespeare nursed a strong desire to control his actors; witness, for example, Hamlet's famous advice to the players about the risks of overacting in act 3, scene 2. It is far less obvious, however, that his dramatic art would have stood to gain anything from a categorical ban on audience address after the mid-1590s. One of Hirsh's own valuable contributions to our understanding of Shakespeare's works – that the Bard probably never used interior monologue, and so never gave the audience direct access to a character's mind – actually gives us grounds to question if the distinction between self-address and audience address could really have been so vital to his dramatic practice. If there is no interior monologue, no direct access to the mind of the character, then self-address and audience address may sometimes convey very similar information. The Iago who delivers his speeches directly to the audience remains enigmatic and mysterious: he cannot be trusted any more than the Iago who engages in self-address. If the audience also senses an uncomfortable analogy between Iago's intimate revelations and his expert manipulation of Othello – as they typically do in the most successful modern productions of the play – then they are likely to trust him even less.

According to Simon Palfrey and Tiffany Stern,[38] Shakespeare's power over his actors would have been partly circumscribed by the conditions imposed by the Elizabethan repertory system. Actors were not only forced to juggle a staggering number of plays in their working memories; they also appear to have learned their lines alone in the study as separate cues, with only minimal textual context and limited time for group rehearsal. So even if Shakespeare *did* try to control the exact mode of delivery, and even if his actors *did* do their very best to comply with the wishes of the master, the pragmatic realities of the stage business would often have wrenched that power out of the hands of author and actor alike, forcing the actors to improvise and clarify their lines as best they could as they went along. Small wonder, then, that the tendency of actors to improvise too flamboyantly comes under fire in *Hamlet*.

Palfrey and Stern even propose that early modern actors would sometimes embrace crowd-pleasing behaviour out of sheer necessity as they stumbled onto the stage and did their best to insert their lines into a larger scene of whose content they were largely ignorant: 'not being told who would speak the next cue on the part, it might be easier to address the audience than risk speaking to the wrong person on a busy stage'.[39] For actors speaking insides, however, this must have been a minimal problem, if indeed it existed at all. Among the 102 entrance insides in the SID, there is not a single speech whose first lines might reasonably be mistaken for dialogue. On those rare occasions when the first lines of the entrance speech are in the grammatical second person, either the character enters reading a letter – as in the following passage from Cymbeline:

How? Of adultery? Wherefore write you not
What monster's her accuser? Leonatus!
O master, what a strange infection
Is fall'n into thy ear!

(*Cymbeline* 3.2.1–4)

– or the lines are demonstrably *not* addressed to another character (as in Edmund's speech 'Thou, nature, are my goddess'). In most situations, any remaining doubts on the part of the actor would have been cleared up as soon as he or she walked onto an empty stage.

Fictional Worlds and Actual Worlds

My next objection to Hirsh's argument for the almost complete dominance of self-address is that it involves a strangely monistic view of the worlds inhabited by the fictional characters and the real-world audience. A basic account of the structure of dramatic communication will be useful as a preparation for this point. In strictly self-addressed speech, characters are enclosed within their internal level of the dramatic fiction, exhibiting no awareness of the audience's attention. Information passes in one direction only, from the characters to the audience. In direct address to the audience, this relationship becomes a two-way process: the characters (and not just the actors, who may stay very much in character) are now aware of the audience and even begin to interact with it.

Such a conversation between a fictional character and an actual spectator, however we may understand its precise mechanisms, must be substantially different from ordinary dialogue from the perspective of both parties. If there were no theatrical convention in place that separated the world of the character from the world of the audience, however implicit and unwritten, then the dramatic fiction would not be possible; there could be no travel in time or space to places like ancient Egypt or Rome. We might even expect a legendary procrastinator like Hamlet to give up his lonely and outnumbered brooding, hold an inflammatory Mark Antony-style speech on the rotten state of Denmark, and lead an army of 3,000 enraged Globe auditors against the helpless and bewildered Claudius. While the exact boundaries between stage and audience are naturally subject to historical and cultural revision, the existence of some sort of boundary between the fictional and the actual is a precondition of drama itself. Even modern experimental plays are fundamentally dependent on the very division that they seek to subvert or even demolish altogether.

I belabour this point because of Hirsh's tendency to downplay or even elide the boundary in Shakespeare's plays between the fictional world and the audience's world. Hirsh writes, for example, that a Shakespearean character

> may give voice to schemes, hopes, regrets, fears, and so on, that the charac-
> ter would not confide even to his closest friend, much less to two thousand
> strangers. Hamlet says certain things to himself that he would not share
> even with Horatio, *much less* with the 'groundlings' (3.2.11) for whom he
> has contempt.[40]

Hirsh is clearly referring to actual groundlings here. He argues elsewhere, with direct reference to the problem of audience address, that it
would make no 'psychological sense' for Hamlet to share his innermost
feelings with a massive crowd: characters who did so would be 'exhibi-
tionists of the crudest sort, the Elizabethan equivalents of guests on the
Jerry Springer show'.[41]

These arguments will make sense only in terms of a dramatic
monism that more or less obliterates the gap between the fictional and
the actual world. From the character's perspective, audience address
(communicating across the internal and external levels) will involve
more or less the same psychosocial dynamic as talking to a fellow
character (communicating on the internal level). It is on the basis of
this dubious psychological assumption – that some things are simply
too sensitive to be shared with a large crowd – that Hirsh disputes
repeatedly that speeches containing very intimate information would
have been audience-addressed. His jocular gloss on a particular speech
in *The Comedy of Errors* is a case in point: 'If soliloquies guarded in
asides were addresses to playgoers, Lucania would have asked, "Why
prat'st thou to these auditors?"'[42]

To dispute this view of the relation between stage and audience is
not to take the opposite view that Shakespeare drew an immutable
line between them, but it does open the door to a viable alternative.
The problem of 'actorial direction' in the delivery of soliloquies and
asides is linked to larger questions about the relation between the
early modern character, the actor, and the audience, and more fundamentally about the relationship between the fictional and the actual
world. In the near-absence of direct evidence from Shakespeare's time,
the 'direction' of the inside must be anchored in a broader theoretical reconstruction, however tentative and speculative, of the relation
between the early modern stage and its audience. To avoid the pitfalls
of reductive historicism, this specific account of the early modern
theatre must in turn be anchored in the more fundamental nature of
drama itself.

Today a strong collective case can be made for a complex, multi-layered, and negotiable view of the relation between character, actor, and audience in dramatic performance. A number of drama theorists have recently employed cognitive theory in order to question Coleridge's classic formulation of fiction as the willing suspension of disbelief. Drawing primarily on the work of theatre historian Julia Walker and cognitive theorists Gilles Fauconnier and Mark Turner, Bruce McConachie argues that spectators do not simply mentally 'suspend' the actual world as they immerse themselves in its fictional counterpart. Instead they cultivate a double consciousness where the actor and the character are blended together in complex and shifting ways:

> This is not an extraordinary ability involving a leap of faith; children playing house have the same capability. And like them, what the mind/brain has blended together, the mind/brain can take apart ... Spectators can slip out of the blend of performance to adjust their bodies in their seats or to mentally note that an actor's costume fits him poorly ... As viewers, we oscillate millisecond by millisecond among blends and singular identities, not between skepticism and faith.[43]

A similar blending characterises the relation between fiction and reality in dramatic performance:

> Performance, it seems, mixes up our usual categories of actuality and make-believe all of the time ... Like other parts of a performance, blended dialogue may contain more or less actuality and fictionality ... In the stretch from naturalistic mumbling to abstract vocalization, the human voice can communicate to audiences along an enormous continuum from actuality to fictionality.[44]

Such cognitive blending will not be entirely subject to envious and calumniating time. It will happen even in realist drama, which strives so hard to eradicate it for the purpose of a complete and self-contained illusion, and it will certainly have existed in Shakespeare's theatre as well. The idea is actually quite similar to S. L. Bethell's argument in the 1940s that Shakespeare's audience had to cultivate a 'dual awareness of play-world and real world'.[45]

Jenn Stephenson makes a similar case for the layered nature of Shakespeare's theatrical space. The spectator's experience of *King Lear* is a

> doubled view of persons and objects inside the newly created fictional world, allowing the audience to perceive in a kind of binocular vision both the imagined fiction and the quotidian material of its creation. One significant quality of thus designated theatrical space is that it steals from actual space to create fictional space.[46]

Like McConachie, Stephenson stresses the flexibility that results from such doubleness: 'Theatrical space oscillates as it is shifted in perception between the actual space of the stage and the fictional space colonized by the play world.'[47] This is what imbues the theatrical performance with its special metatheatrical potential: 'The characteristic phenomenological duality of fictional space and the objects within that space gives rise to a self-aware metatheatrical perception that is ubiquitous and deeply ingrained in the elemental fabric of the theatrical system.'[48]

MacConachie and Stephenson both regard the formation of this double consciousness, this blending of the actual and the fictional, as an inescapable aspect of theatre itself. Indeed, it is easy to think of examples where Shakespeare seems to heighten this blending of the actual and the fictional quite deliberately. In *The Tempest* Trinculo delivers the following soliloquy:

> Were I in England now, as once I was, and had but this fish painted, not a holiday fool there but would give a piece of silver: there would this monster make a man; any strange beast there makes a man: when they will not give a doit to relieve a lame beggar, they will lay out ten to see a dead Indian.
>
> (*The Tempest*, 2.2. 27–33)

Such a speech seems designed to produce at least a small cognitive surprise, a brief disorientation in time and place, forcing Jacobean theatre-goers to check their bearings rapidly before re-immersing themselves in the play-world. This play is Shakespeare's most formally conservative work, and yet he saw fit to foreground the overlap in theatrical space between the fictional and the actual world. A second example can be culled from *Twelfth Night*, act 3, scene 3, where Shakespeare inserts a wry product placement for a local inn:

> Hold, sir, here's my purse.
> In the south suburbs, at the Elephant,
> Is best to lodge: I will bespeak our diet,
> Whiles you beguile the time, and feed your knowledge
> With viewing of the town: there shall you have me.
>
> (*Twelfth Night*, 3.3.38–42)

This is another example of how Shakespeare actively foregrounds the cognitive blending that characterises all dramatic art to various degrees: for a brief moment the stage is both South Bank and Capital of Illyria.

I personally find it too vague to dub these gestures metatheatrical or (especially) metadramatic since these terms are open to widely divergent interpretations.[49] It is more precise to regard them as a particular form of *metalepsis*, defined as the transgression of the conventional boundary between the internal and the external level of communication (or in narrative fiction, between the diegetic and extradiegetic level). Shakespeare's characters sometimes deliver a specific type of metaleptic speech where references to the character's world can be, *but need not be*, extended from the play-world to the actual world inhabited by the audience. The effect of such extended references, should the audience wish to pursue them, is to inflate rather than deflate the fictional space by allowing it to extend outwards and encompass the actual world inhabited by the audience. The common denominator in Shakespeare's classic metaleptic statements about 'this great globe itself' or references to the world as a 'stage' is this kind of optional inclusiveness. The 'globe' could be taken to mean the fictional world, or the Globe playhouse, or the actual world, or all three at once, and in a blended theatrical space the integrity of the self-contained fictional world would not be threatened. The same goes for the Elephant in the theatrical room above.

When Shakespeare works metaleptically, therefore, he usually does so in two ways (with some striking exceptions that I will return to later on in this chapter). He typically works by *implication*, so that his characters are making statements about *their own* world, and it is up to the audience or reader to extend or not extend their meaning, possibly with the help of the actors. He also works centrifugally by means of *inclusion*, in that the theatrical metaphor can be extended outwards to encompass the actual world.

The most plausible hypothesis about the nature of Shakespeare's theatrical space, as I see it, can be arrived at by combining these theoretical considerations with the absence of a normative Elizabethan or Jacobean theory of acting. Edward Burns has suggested, convincingly in my view, that Shakespeare's contemporaries would not really have needed such a theory 'since all the essentials of the trade were covered by the art of rhetoric, speaking to move, delight, and persuade'.[50] Since there was no contract comparable to the fourth wall of classical realism, the audience's relationship to the fictional events on the stage would simply have been left undefined and open to continual revision.

Such vagueness should not be understood as a failure on the part of these dramatists to theorise or regulate their own activity. On the contrary, it would have been highly functional, allowing for a rich range of blended theatrical effects, a multiplicity of shifting relations between actor and audience, fiction and reality. Nor would such flexibility necessarily have undermined the integrity of the stage fiction with respect to the actual world, since, as we have seen, even the boldest metaleptic statements in Shakespeare tend to make perfect sense as statements about a self-contained dramatic world (with a few notable exceptions that I will return to below).

If anything, Shakespeare appears to have practised the noble art of having it both ways in order to maximise the dramatic impact of his art. The important consequence for my purposes here – because it brings us directly back to the immediate problem of actorial direction – is that an audience accustomed to such frequent back-and-forth, to such blending of layer upon layer, of the fictional upon the actual, would naturally have regarded their relationship with the fictional characters as equally negotiable. Soliloquists might briefly acknowledge the audience's presence, but perhaps only for special reasons and under specific circumstances, before returning to their self-addressed ways.

What I'm picturing here is an early modern theatrical convention where a firm but flexible line divides the stage characters from the audience; where the dominant mode of delivery for insides is self-address, as Hirsh argues convincingly; but where the characters will often complement their habitual self-talk with direct address to the audience. The central factor that seems to underpin the intrusion of direct audience address, I have argued, is *detachment* of a structural, mental, and conventional nature.

I would now like to consider a final problem: whether Shakespeare's use of audience address in the early comedies was really as deflationary as Hirsh submits. To this end it will be useful to descend from the empyreal heights of dramatic theory and grapple systematically with some concrete examples from one of these early comedies, *The Two Gentlemen of Verona*. My main argument will be twofold: that Shakespeare's use of audience-addressed soliloquies is more frequent and less deprecating than Hirsh allows for, and also that it involves a more direct and intimate link between the fictional character and the actual audience than scholars such as Robert Weimann have recognised.

The Two Gentlemen of Verona: Launce Addresses the Audience

The Two Gentlemen of Verona is often considered an apprentice piece on Shakespeare's part, but many scholars have also held that its most successful passages – the comic speeches delivered by Launce and Speed – anticipate important aspects of Shakespeare's later art.[51] A brief look at the SID shows that the sheer quantity of soliloquies and asides in this play constitutes a striking departure from Shakespeare's habitual practices. *Verona* contains more than 16 per cent insides. This is more than twice the Shakespearean average of around 7 per cent, and much higher than any other Shakespeare play except its fellow outlier, *Cymbeline* (17 per cent). The author's conscious intentions may be lost in the dark backward and abysm of time, but it is still a fact that *Verona* afforded him an unusual amount of space to explore the potentials of insides in general and soliloquies in particular.

In this section I want to examine the three soliloquies spoken by Launce, with an eye to how their satirical counterpoint to the main plot interrogates the underlying conditions of Shakespeare's dramatic art. The notion that Shakespeare intended Launce as a vehicle for the satire of dramatic conventions is strengthened indirectly by his affinity with a different character of roughly the same name, Lancelot Gobbo of *The Merchant of Venice*. In one of Gobbo's classic speeches, the good and bad angel of the medieval morality play are rewritten as a comic tug-of-war between his 'conscience' and the 'fiend' (*Merchant*, 2.2.1–30). As soon Shakespeare put pen to paper and started writing lines for a character called something like 'Launcelot', 'Launce', or 'Lance', he also started playing around with the shortcomings and inherent absurdities of his own dramatic medium. To this we can add that *The Two Gentlemen of Verona* is one of only three Shakespeare plays that contain explicit discussions of the nature of acting.[52]

My first and simplest objective here will be explore Launce's three soliloquies for clues about how they might have been spoken on the Elizabethan stage. Hirsh singles out only Launce's first soliloquy – his famous leave-taking speech, which includes the account of his dog's hardened heart – as an instance of audience address, but my interpretation will confirm Weimann's opinion that all three are audience-addressed (though not all of them exclusively so).

My main reason for studying the three soliloquies together, however, is their aggregate literary function. Shakespeare's comic employment of audience address in these speeches consistently targets the intrinsic absurdity of a literary convention where someone who is not who he is (actor, character) communicates directly with people who are not really there (audience) or cannot understand what is being said (such as dogs). Launce's audience-addressed soliloquies in *Verona* are not deflationary or distancing, as Hirsh would have it, but allow for a festive interrogation of the deeper conditions, not just of the theatrical medium in general, but of the specific medium of the audience-addressed soliloquy.

While I thus agree wholeheartedly with Robert Weimann's view that Launce's speeches involve an 'exuberant probing into the limits of dramatic representation',[53] my interpretation of this probing will differ markedly from his. It is, as we saw above, a cornerstone of

Weimann's distinction between *locus* and *platea* that the actor playing Launce would partly detach himself from the character he played and collude directly with the audience, coming to laugh both *within* and, so to speak, *above* his character. Nora Johnson notes that 'Launce is for Weimann a paradigmatic moment of union in division; actor slips out of character to laugh with his audiences about the stupidity of Launce', resulting in a 'composite figure' that joins together the individual and the collective, the fictional and the actual.[54]

In contrast to Weimann, I will argue that Shakespeare endows his fictional clown with more integrity. The central miracle encoded in Launce's audience-addressed soliloquies is not that the *actor* partly transcends his *character* at the latter's expense (though it is likely that Will Kempe frequently did so, to Shakespeare's chagrin), but that Launce the *character* can magically transcend the confines of his own fictional play-world and address someone who is not technically there. As we shall see, this absurd contract even allows him to reveal secrets to the audience that he cannot reveal to himself, and the audience is invited to laugh at their own complicity in this game of make-believe.

As we saw above, James Hirsh lists Launce's first soliloquy (2.3.1–31) – the leave-taking speech, where he describes his parting from his family and elaborates on his dog Crab's singularly unsentimental nature – as one of three audience-addressed speeches in Shakespeare's early comedies. Hirsh appears to do so mainly on the basis of Launce's offer to illustrate this moving scene by means of a few simple utensils: 'I'll show you the manner of it.' Another conspicuous signal of audience address in the same speech that Hirsh does not mention is Launce's use of the relational marker 'Now, sir' (2.3.19). Since Hirsh mentions neither the second nor the third soliloquy in a list of audience-addressed speeches that is meant to be exhaustive, it follows that he must classify the other two soliloquies as self-addressed (according to his principle that all soliloquies will be self-addressed unless accompanied by unambiguous signals to the contrary).

A closer look at the second and third soliloquies uncovers strong evidence of audience address there too. Since Launce has already addressed the audience in the first soliloquy they will naturally expect something similar when he next enters the stage alone in act 3, scene 1. This expectation is confirmed immediately by his opening words: 'I am but a fool, look you'. The relational marker 'look you' is used on and off in Shakespeare's works, and even *overused* for satiric purposes when Fluellen delivers a rapid volley of 'look yous' in *Henry V* (3.2.96–103). A SID text query shows that Shakespeare's other soliloquists frequently employ imperative constructions as they reason with themselves, but they never say 'look you' to themselves. The same formulation returns towards the end of the second soliloquy when Launce completes his unpoetic blazon of the milkmaid: 'look you, a sweet virtue in a maid with clean hands' (3.1.275–6). It seems unlikely that Launce should say 'look you' to himself when he has just used it to address the audience.

The evidence for audience address is even stronger in Launce's third soliloquy, the one on his altruistic cover-up for Crab's multiple misdemeanours. Here Launce once again begins his speech with another 'look you' while talking about his dog in the third person. The anecdote about Crab pissing under the Duke's table is then introduced by yet another relational marker: 'You shall judge' (16). This second-person construction certainly cannot be addressed to the dog (who is still being discussed in the third person) or to Launce himself (since it makes little sense for him to ask himself to judge his own story). The third soliloquy also differs from the other two in not being consistently audience-addressed, or at least not directly so. The first, audience-addressed part consists in Launce's retelling of the painful incident at the Duke's palace:

Enter LAUNCE with his dog.
LAUNCE When a man's servant shall play the cur with him, look you, it goes hard: one that I brought up of a puppy; one that I saved from drowning, when three or four of his blind brothers and sisters went to it. I have taught him, even as one would say precisely 'Thus I would teach a dog'. I was sent to deliver him as a present to Mistress Silvia, from my master; and I came no sooner into the dining-chamber, but he steps me to her trencher and steals her capon's leg. O, 'tis a foul thing when a cur cannot keep himself in all companies: I would have (as one should say) one that takes upon him to be a dog indeed, to be, as it were, a dog at all things. If I had not had more wit than he, to take a fault upon me that he did, I think verily he had been hanged for't; sure as I live he had suffered for't. You shall judge: he thrusts me himself into the company of three or four gentleman-like dogs, under the Duke's table; he had not been there (bless the mark) a pissing while, but all the chamber smelt him. 'Out with the dog', says one; 'What cur is that?' says another; 'Whip him out', says the third; 'Hang him up', says the Duke. I, having been acquainted with the smell before, knew it was Crab; and goes me to the fellow that whips the dogs: 'Friend', quoth I, 'you mean to whip the dog?' 'Ay, marry, do I', quoth he. 'You do him the more wrong', quoth I; ''twas I did the thing you wot of'. He makes me no more ado, but whips me out of the chamber. How many masters would do this for his servant? Nay, I'll be sworn I have sat in the stocks, for puddings he hath stolen, otherwise he had been executed; I have stood on the pillory for geese he hath killed, otherwise he had suffered for't.

(4.4.1–33)

Towards of the end of the speech, Launce turns away from the audience to engage in the following 'dialogue' with Crab:

> Thou think'st not of this now. Nay, I remember the trick you served me, when I took my leave of Madam Silvia: did not I bid thee still mark me, and do as I do? When didst thou see me heave up my leg, and make water against a gentlewoman's farthingale? Didst thou ever see me do such a trick?
>
> (33–8)

It is vital to find our fictional bearings here. In the course of this soliloquy, Launce first addresses a crowd of people who are not really there (the audience) and then addresses a creature who can neither understand his words nor respond to them (his dog). In both parts of the speech we find a dramatic discourse characterised by blatant disregard for its own impossibility.

This brings us to a second aspect shared by these three soliloquies: their interrogation of dramatic conventions. By having Launce address his dog in the third soliloquy, Shakespeare produces a richly layered satire. The audience will be amused partly by Launce's overestimation of his dog's mental capacities, partly by the dog's incapacity to act his part, and perhaps also by a human propensity to talk to animals as if they could really understand us. It is a *commedia dell'arte* routine that would have been destined to succeed no matter how it was played out on the Elizabethan stage.[55]

The parodic object of Launce's first soliloquy – the leave-taking speech – is something else, namely what contemporary writers on drama and rhetoric called the art of *personation*, adopting the role of another person (or, in this case, a dog).

> LAUNCE Nay, 'twill be this hour ere I have done weeping. All the kind of the Launces have this very fault. I have received my proportion, like the prodigious son, and am going with Sir Proteus to the Imperial's court. I think Crab my dog be the sourest-natured dog that lives: my mother weeping; my father wailing; my sister crying; our maid howling; our cat wringing her hands, and all our house in a great perplexity; yet did not this cruel-hearted cur shed one tear. He is a stone, a very pebble stone, and has no more pity in him than a dog. A Jew would have wept to have seen our parting. Why, my grandam, having no eyes, look you, wept herself blind at my parting. Nay, I'll show you the manner of it. This shoe is my father. No, this left shoe is my father; no, no, this left shoe is my mother; nay, that cannot be so neither. Yes, it is so, it is so: it hath the worser sole. This shoe with the hole in it is my mother; and this my father. A vengeance on't, there 'tis. Now, sir, this staff is my sister; for, look you, she is as white as a lily, and as small as a wand. This hat is Nan our maid. I am the dog. No, the dog

is himself, and I am the dog. O, the dog is me, and I am myself. Ay; so, so. Now come I to my father: 'Father, your blessing.' Now should not the shoe speak a word for weeping; now should I kiss my father; well, he weeps on; now come I to my mother. O, that she could speak now, like a wood woman! Well, I kiss her. Why, there 'tis: here's my mother's breath up and down. Now come I to my sister: mark the moan she makes. Now the dog all this while sheds not a tear; nor speaks a word; but see how I lay the dust with my tears.

(2.3.1–31)

Launce turns out to be an inept theatrical director and a terrible casting agent, but the problem is exacerbated when he moves from having inanimate objects stand in for living beings and decides to personate his dog. The result is a richly blended performance where Launce (a fictional character) is suddenly both himself (an actor) and his dog (the actor's role). This is another example of how Shakespeare actively exploits the dramatic blending or overlay of distinct identities, with the humour resulting mainly from Launce's failure to untangle the different layers from each other. He fails to *stay in character* because he cannot reconcile his dual identities as human actor and theatrical dog, and so a performance that was meant to clarify a simple anecdote becomes a weirdly inconsistent hybrid that resolves nothing: 'I am the dog. No, the dog is himself, and I am the dog. O, the dog is me, and I am myself. Ay; so, so' (2.3.21–3).

Here Shakespeare embraces the inclusive and optional metaleptic mode I discussed above. He leaves it to his audience to complete the additional blended layer, where an *actor* is playing the *role* of a *character* who tries to *act* but fails to separate himself from his *role*. How all this played out on the Elizabethan stage would have been highly dependent on the nature of the actor's performance (most probably Will Kempe in the original production). It is possible, as Robert Weimann has argued repeatedly, that the original Launce not only became the object of the audience's laughter here but also the 'laughing subject of his own mirth'[56] because Kempe detached himself partly from his role and colluded with the audience. Or as Weimann puts it in a later work co-authored with Douglas Bruster, '[t]he clown's own laughter is *with* the audience and therefore *at* his own comic representation'.[57]

This is, however, hardly a necessary conclusion since the splitting of roles is already rampant on the internal level of the dramatic fiction: the central joke is that Launce the character fails to stay in character in the attempt to personate his dog. What is more, Weimann's partial dissociation between actual actor and fictional character does a poor job of accounting for Launce's second soliloquy, the one where he reveals his love for the milkmaid. It is a shame that Weimann hardly even mentions this speech since it harbours a much deeper comment on the absurdity of a specific dramatic device – the soliloquy – whereby fictional characters smuggle inside information about their fictional play-world to the actual spectators before the stage.

The second soliloquy on the milkmaid is structured as a sequence of seemingly inadvertent confessions where Launce's desire to *withhold* his personal secrets is quickly trumped by his blatant incapacity to *keep* them:

> LAUNCE I am but a fool, look you, and yet I have the wit to think my master is a kind of a knave; but that's all one, if he be but one knave. He lives not now that knows me to be in love, yet I am in love, but a team of horse shall not pluck that from me; nor who 'tis I love; and yet 'tis a woman; but what woman I will not tell myself; and yet 'tis a milkmaid; yet 'tis not a maid, for she hath had gossips; yet 'tis a maid, for she is her master's maid, and serves for wages. She hath more quali-ties than a water-spaniel, which is much in a bare Christian. [taking out a paper] Here is the cate-log of her conditions. 'Imprimis, she can fetch and carry': why, a horse can do no more; nay, a horse cannot fetch, but only carry, therefore is she better than a jade. 'Item: She can milk': look you, a sweet virtue in a maid with clean hands.
>
> (3.1.261–76)

Just as Launce's weepy-eyed first soliloquy provided a comic mirror-image of a heart-breaking farewell in the previous scene, so the second soliloquy sets up a satirical counterpoint to the pangs of love voiced by Proteus and Valentine. This satire comes across most overtly in Launce's watered-down version of conventional poetic blazon, which now consists in a list of extremely trivial facts about the beloved (lines 269–76). By dragging the high-flown but conventional rhetoric of love down to his own level, Launce throws an unfavourable light on the seemingly immutable class distinctions that elevate the aristocratic discourse of love over that of the commoner. There may even be an additional sense in which the speech questions the special nature of love itself, as Shakespeare does elsewhere in *Verona* and in other plays written around the same time (such as the first act of *Romeo and Juliet*). Love is far from a *trivial* phenomenon in Launce's account – which would remove the need for secrecy – but it certainly seems *mundane*.

A crucial aspect of Shakespeare's satire in the second soliloquy is that a theatrical convention normally reserved for the communication of inside information (the soliloquy) is used to communicate things that really do not seem to be very special. There is an absurd clash between the audience's expectation of juicy *soliloquised particulars* and Launce's strikingly *general*, not to say *generic*, description of his beloved milkmaid. But even this collision between form and content seems almost epiphenomenal when we consider how Shakespeare's interrogation of this theatrical convention strikes at the very idea of a fictional character talking to a real-life audience.

Launce's second soliloquy is, as we have seen, just as audience-addressed as the first, which means that the audience expects to receive a direct transmission of privileged information from which Launce's fellow characters are barred. This expectation is quickly confirmed when he begins to reveal highly confidential information about his love life: 'He lives not now that knows me to be in love, yet I am in love, but a team of horse shall not pluck that from me' (263–5). Launce-the-character clearly thinks of talking to the audience as a special kind of intimacy since he first confesses his love and then asserts that no one can drag it from him.

Since Launce is a fictional character addressing a real-life audience, there is a strong sense in which his secret isn't really being heard by anyone. There is no one there in Verona to hear him. Talking to the audience enables Launce to keep his secrets on the internal level of the dramatic fiction, presumably because the audience is not part of his own world and so can never be expected to intervene in his business. The situation is reminiscent of the epigraph from Dante that Eliot affixed so famously to 'The Lovesong of J. Alfred Prufrock': Launce can confess his deepest secrets to his audience without any fear of infamy because he knows that they will never be shared with the world of the living.

This otherworldly revelation provides an important context for our interpretation of Launce's next confession, where an almost identical linguistic structure is applied to the soliloquist's relationship to his own secrets: 'but what woman I will not tell myself; and yet 'tis a milk-maid'. The verbal meaning of this strange utterance may seem slightly ambiguous – we cannot be absolutely sure if he refuses to '*tell the secret himself*' or to '*tell it to himself*' – but it is almost certainly a reflexive construction. Launce is declaring that he will not talk to himself about his love. We find a similar line in a later play, William Rowley's *A Shoemaker, A Gentleman* (1638), where Leodice poses a rhetorical question to herself – 'I am alone, and why / Should I feare to tell my self my thoughts' – and then remarks, as she hears the Nurse approaching: 'So, I am well called out of my contemplation.'[58] The strange thing about Launce's speech, however, is that he not only addresses the audience directly but explicitly *contrasts* his audience-addressed speech with self-addressed speech: he vows not to address to himself what he is currently addressing to the audience.

It is certainly possible to interpret Launce's decision not to 'tell himself' merely as a ludicrous failure until we remember that he hasn't *literally* told himself anything; he has addressed a personal secret to the audience, and we have then inferred that he has also informed himself of the same thing indirectly. This inference will, in turn, be reasonable only on the assumption that there is an overlap between talking to oneself and talking to the audience, that these activities amount to more or less the same thing. Since Launce's speech explicitly juxtaposes these two types of dramatic discourse, and since his refusal to tell *himself* mirrors his previous refusal to tell *others* so closely, a more literal and more radical interpretation insinuates itself. We must consider the notion that Launce is keeping the secret from himself in the process of revealing it to the audience:

I will not tell a living soul that I'm in love, yet ...   [revealed to the audience]

I will not tell myself who she is, yet ...   [revealed to the audience]

The notion of telling the audience something that he knows but cannot express to himself is a curious one. It sounds suspiciously like unlearning the alphabet or wilfully forgetting one's own name. Under what conditions could a dramatic character meaningfully be said to keep a secret from himself in the act of sharing it with the audience?

Launce can express vital secrets about his own person and still withhold them from himself on one condition: talking to the audience must be entirely distinct from talking to himself or to other characters. This will, in turn, be possible if audience address enables him to transcend momentarily the world that is real to him (his fictional Verona). If the audience is not really real to Launce in the same way that other characters are real to him – which, as we have seen, seems likely – then he cannot *really* be said to be talking to the audience in the first place. There is thus a coherent sense in which he cannot bring himself to utter certain words to himself but can still speak them freely to the audience without actually having said them. The audience becomes the ultimate confessor, someone with whom you can share things without really sharing them. In the early 1590s, in a public theatre that was gradually finding its bearings and mixing radical metaleptic ideas with residual practices, such an act would have been only marginally more absurd than the idea of a clown standing in Verona and directly addressing a crowd in London.[59]

Considered in this way, Launce's comic refusal to tell his secret to himself becomes a wonderful satire of the absurdity that is the audience-addressed soliloquy. It is a logical consequence of the convention that

soliloquies and asides supply the audience with privileged inside information about a play-world to which they do not belong. Such a radical
reckoning can perhaps only be put into the mouth of a Clown, whose
bumbling failure to respect different levels of dramatic discourse does
not threaten the broader integrity of Shakespeare's artistic vision.

Shakespeare writes an even more daring version of such comic
metalepsis when the Fool in *King Lear* steps out of his fictional space
and reveals facts about the future that he cannot possibly know: 'This
prophecy Merlin shall make, for I live before his time' (*King Lear*,
3.2.95). When he utters this speech – which is not formulated 'in the
midst of the action' since it constitutes a scene-ending exit speech –
the Fool has clearly stepped outside the confines of the internal level
of the dramatic fiction. He is exhibiting a knowledge of future events
that is simply incompatible with the limited perspective of the individual character on the internal level of the fiction. If the Fool in *Lear*
can reveal things to the audience that he cannot possibly know, then
it's not such a huge step for Launce to reveal things that he cannot
admit to himself. If this reading is correct, it forces us to revise Robert
Weimann's account as follows: it is Launce the *character*, and not the
actor playing Launce, who detaches himself momentarily from his play-
world and colludes directly with the audience.

It might perhaps be objected here that I am tracing super-subtle, fine-
grained nuances in Launce's speech that belong more to the academic
study than to the stage. Could this self-detached intimacy with the
audience really have been communicated successfully in actual performance? Wouldn't powerful metaleptic implications of this kind have
been entirely lost on Shakespeare's audience, even if we should happen
to accept them on purely textual grounds?

This line of reasoning is, ironically, too fixated on the text, since
things that are quite lucid on the stage can often become ambiguous and
obscure on the written page. We will, of course, never know for certain
if or *how* the line 'I will not tell myself' was spoken by Will Kempe on
the Elizabethan stage,[60] but it would not have been difficult to deliver it
effectively as the metaleptic joke I have sketched here. All Kempe would
have needed to do was deliver it with the same conventional technique
normally used for solo asides. It would have been enough to hold his
hand to the side of his mouth, perhaps accompanied by a comic pause
that allowed the absurd implications to reverberate across the stage.
Such a shift from standard audience address to the close secrecy of the
guarded aside would have sent a clear signal to anyone who grasped
the most basic conventions of Elizabethan drama. The audience would
have understood that the character was now conveying an even deeper

secret than in the rest of his audience-addressed soliloquy: *I just told you things about myself that I can't reveal to my fellow characters. Now I'm telling you something so secret that I can't even utter it to myself.*

In the course of a single speech, Shakespeare manages to satirise both the general dramatic convention that he is employing (the soliloquy) and one of its specific forms (direct audience address). Launce uses a type of speech designed for the transmission of important secrets or vital information to convey a message that comes across as exceedingly mundane. This mundane 'secret' seems so momentous and weighty that he cannot even tell it to himself, but it is perfectly fine to reveal it directly to the audience, presumably because they are not really there at all. The point is subtle on the page, but it would have been easy enough to convey on the stage.

We will probably never know for certain just how Shakespeare's soliloquies and solo asides were spoken on the Elizabethan and Jacobean stage, but a close consideration of the existing evidence points in the direction of a mixed approach involving several different techniques. My main argument in this chapter has been that Shakespeare's insides were predominantly self-addressed, *pace* James Hirsh, but with the crucial addition that this was a *dominant* and not a *near-exclusive* mode of address. Hirsh is probably right that Shakespeare wrote directly audience-addressed speeches with considerable discretion, but this type of address was probably much more widespread on the Shakespearean stage than Hirsh's dichotomous view allows for. Such flexibility and variability would have made perfect sense in a cognitively blended theatrical space that had not yet been fully theorised and so could put into play a multiplicity of relations between the fictional and the actual world. Launce's decision to reveal his amorous secret to the audience but not to himself is a particularly rich example of how this freedom and flexibility could be mined for rich ironic effects without actively disrupting the medium.

If we condense all demonstrable, probable, and putative instances of Shakespearean audience address into a single word, then that word surely has to be *detachment*. This detachment can be *structural*, as when characters deliver entrance and exit speeches that place them at one remove from the rest of the action. The detachment can be *mental*, ranging from the festive and inclusive humour of Launce and the comic relief offered by Polonius or the Porter to the black sarcasms spoken by characters who have disengaged themselves entirely from human loyalty and decency (such as Iago or Richard of Gloucester). Or it can be *conventional*, as when Launce cuts through the dividing line between his play-world and the audience's actual world.

In some cases, as when Iago taunts his audience with an extended rhetorical question, it is more or less impossible for a modern interpreter to say whether the speech is meant to be audience-addressed or self-addressed. In the next chapter we will examine another interesting ambiguity surrounding Shakespeare's insides: the sometimes porous boundary between soliloquies or solo asides and ordinary dialogue.

Notes

1. Andrew Gurr, *The Shakespearean Stage, 1574–1642*, 2nd edn (Cambridge: Cambridge University Press, 1980), 101. Gurr draws primarily on S. L. Bethell's *Shakespeare and the Popular Dramatic Tradition* (Durham, NC: Duke University Press, 1944). The best analysis to date of the transition from direct address to soliloquy on the English stage is Michelle Markey Butler's PhD dissertation '"All hayll, all hayll, both blithe and glad": Direct Address in Early English Drama, 1400–1585' (Duquesne University, 2003), esp. ch. 6.
2. Janette Dillon, 'Elizabethan Comedy', in *The Cambridge Companion to Shakespearean Comedy*, ed. Alexander Leggatt (Cambridge: Cambridge University Press, 2001), 47–63.
3. Hirsh, *History of Soliloquies*, 62.
4. Hirsh, *History of Soliloquies*, 43.
5. Hirsh, *History of Soliloquies*, 43.
6. See Richardson, 'Point of View in Drama', 204.
7. Hirsh, *History of Soliloquies*, 202.
8. Hirsh, *History of Soliloquies*, 45–6.
9. James Hirsh, 'The "To be, or not to be" Speech: Evidence, Conventional Wisdom, and the Editing of Hamlet', *Medieval and Renaissance Drama in England* 23 (2010): 34–62.
10. James Hirsh, 'The Origin of the Late Renaissance Dramatic Convention of Self-Addressed Speech', *Shakespeare Survey* 68 (2015): 131–45.
11. Hirsh, *History of Soliloquies*, 221.
12. 'Shakespeare Factory Performance Vision.' <http://shakespearefactory.org/?page_id=314>, accessed 31 March 2015.
13. Bridget Escolme, *Talking to the Audience: Shakespeare, Performance, Self* (Abingdon: Routledge, 2005), 16.
14. Escolme, *Talking to the Audience*, 64.
15. Erika T. Lin, 'Performance Practice and Theatrical Privilege: Rethinking Weimann's Concepts of Locus and Platea.' *NTQ* 22:3 (2006): 283–98, 288.
16. Hirsh, *History of Soliloquies*, 198.
17. Ken Hyland, 'Persuasion and Context: The Pragmatics of Academic Discourse', *Journal of Pragmatics* 30 (1998): 437–55, 444.
18. SID text query for the words *see* and *look*.

19. See Leah S. Marcus, *Unediting the Renaissance: Shakespeare, Marlowe, Milton* (London: Routledge, 1996) and Robert Weimann, *Author's Pen and Actor's Voice: Playing and Writing in Shakespeare's Theatre* (Cambridge: Cambridge University Press, 2000).

20. Andrew Gurr, for example, subscribes to S. L. Bethell's view that '[l]ike explanatory prologues, the explanatory soliloquy or aside to the audience was a relic of the less sophisticated days that developed into a useful and more naturalistic convention of thinking aloud, but never entirely ceased to be a convention' (Bethell, *Shakespeare and the Popular Dramatic Tradition*, cited by Gurr in *The Shakespearean Stage*, 101).

21. Williams, 'On Dramatic Dialogue and Monologue', in *Writing in Society*, 44–5.

22. A. C. Bradley, *Shakespearean Tragedy: Lectures on Hamlet, Othello, King Lear, Macbeth*, 1904 (London: Macmillan, 1957), 56.

23. Hirsh, *History of Soliloquies*, 201.

24. Bradley, *Shakespearean Tragedy*, 56.

25. Hirsh, *History of Soliloquies*, 202.

26. Hirsh, *History of Soliloquies*, 84.

27. David Wiles, *Shakespeare's Clown: Actor and Text in the Elizabethan Playhouse* (Cambridge: Cambridge University Press, 2005), 102–3.

28. Hirsh, *History of Soliloquies*, 199–200.

29. Wolfgang Riehle goes further, arguing that 'in all of Iago's soliloquies in the first two acts there is a marked dichotomy between his consciousness of the spectators, *whom he addresses*, and his concentration on himself until he has generated the plan for his intrigue' (italics mine). 'Shakespeare's Reception of Plautus Reconsidered', in *Shakespeare and the Classics*, ed. Charles Martindale (Cambridge: Cambridge University Press, 2004), 109–21, 113.

30. Weimann, *Author's Pen and Actor's Voice*, 196.

31. *Literature Online* full-text search for the phrase 'how say you by', search parameters set to 'drama' and '1550–1650' including variant spellings.

32. SID coding query for **tuism**. **Tuism** is used, for example, when Mark Antony urges himself to commit suicide in *Antony and Cleopatra*; when Orlando vows to write his mistress's name on the trees of the forest; when York tells himself to bide his time in *2 Henry VI*; when the Queen in *Richard III* tells herself to withdraw; when Master Ford confronts himself with his cuckoldry; when Petruchio tells himself to speak out, Thersites confronts his own anger, Julia deplores her own ingratitude, Leontes tells himself to leave Polixenes alone, and so forth. There is a massive difference between these speeches and Polonius's glib assertion of his own excellent judgement. Shakespeare's speakers of insides typically assert their own position by means of a related trope – **illeism**, the act of speaking of oneself in the third person, which will also be discussed in Chapter 3.

33. William Shakespeare, *Hamlet*, Arden 3, ed. Ann Thompson and Neil Taylor (London: Methuen, 2006), 2.2.184n.

34. Lin, 'Performance Practice and Theatrical Privilege:'.

35. Nova Myhill, '"Hark, a word in your ear": Whispers, Asides, and Interpretation in *Troilus and Cressida*', in *Who Hears in Shakespeare?*

Shakespeare's Auditory World, Stage, and Screen, ed. Laury Magnus and Walter W. Cannon (Lanham, MD: Fairleigh Dickinson University Press, 2012), 163–80, 164.

36. Larry S. Champion, *The Evolution of Shakespeare's Comedy: A Study in Dramatic Perspective* (Cambridge, MA: Harvard University Press, 1970), 7–8.

37. Hirsh, *History of Soliloquies*, 24–5, 217. Hirsh revisits the same argument in his 2015 article: if 'soliloquies had gone back and forth between self-address and audience address … it would have been necessary to establish unambiguously in each case the transition from self-address to audience-address, but evidence for these hypothetical transitions is conspicuous by its absence'. Hirsh, 'Origin of the Late Renaissance Convention of Self-Addressed Speech', 141.

38. Simon Palfrey and Tiffany Stern, *Shakespeare in Parts* (Oxford: Oxford University Press, 2007). Their argument about the fragmented nature of the rehearsal process has been revised usefully with reference to recent theories of social cognition in Evelyn Tribble's 'Distributing Cognition in the Globe', *Shakespeare Quarterly* 56: 2 (2005): 135–55.

39. Palfrey and Stern, *Shakespeare in Parts*, 75.

40. Hirsh, *History of Soliloquies*, 27.

41. Hirsh, *History of Soliloquies*, 228.

42. Hirsh, *History of Soliloquies*, 205.

43. McConachie, *Engaging Audiences*, 44.

44. McConachie, *Engaging Audiences*, 49.

45. Bethell, *Shakespeare and the Popular Dramatic Tradition*, 27.

46. Stephenson, 'Spatial Ambiguity', 25.

47. Stephenson, 'Spatial Ambiguity', 26.

48. Stephenson, 'Spatial Ambiguity', 27.

49. As Meredith Anne Skura puts it in *Shakespeare the Actor and the Purpose of Playing* (Chicago: University of Chicago Press, 1993), x, metadramatic readings 'are interested in the way in which the plays are about their own creation'.

50. Edward Burns, *Character: Acting and Being on the Pre-Modern Stage* (New York: St. Martin's Press, 1990), 9–10.

51. Some fifty years ago, Harold F. Brooks noted how Shakespeare used the speeches of Launce and Speed to develop his play 'by means of comic parallels that illustrate and extend its themes'. See 'Two Clowns in a Comedy (To Say Nothing of the Dog): Speed, Launce (and Crab) in *The Two Gentlemen of Verona*', reprinted in *Two Gentlemen of Verona: Critical Essays*, ed. June Schlueter (New York: Garland, 1996), 71–8, 71.

52. Skura, *Shakespeare the Actor*, 158.

53. Weimann, *Author's Pen and Actor's Voice*, 193.

54. Nora Johnson, *The Actor as Playwright in Early Modern Drama* (Cambridge: Cambridge University Press, 2003), 4–5.

55. Meredith Skura summarises Bert O. States's view that Launce's dealings with his dog are emblematic of 'theater's ontological frisson … The excitement audiences always feel at theatre, States argues, depends on a condition epitomized by the fact that at any moment a real dog can misbehave drastically … the clown, who lives always at the edge where the illusional

world falls off into the audience's, makes his position even more precarious with the dog' (Skura, *Shakespeare the Actor*, 160–1).

56. Robert Weimann, *Shakespeare and the Popular Tradition in the Theater: Studies in the Social Dimension of Dramatic Form and Function*, ed. Robert Schwartz, 1978 (Baltimore: Johns Hopkins University Press, 1987), 257.

57. Robert Weimann and Douglas Bruster, *Shakespeare and the Power of Performance: Stage and Page in the Elizabethan Theatre* (Cambridge: Cambridge University Press, 2008), 83.

58. William Rowley, *A Shoo-maker a Gentleman* (London, 1638). *Literature Online*.

59. 'Although the Elizabethan theatre was moving towards a more illusionistic relation between beholders and actors, audiences were, by our standards, comparatively alienated from the dramatic illusion, rendered more frequently conscious of both the play as play and of itself as audience.' John Timpane, '"I am but a foole, looke you": Launce and the Social Functions of Humor', in Schlueter, *Two Gentlemen of Verona*, 189–211, 205.

60. Kathleen Campbell makes an ambitious case for Kempe's co-authorship of the Launce character in 'Shakespeare's Actors as Collaborators: Will Kempe and *The Two Gentlemen of Verona*', in Schlueter, *Two Gentlemen of Verona*, 179–87.

Chapter 2

Divergence

> A speech which is not spoken on an empty stage may yet be nearer to soliloquy than dialogue.
>
> M. C. Bradbrook[1]

Chapter 1 explored an important question about Shakespeare's insides: the problem of their direction. I argued for a softer version of James Hirsh's argument for the dominance of self-address in the delivery of asides and soliloquies which allowed for principled variations in Shakespeare's dramatic practice. On the first page of that chapter I also raised a second question that has so far gone unanswered:

> Can we always know if a Shakespearean actor or character intends to address another character? Will there not be hybrids and borderline cases?

A canon as vast as Shakespeare's is likely to contain many ambiguous speeches, some of which will disturb the modern researcher's attempt at quantification, and some of which may even have been written with the direct intent of *being* ambiguous. This chapter will explore some situations and conditions where speech becomes difficult to categorise on the internal level of the dramatic fiction, with a focus on those instances where this lack of clarity becomes particularly productive.

The central problem here is how to decode the putative intentions of fictional beings that do not exist independently from the text. At first sight, this looks like the sort of nightmares suffered by the orthodox psychological behaviourists of the twentieth century. If even real human minds are impenetrable black boxes, then how can we possibly hope to gaze into the mind of someone who does not even exist? The analogy between psychological and textual interpretation is instructive, for in both cases the question revolves around our limited capacity to pierce beneath a visible surface and uncover underlying structures, motivations, or intentions.

Traditional behaviourism is now seriously out of date as a psychological theory because its super-strict concern with observed, measurable behaviour not only bracketed but actively suppressed so many important questions from the scientific discourse about the mind. More recent cognitive theorists have joined ranks in stressing the continuity between everyday acts of interpretation – where our lives would quickly become intolerable if we did not infer internal mental processes from external behaviour – and what happens in dramatic performance:

> What happens cognitively when spectators project themselves into the emotional life of an actor/character on stage? Sometimes this process is called 'identification,' but this vague and encompassing word usually mixes empathy with sympathy, terms that most cognitive psychologists prefer to separate. Before spectators form a sympathetic response to actor/characters in most dramatic situations, they must ascribe beliefs, desires, intentions, and emotions to them; they must be able to 'read their minds.' To do this, spectators simulate the experiences of actor/characters in their own minds. Simulation, for many cognitive psychologists, is synonymous with empathy. How spectators read the minds of actor/characters is fundamentally no different from how people intuit each other's attitudes and intentions in real life … Our attributions of states of mind to others are not always accurate, but most people can gain a general sense of what others are experiencing by simulating that experience for themselves.[2]

Seen from this perspective, the reconstruction of fictional minds is both problematic and absolutely necessary. And yet for several decades, many professional Shakespeare critics were held in thrall by a strange theoretical dichotomy between a prescribed anti-intentionalist 'structural' view (that characters are textual constructs that have no independent existence and can only be understood as functions of a larger system) and a caricatured 'essentialist' view (in this case, the naïve notion that characters might somehow exist independently from the marks on the page).

The way around this false dichotomy is to say that literary characters are textual constructs whose design requires substantial, though often uncertain, inferences on the part of audiences or readers in order to be concretised:

> Fictional characters can be described as possible persons carrying out possible actions in a possible world. We know that Achilles and Hamlet and Winnie the Pooh don't exist in the actual world, but we also know that a competent grasp of fiction entails understanding that the wrath of Achilles or the story of Eeyore's tail are intended to be taken up as real situations involving real persons in a possible world. Our knowledge that stuffed donkeys don't actually care about what happens to their tails is not relevant to the situation.[3]

This reconstruction of fictional minds in drama sets in motion an indefinite number of inferential processes based on the character's speech and actions, descriptions by other characters, incomplete textual information (does a character stand aside?), contextual factors (timing), and conventions with varying degrees of fixity (is this a formal elegy?). Some of these inferences will be unproblematic ('Hamlet is quite upset in act 2, don't you think?') while others will be more controversial or simply wrong ('Hamlet is driven by incestuous desire for Claudius'). It has always been a central task for Shakespeare criticism to mine the rich continuum between these uninteresting poles, to separate the plausible and the compelling from the ill-founded or specious.

I will begin this chapter with an analytical survey of situations in Shakespeare's plays where the distinction between inside and dialogue becomes particularly tenuous, usually because it is hard to gauge the speaker's fictional intentions from the printed page. In some cases this uncertainty may have direct consequences for how the audience understands a character or scene in performance, and the text more or less forces the actor or director into a binary choice between different interpretations. In other situations the ambiguity is better described as a dramatically productive transgression of the conventional boundary between inside and dialogue. Characters may, for example, speak dialogue as if they were really talking to themselves, or there may be some other complicating factor that undermines the distinction between talking to oneself and talking to others, and this may sometimes give rise to rich dramatic effects.

The chapter then gives extended attention to two particularly fruitful divergences from Shakespeare's standard practice: how the conventions governing insides are affected by the intrusion of magic in *The Tempest* and by the early modern discourse of royalty in *Richard II*. In both plays we find a powerful protagonist with rhetorical boundary issues that either transcend (Prospero) or dismantle (Richard) the ordinary conventions between private and public speech. Prospero is endowed with magic powers that allow him to transcend the normal conventions of Shakespearean drama: he can overhear guarded speech and address his spellbound enemies face to face without exposing himself to their gaze or hearing. In *Richard II*, the protagonist's striking failure to adapt his speech to the situation, his tendency to speak as if he were alone when in the company of other people, has important sociohistorical and political dimensions. It is rooted in a disastrous conflation of his greedy body natural with his role as head of the body politic. In both plays, I will argue, the protagonist's divergent speech makes a central contribution to the play's total meaning and effect.

Ambiguous Insides

In some Shakespearean speeches, the direction of the actor's delivery (as discussed in Chapter 1) may not necessarily *diverge* from the standard convention, but it does become *uncertain* on the printed page. One situation that tends to give Shakespeare's editors extra grey hairs is when the content of a speech seems particularly controversial on the internal level of the dramatic fiction: is this something that the character can be expected to say openly, or does it make more sense as a solo aside? Due to the paucity of stage directions in the original printed texts, modern editors are often forced to make difficult choices on the basis of limited information. In some cases the ambiguity is also actively encoded in the original sixteenth- and seventeenth-century publications of Shakespeare's works, suggesting that the same speeches could be performed – or, at the very least, interpreted – very differently in Shakespeare's own time.

A good example is Claudius's entrance speech in act 4, scene 3, of *Hamlet*, where the King analyses the current crisis and deliberates about future actions:

> KING I have sent to seek him and to find the body.
> How dangerous is it that this man goes loose!
> Yet must not we put the strong law on him
> He's lov'd of the distracted multitude,
> Who like not in their judgement but their eyes,
> And where 'tis so, th'offender's scourge is weigh'd,
> But never the offence. To bear all smooth and even,
> This sudden sending him away must seem
> Deliberate pause. Diseases desperate grown
> By desperate appliance are reliev'd,
> Or not at all.
>
> (4.3.1–11)

The editors of the First Folio thought this was a soliloquy ('*Enter king*') while the Second Quarto rendered it as dialogue by having Claudius enter with '*two or three*' attendants. The Folio and Quarto versions may well be records of separate performances where the scene was handled differently, leaving us with two different versions of the degree of complicity between Claudius and his followers, and forcing modern editors to pick their favourite version. As we shall see in the extended discussion of *Richard II* towards the end of this chapter, such considerations about what a character can be expected to share with others can have important consequences for our interpretation of a Shakespeare play.

Another factor that may render a Shakespearean speech ambiguous – dialogue or inside? – is its precise timing. This is partly because Shakespeare's original editors were not always careful about where they placed their sparse stage directions in the text, and partly because the exact timing of a particular utterance or action must be resolved in performance. One example is the timing of exits, as when the worn-out Hector and Achilles have reached a first stalemate on the battlefield in *Troilus and Cressida*:

> ACHILLES   I do disdain thy courtesy, proud Trojan.
>   Be happy that my arms are out of use:
>   My rest and negligence befriends thee now,
>   But thou anon shalt hear of me again,
>   Till when, go seek thy fortune.   *Exit.*
> HECTOR   Fare thee well.
>   I would have been much more a fresher man,
>   Had I expected thee.
>   *Enter* TROILUS.
>
>   (5.6.15–21)

The actor playing Achilles must probably exit before Troilus enters to avoid crowding the stage and diverting the audience's attention from Hector's final line, but the act of leaving the stage is always a more gradual phenomenon than the sudden onset of a printed stage direction. It is hard to say whether Shakespeare intended Hector's line as dialogue (spoken to Achilles's back) or as an inside, and the matter can only be resolved in performance. Depending on how the scene is played, Hector will be justifying his temporary weakness either to his sworn enemy or to himself by means of self-address.

A more ominous version of this problem may apply when actors time their characters' exits from the world of the living. One horrifying example is Gloucester's sarcastic treatment of the dying King Henry, which we looked at briefly in Chapter 1:

> RICHARD I'll hear no more: die, prophet, in thy speech.
>   *[Stabs him.]*
>   For this, amongst the rest, was I ordain'd.
> KING HENRY Ay, and for much more slaughter after this.
>   O God, forgive my sins and pardon thee! *[Dies.]*
> RICHARD What, will the aspiring blood of Lancaster
>   Sink in the ground? I thought it would have mounted.
>   See how my sword weeps for the poor king's death.
>   O, may such purple tears be always shed
>   From those that wish the downfall of our house!
>   If any spark of life be yet remaining,
>   Down, down to hell; and say I sent thee thither –
>   *[Stabs him again.]*

> I, that have neither pity, love, nor fear.
>
> (5.6.56–69)

In this particular case, the detailed stage directions are authoritative enough since they come right out of the First Folio. They reassure the reader of the play-text that Henry dies quickly and can only be addressed apostrophically by the time that Richard stabs him for the second time. But in performance, where there can be no such clarity, and where Henry may still exhibit those sparks of life, Richard's sarcastic desecration of Henry's body as he ushers him to hell becomes almost unimaginably cruel.

So far we have considered some simple examples of stage business where the character's communicative intention becomes unclear. A Shakespearean line can, however, also be spoken with the manifest intention of *being* ambiguous; that is, the character may speak in a way that actively blurs the sharp dividing line between dialogue and self-addressed speech. One reason can be that characters are torn between a strong desire to express a particular point of view and an equally strong incentive to suppress it. As a consequence, they end up doing neither, muttering something that is so vague that they cannot be taken to task for it.

In his classic 'dramaturgical' account of social interaction, Irving Goffman groups this type of speech under the rubric of *realigning actions*. Goffman adapts the language of the theatre to the study of group dynamics because it helps him explore the ways

> in which the individual in ordinary work situations presents himself and his activity to others, the ways in which he guides and controls the impression they form of him, and the kinds of things he may and may not do while sustaining his performance before them.[4]

Goffman's use of the word 'audience' in the following passage should not be confused with a *theatrical* audience, since it simply stands for other persons who interact with the 'performer' (in drama, this translates into other characters):

> [P]erformers rarely seem content with safe channels for expressing discontent with the working consensus. They often attempt to speak out of character in a way that will be heard by the audience but will not openly threaten either the integrity of the two teams or the social distance between them. These temporary unofficial, or controlled, realignments, often aggressive in character, provide an interesting area for study ... The communicator has the right to deny that he 'meant anything' by his action, should his recipients accuse him to his face of having conveyed something unacceptable, and the recipients have the right to act as if nothing, or only something innocuous, has been conveyed.[5]

Shakespeare gives us a lucid example of this phenomenon in act 4, scene 1, of *Othello*, when the protagonist's disastrous inability to confront Desdemona about her supposed infidelity has gradually compressed his heart into a smouldering coal. When the newly arrived Lodovico enters together with Desdemona, Iago, and some attendants, Othello barely manages to maintain his façade and quickly withdraws upstage to read a letter from Venice as the other characters catch up on recent events:

> IAGO I am very glad to see you, signior.
>   Welcome to Cyprus.
> LODOVICO I thank you. How does lieutenant Cassio?
> IAGO Lives, sir.
> DESDEMONA Cousin, there's fall'n between him and my lord
>   An unkind breach: but you shall make all well.
> OTHELLO Are you sure of that?
> DESDEMONA My lord?
> OTHELLO [*Reads.*] *This fail you not to do, as you will* –
> LODOVICO He did not call; he's busy in the paper.
>   Is there division 'twixt my lord and Cassio?
>
> (4.1.224–30)

Othello both speaks and does not speak to the other characters here, suppressing his outburst barely enough to disguise it as a simple mis-understanding. As his anger increases, his short outbursts then become more and more uncontrolled, each time generating another puzzled 'My lord?' from Desdemona (4.1.227, 233, 237) until he finally strikes her in the face and pours out his hatred for his supposedly adulterous wife before the flabbergasted Lodovico.

This example from *Antony and Cleopatra* seems to fall somewhere between a realigning action and a solo aside:

> CLEOPATRA Is't not denounced against us? Why should not we
>   Be there in person?
> ENOBARBUS Well, I could reply:
>   If we should serve with horse and mares together,
>   The horse were merely lost; the mares would bear
>   A soldier and his horse.
> CLEOPATRA   What is't you say?
> ENOBARBUS Your presence needs must puzzle Antony,
>   Take from his heart, take from his brain, from's time
>   What should not then be spared. He is already
>   Traduced for levity, and 'tis said in Rome
>   That Photinus, an eunuch and your maids
>   Manage this war.
>
> (3.7.5–15)

Enobarbus's first line is best described as an offensive version of his second line, where the same argument is presented in more palatable form that will speak to Cleopatra's vanity. His explicitly hypothetical formulation ('I could reply') can be taken to suggest that he is muttering the first line under his breath, in such a way that it is half overheard by Cleopatra, who then asks him to repeat it. It is, however, also possible that Enobarbus is sticking his neck out by speaking the first line straightforwardly as dialogue, at which point Cleopatra simply asks him to explain his meaning. The editors of Shakespeare's plays have not managed to agree on a single interpretation.

The phenomenon of 'realigning actions' illustrates the importance of not allowing our analytical categories to impose themselves too harshly on the potential fluidity of Shakespeare's original dramatic practice. We have no reason to assume that his actors did not deliver some of the speeches that are now termed 'solo asides' in the same way as Othello does above: as half-muffled taunts, indiscretions, or even protests, producing an equally subtle response on the part of other characters that never had a chance of making it into the printed text. How many of Hamlet's interjections during the performance of the Mousetrap were originally meant to be dialogue, solo asides, or half-suppressed mutterings that were picked up and put to the side by Gertrude and Claudius? It is hard to say. We must simply accept that the act of drawing the line between aside and dialogue will sometimes be a shot in the dark. Fortunately, asides are generally so short that they will seldom have a major impact on the overriding word count for insides versus dialogue.

A Shakespearean speech may also become ambiguous because the basic distinction between self-address and dialogue has somehow lost its meaning for the speaker. Consider, as a choice example, the most famous monologue from Shakespeare's Scottish play. Macbeth has just entered the stage in the company of Seyton and an unspecified number of soldiers, and there is no textual indication that he 'stands aside' after receiving the news of his wife's death:

> To-morrow, and to-morrow, and to-morrow,
> Creeps in this petty pace from day to day,
> To the last syllable of recorded time;
> And all our yesterdays have lighted fools
> The way to dusty death. Out, out, brief candle!
> Life's but a walking shadow, a poor player,
> That struts and frets his hour upon the stage,
> And then is heard no more; it is a tale
> Told by an idiot, full of sound and fury,
> Signifying nothing.
>
> (5.6.19–28)

James Hirsh gives a good account of this speech from the perspective of delivery:

> It is unlikely that Macbeth says these words, except perhaps the first two lines, for the edification of his servant. Nor is it likely that Macbeth guards his speech from the hearing of Seyton. The speech contains no specific admissions of crimes, and someone who expresses a nihilistic attitude – nothing matters – is unlikely to care if someone overhears a non-incriminating self-addressed speech.[6]

One can rightly ask if self-address itself remains a meaningful term here, if Macbeth isn't simply speaking into thin air, to everyone and to no one. Keeping secrets to himself or engaging in private rumination has become meaningless because life itself has become meaningless. As Macbeth himself notes elsewhere, he has ceased to exist as a moral being by wading so far into a sea of blood that it is just as onerous to go back as to continue towards the other shore. There is a striking parallel here with Hamlet's classic soliloquy on the relative merits of being and non-being. The perception of life as fundamentally futile leads to detachment from self, producing a pure thematic abstraction that strips away all the individual fears, hopes, and desires that have characterised the speaker's previous soliloquies.

There is also a more specific reason why Macbeth can speak like this with full confidence that Seyton and his other followers will stand patiently and wait. He is the king and they are his servants. As we shall see repeatedly in the course of this chapter, the speaker's social class or status is often a central factor when Shakespeare worries the line between dialogue and inside.

On some occasions in the complete plays, a character will respond to the death of a high-status figure with a kind of improvised elegy that frays at the distinction between public dialogue and the personal mode of soliloquy. These speeches are diametrically opposed to Macbeth's speech above in that they seek to establish, not the *meaninglessness* of human existence, but the tremendous *value* of a single, irreplaceable life. It is in the nature of such speeches to bridge or perhaps even deny the gap between private feelings and public sentiments, between the spontaneous overflow of feelings and the conventional payment of respects. When a single human life is perceived to have touched countless other lives, the concerns of the few become the concerns of the many, at which point the personal, individual grief of the speaker extends outwards in sympathy with his fellow men – provided, of course, that it is sincere. For when the boundary between inside and dialogue is muddled, so is the question of the speaker's sincerity. A sense of theatricality may easily insinuate itself into the speaker's words because we have no external means to distinguish a powerful burst of emotion from rhetorical self-display.

This is how Octavius Caesar responds to the death of Antony:

> O Antony,
> I have followed thee to this; but we do launch
> Diseases in our bodies. I must perforce
> Have shown to thee such a declining day
> Or look on thine. We could not stall together
> In the whole world. But yet let me lament
> With tears as sovereign as the blood of hearts
> That thou, my brother, my competitor
> In top of all design, my mate in empire,
> Friend and companion in the front of war,
> The arm of mine own body, and the heart
> Where mine his thoughts did kindle, that our stars,
> Unreconcilable, should divide
> Our equalness to this. Hear me, good friends –
> > *Enter an* Egyptian.
> But I will tell you at some meeter season.

(5.1.35–49)

At first sight, the speech might seem like a clear-cut example of a heart-felt self-addressed inside, followed by an interrupted attempt at dialogue. Octavius first delivers a private elegy on his admired enemy and then turns to his war council to deliver a more public elegy that is interrupted by the arrival of the Egyptian messenger. Yet none of the three editions used systematically in this study (Arden, RSC, Norton) identifies the speech as in any way distinct from the dialogue that precedes it.

It could be that Shakespeare simply wants us to see a new side of Octavius and to deepen our sense of tragic loss at Antony's demise. But the pathos of the initial elegy is disturbed by the fact that it is not a soliloquy; Octavius is never alone on the stage, and he never leaves the eyes (or perhaps even the ears) of his war council as he delivers his speech. The elegy therefore comes to function – intentionally or not – as a form of personal display where the dead Antony becomes a mirror of Octavius's own greatness in the eyes of an onlooker:

> [AGRIPPA]   Caesar is touched.
> MAECENAS
> > When such a spacious mirror's set before him,
> > He needs must see himself.

(5.1.33–5)

Since the audience knows full well by now that they have a highly pragmatic and coolly calculating figure before them, they are also likely to find it suspect that the arrival of the Egyptian messenger should purge

Octavius of his newfound sentimentality so very quickly. After post-poning the thought of Antony to a meeter season Octavius is immedi-ately back to his usual self, and as the scene draws to a close we find him forging political plans and controlling his public image:

> Go with me to my tent, where you shall see
> How hardly I was drawn into this war,
> How calm and gentle I proceeded still
> In all my writings. Go with me and see
> What I can show in this.   *Exeunt.*
>
>   (5.1.73–7)

When we now turn to more detailed and extended examinations of divergent speeches in *The Tempest* and *Richard II*, two aspects of this discussion will remain central. How is the audience's perception of the boundary between inside and dialogue affected by the personal qualities of the speaker and by issues of status and power? I will be particularly interested in the reciprocal relationship between these two factors: that is, how personal qualities affect the exercise of power and vice versa.

The Tempest: Playing Rough with Magic

According to James Hirsh, the dominance of self-address on the English Renaissance stage was probably rooted in respect for 'the frustrating inaccessibility of the minds of others and of parts of one's own mind'. Later writers would be less embarrassed to delve into the content of individual minds and conjure up their most intimate thoughts as inte-rior monologues because 'it no longer seemed an arrogation of divine authority to provide readers and playgoers with the fantasy experience of reading minds'.[7] As we have seen, Hirsh's general argument about Shakespeare's soliloquies and asides is sound, even if it probably needs to be modified to allow for a number of principled intrusions of direct audience address. I would now like to consider an additional complica-tion: the fact that Shakespeare sometimes endows his characters with magic powers that transcend or subvert ordinary human cognition. In one extravagant case, *The Tempest*, he even allows his protagonist to transcend magically the conventions that regulate soliloquies, asides, and ordinary dialogue.

Some of the dramatic complications caused by magic in Shakespeare's plays are of a fairly academic nature. It would probably not have mat-tered greatly to a practising dramatist or actor whether Oberon was *intending to be heard* in some special, occult sense when he squeezed the love juice on the sleeping Titania's eyes:

> What thou seest when thou dost wake,
> Do it for thy true love take;
> Love and languish for his sake.
> Be it ounce, or cat, or bear,
> Pard, or boar with bristled hair,
> In thy eye that shall appear
> When thou wak'st, it is thy dear:
> Wake when some vile thing is near.

> (2.2.26–33)

Such burning questions are the province of early modern magi or modern-day coders of Shakespearean soliloquies (who cannot rule out that Oberon is intending to be *heard* on some level by the sleeping Titania).

A little earlier in the same scene, however, Oberon's magic has already created problems of a more practical nature by altering the conventional relationship between the characters on the stage. When Demetrius and Helena enter the stage in act 2, scene 1, Oberon delivers the following solo aside: 'But who comes here? I am invisible; / And I will overhear their conference' (2.1.186–7). Shakespeare cannot render Oberon invisible without clarifying this to the audience, and Oberon's somewhat awkward line is clearly intended to preclude confusion in this area. In this way, a shift on the internal level of the fiction induces an authorial response on the external level, most likely in the form of direct audience address. (Some scholars might consider this an arguable claim, but I think one has to squint very hard in order to see Oberon informing himself by means of self-address of his own invisibility and his future plans.)

These practical complications in *A Midsummer Night's Dream* are still quite trivial compared to what we find in Shakespeare's crowning achievement as a single author, *The Tempest*. The play has been subject to many productive readings over the years, from courtly wedding celebration to colonial critique, many of which should be regarded as complementary rather than competing accounts. For example, Shakespeare certainly 'capitalizes on the popular appeal of Hermetic magic, as well as its application in the court masque, knowing James I's fascination for the subject',[8] but the figure of Prospero is also carved quite clearly in the author's own image:

> Nowhere does Renaissance art speak of its powers with more confidence than in *The Tempest*, where its greatest dramatic poet, figured as an exiled duke-magician instructing kings and their heirs on a desert island, proudly catalogues the accomplishments of his theatrical magic in a list that invokes with eerie memories the entire Shakespearean oeuvre.[9]

In the last decades of the twentieth century – when so many Shakespeare scholars were in thrall to various anti-intentional philosophies that minimised the role of the biographical author – it was common practice to cast aspersions on this time-honoured reading of the play, but *The Tempest* simply begs to be seen as the culmination of Shakespeare's double vision with respect to his own work. As Katherine Duncan-Jones puts it, 'Prospero's island ... is obviously an image of the play-house and its backstage equipment.'[10] The play is his celebration of an artistic power that raises the dead from their graves and conjures forth magnificent cloud-capped towers, coupled with an intense awareness of its illusory and even morally problematic nature. To grasp the nature of the play's striking divergence from the basic speech conventions of Shakespeare's theatre as fully as possible we must first consider three central aspects: its metaleptic nature, its redemptive structure, and its problematic protagonist.

The extended analogy between art and magic in *The Tempest* unfolds within the same metaleptic framework discussed in the previous chapter: its central thematic statements project themselves outwards in concentric circles from the internal level of the fiction to the external level of the actual world. The personal pronoun in Prospero's assertion that '[w]e are such stuff as dreams are made on' can refer just to the literary characters on the internal level (Prospero's awareness of his own mortality and that of other characters that occupy his world); it can be seen as a reference to the dramatic fiction on the external level (a metaleptic statement of his own dreamlike nature *qua* literary character); and it can be a thematic statement on the external level (about the brevity and unreality of human life). The stage is a fictional microcosm, autonomous and complete unto itself, but it also stands in a mutually illuminating relation to the macrocosmic world occupied by the audience.

Considered together with the analogy between art and magic, *The Tempest*'s redemptive structure invites many biographical speculations. Was the play at least partly a fictionalised response to various personal obstacles and disappointments in Shakespeare's own lifetime? Written around the time of his own return to Stratford, it tells the prototypical story of a hero's return from exile.[11] After having written a large swathe of plays that jump back and forth in time and place, and sometimes apologising for doing so in the printed text, our author finally respects the classical unities of time, place, and action. A Stratford boy who got his lover pregnant before wedlock and who now has teenage daughters of his own allows his protagonist to control his daughter's sexuality by means of meticulously varied tactics (from active remonstrations in 4.1.13–23 to a masque in celebration of Hymen). The list could be made longer. Seen in this way, *The Tempest* is not merely a general piece of metatheatre but an act of fictionalised wish-fulfilment.

The Tempest may end as a story of redemption and forgiveness, but it is also a fantasy of personal power and vindication. Katherine Duncan-Jones calls the play 'a wish-fulfilment dream of absolute control'.[12] Many other scholars have pointed to similar undercurrents in the portrait of Prospero. Frank Kermode comments on his 'peremptoriness, arrogance, and ill temper', which he feels is outgunned only by Caliban's unique 'idiolect',[13] while Jonathan Bate finds him 'more interested in the power-structure than in the substance of what he teaches. It is hard to see how making Ferdinand carry logs is intended to inculcate virtue: its purpose is to elicit submission.'[14] As Patrick Colm Hogan notes perceptively, 'the mere fact that Prospero is so adept at magic taints his actions and his character. His power is too close to witchcraft, too near to demonic practices.'[15]

The Tempest takes these various strands (the analogy between art and magic, the layered metalepsis, the all-powerful protagonist, the painful tension between redemption and personal vindication) and weaves them into a unique textual fabric. As we shall see, Prospero's magic allows Shakespeare to suspend the basic speech conventions that normally govern his dramatic art on the internal level of theatrical communication – the mind's lack of access to other minds, the sharp divide between soliloquy and dialogue, and the guarding of asides from eavesdroppers – on behalf of his *almost* omnipotent and *almost* omniscient protagonist.

Prospero wields such power on his island that one might be forgiven for deeming him omniscient, even if he does have moments of absent-mindedness:

> PROSPERO [aside] I had forgot that foul conspiracy
>   Of the beast Caliban and his confederates
>   Against my life: the minute of their plot
>   Is almost come.
>
> (4.1.139–42)

In the first four acts we learn that his magic is subject to the same mental restrictions that apply more generally to Shakespeare's own theatrical conventions. He can command the elements, he has spirits that supply him with rich intelligence about all events on his island, but he probably cannot delve into another character's mind to see what that person is thinking. This impression is reinforced by Caliban's remark that 'his spirits hear me, / And yet I needs must curse' (2.2.3–4), suggesting that

Caliban's *thoughts* might not be open to the same kind of scrutiny. We find the same idea in Stephano's drunken insistence that 'thought is free' (3.2.125). Prospero's spirits may extend the range of his hearing considerably, but he never seems to see directly what Caliban or anyone else is thinking.

In act 5, scene 1, however, Shakespeare endows his protagonist with another powerful skill that suspends the basic principles of his own stagecraft: the capacity to regulate the boundaries of speech and perception on the internal level of the dramatic fiction. He cannot *see* what the other characters see, but he can certainly *bend* it to his own purposes. The scene begins with Prospero taking stock of a situation that has now been brought entirely under control:

> PROSPERO Now does my project gather to a head.
>   My charms crack not, my spirits obey, and Time
>   Goes upright with his carriage.
>
> (5.1.1–3)

After promising to follow Ariel's example and take pity on his enemies, Prospero delivers the legendary soliloquy cataloguing his wondrous feats of magic. This speech worries the ordinary conventions of speech in Shakespeare's plays from the very first line. Since it is spoken by a solitary character it should really be a self-addressed speech where the speaker simulates dialogical address by means of **apostrophe**, but it seems more plausible to suggest that Prospero's magic enables him to transcend magically the acoustic confines of the stage and speak directly to a world of unseen elves and spirits. As Prospero speaks, the thought of his magical feats gradually causes him to lose his focus, so that what began as a supernatural dialogue with unseen interlocutors turns into an introspective, self-addressed contemplation of his own art:

> Ye elves of hills, brooks, standing lakes, and groves;
> And ye that on the sands with printless foot
> Do chase the ebbing Neptune, and do fly him
> When he comes back; you demi-puppets that
> By moonshine do the green sour ringlets make,
> Whereof the ewe not bites; and you whose pastime
> Is to make midnight mushrooms, that rejoice
> To hear the solemn curfew; by whose aid –
> Weak masters though ye be – I have bedimm'd
> The noontide sun, call'd forth the mutinous winds,
> And 'twixt the green sea and the azur'd vault
> Set roaring war: to the dread rattling thunder
> Have I given fire, and rifted Jove's stout oak
> With his own bolt; the strong-bas'd promontory
> Have I made shake, and by the spurs pluck'd up

> The pine and cedar: graves at my command
> Have waked their sleepers, op'd, and let 'em forth
> By my so potent Art.

Prospero then announces his imminent abjuration of his powers:

> But this rough magic
> I here abjure; and, when I have requir'd
> Some heavenly music, – which even now I do, –
> To work mine end upon their senses that
> This airy charm is for, I'll break my staff,
> Bury it certain fadoms in the earth,
> And deeper than did ever plummet sound
> I'll drown my book.
>
> (5.1.33–57)

It has become a critical commonplace that Prospero considers his own art to be 'rough' in the sense of 'rudimentary, crude, imperfect' (*OED* 8.a),[16] and some scholars have done their bit in mapping its limitations.[17] The problem is, however, that reading 'rough' as 'crude' makes the passage a volte-face compared to the proud feats of magic that Prospero has just described. Nor is there any evidence elsewhere in the play that he considers his own art to be either limited or crude. The main effect of the Epilogue is rather to contrast the naked, power-less, and vulnerable human being who now stands shorn of his powers before the audience with the spectacular being that so dominated the previous five acts. Given what we know about Prospero it seems far more apposite to read 'rough' as Shakespeare typically uses this word when describing human actions, in the sense of 'characterised by vio-lence or harshness, esp. towards someone' (*OED* 11.a).[18] As Prospero puts it, his moral project is to side with his 'nobler reason' against his 'fury' (5.1.30), hoping that rational detachment from vindictive feelings will open up a tiny crack for fellow feeling to creep in.

In act 5, Prospero finally begins to 'work his end upon the senses' of the shipwrecked characters after having stayed in the background for the most part of the play. When they are brought in by Ariel he has them 'spell-stopped' (61) and can speak to them freely without expect-ing any response:

> *Here enters* ARIEL, *before; then* ALONSO, *with a frantic gesture, at-tended by* GONZALO; SEBASTIAN *and* ANTONIO *in like manner, attended by* ADRIAN *and* FRANCISCO: *they all enter the circle which Prospero has made, and there stand charm'd; which Prospero observ-ing, speaks:*

> A solemn air, and the best comforter
> To an unsettled fancy, cure thy brains,

Now useless, boil'd within thy skull! There stand,
For you are spell-stopped.
Holy Gonzalo, honourable man,
Mine eyes, ev'n sociable to the show of thine,
Fall fellowly drops. The charm dissolves apace;
And as the morning steals upon the night,
Melting the darkness, so their rising senses
Begin to chase the ignorant fumes that mantle
Their clearest reason. O, good Gonzalo,
My true preserver, and a loyal sir
To him thou follow'st! I will pay thy graces
Home both in word and deed. Most cruelly
Didst thou, Alonso, use me and my daughter:
Thy brother was a furtherer in the act.
Thou art pinch'd for't now, Sebastian. Flesh and blood,
You brother mine, that entertain'd ambition,
Expell'd remorse and nature; who, with Sebastian, –
Whose inward pinches therefor are most strong, –
Would here have kill'd your King; I do forgive thee,
Unnatural though thou art. Their understanding
Begins to swell; and the approaching tide
Will shortly fill the reasonable shore,
That now lies foul and muddy. Not one of them
That yet looks on me, or would know me: Ariel,
Fetch me the hat and rapier in my cell:
I will discase me, and myself present
As I was sometime Milan: quickly, spirit;
Thou shalt ere long be free.

(5.1.58–87)

When we consider this long speech in its dramatic context, the most striking aspect is its apparent redundancy. Only a few lines later (112–83), the six characters have been released from the spell, at which point Prospero once again confronts them with their past actions and forgives the ones that need to be forgiven. Why does Shakespeare give us two almost identical acts of reckoning and reconciliation?

Let me first clear up a frequent misunderstanding about the long speech I have just cited. The 'scene-by-scene analysis' in the RSC edition of *The Tempest* glosses the passage in this way:

> Ariel returns with the courtiers who enter Prospero's magic circle. He addresses each in turn; quieting Alonso's distress, blessing Gonzalo's kindness, and even forgiving his brother, Antonio. *They don't recognise him dressed as he is*, so he sends Ariel for his hat and rapier.[19]

The italicised passage is a fairly common misreading. It is not, as the RSC editor has it, that the other characters do not *recognise* Prospero at this stage; thanks to the charm that surrounds them inside the magic circle, they can neither *see* nor *hear* him even though he stands directly before them. Prospero makes this eminently clear to the audience towards the end of the speech: *Not one of them that yet looks on me, or would know me.* The fact that Shakespeare gives Prospero the same type of clarifying comment that we found in *A Midsummer Night's Dream* – '*I am invisible, and I will overhear their conference*' (Oberon) – constitutes direct proof that Prospero is meant to stand directly before the other characters, withheld from their perception by the magic charm. As in *A Midsummer Night's Dream*, Shakespeare would hardly have added this clarification unless it was deemed an important clue to the audience, and yet the line is rarely mentioned in scholarly discussions of this scene.[20]

It is also evident that all six characters are meant to be subject to the same spell, as indicated towards the end of one of the longest stage directions in Shakespeare: '*they all enter the circle which Prospero has made, and there stand charm'd.*'. It is true that the guilty characters (Antonio, Sebastian, Alonso) are also '*distracted*' and enter '*with a frantic gesture*' while the other three (Gonzalo, Adrian, Francisco) do not suffer the same type of agony, but the absolutes in Shakespeare's formulations (*they all* stand charmed, *not one* looks on me or would hear me) establish clearly that Prospero has closed down everyone's powers of perception. If the three characters who are not 'distracted' could actually see and hear Prospero at this point, then they would surely recognise him immediately from the content of his speech.

It is apparent, then, that Prospero's magic has suspended one of the most basic conventions of speech and action in Shakespeare's theatre. Unlike an ordinary human being or a normal Shakespearean character, he can stand directly before six others and address them directly without being either seen or heard. This is not the only curious divergence from Shakespeare's ordinary stagecraft in the speech. Prospero probably cannot read minds, but he can certainly control them, and there is even a lurid sense in which his magic seems to pierce into the inward person. His favourite punishment for wrongdoers throughout the play is that of *pinching* (1.2.330, 2.2.4), but when he now turns to Sebastian he notes that the latter's '*inward* pinches ... are most strong' (5.1.77, italics mine). There can be no certainty about the nature of these inward pinches; perhaps Prospero is simply subjecting Sebastian's entrails to a special type of physical agony on account of his treachery. There is, however, at least a potential sense in which his magic pierces deep into Sebastian's guts, perhaps even into his guilty mind.

Prospero's speech before the spell-stopped characters is not redundant because it functions as a dramatic rehearsal for his real performance later in the same scene. It allows him to straddle the roles of author, director, and character on the internal level of the fiction. He can confront the others without actually confronting them: he can speak directly and openly to them without being either gainsaid or questioned. The speech is thus a strangely one-sided forerunner to the reconciliation scene that allows Prospero to test his own capacity for forgiveness and gradually come to terms with twelve years of anger and pain before achieving his real redress. As we have seen, forgiveness does not come easily to Prospero, and he has so far had slender recourse to the sympathetic passions that Shakespeare typically places at the heart of moral action. Thanks to its suspension of the normal rules for soliloquies and asides, his theatrical rehearsal allows him to try out his lines without giving anything away before the actual performance. It also allows him to reap some of the psychological benefits of an extended confrontation without having to expose himself in return.

In Chapter 1 we saw how the path between the actual and the fictional world opened up by direct audience address enabled Launce to share secrets without really sharing them (because he shared them with an audience that was not part of his world). In *The Tempest*, the magic suspension of the boundary between dialogue and inside has a very similar effect on the internal level of the dramatic fiction: it enables Prospero to confront his enemies without really confronting them. Considered from this perspective, his dress rehearsal also embodies a central function of fiction itself: to prepare us for reality's hard knocks by allowing us to grapple emotionally and intellectually with their simulacrum.

If Prospero also comes to gaze directly into the inward pinches of Sebastian's mind or soul, which his references to the *inward pinches* could be taken to suggest, then he even enjoys a type of psychological insight that neither Shakespeare nor his fellow dramatists could arrogate to themselves: the capacity to render the secrets of the heart visible. Prospero attains power not only over his enemies, over his kin, and over the elements, but also over the troublesome chasm between mind and matter that prevents us from ever knowing what others are really thinking. Unlike the writers of the eighteenth century and beyond, who performed this magical feat by means of interior monologue, Shakespeare does not offer his tremendous gift to the audience: instead, he gives it to his protagonist. If that is the case, then Prospero's greatest exercise of power is to gain access to the one thing that no ordinary human or literary character could possibly ask for. But this radical interpretation must, I think, remain merely a tantalising possibility because it hinges on the precise interpretation of a single word ('inward').

There is still more to Prospero's power over theatrical conventions in this remarkable scene. A little further on, when he has finally revealed himself to the others, his magic allows him to override a more specific speech convention in Shakespeare's dramatic practice. As we have seen with the help of James Hirsh, a basic convention for asides in Shakespeare's theatre was that guarded speech would not be overheard if the speaker was aware of the eavesdropper's presence. But when Sebastian mutters an aside in full presence of Prospero, the latter clearly overhears him, presumably thanks to preternatural powers of perception:

> [PROSPERO] But you, my lords ...
> SEBASTIAN [aside] The devil speaks in him.
> PROSPERO.   No.
>
> (5.1.131)

To my knowledge, there is no other instance in Shakespeare of a character being overheard by the very same person from whom he guards his speech. Once again Prospero's magic produces a divergence from ordinary theatrical practices that infuses him with superhuman powers. The dramatic contrast between what Bertram Evans calls levels of discrepant awareness[21] could hardly be greater, since, in the words of Cosmo Corfield, Prospero's own 'soliloquies and asides (his most characteristic form of utterance) isolate his mental processes from the other characters'.[22]

It has always been a central question for the criticism on *The Tempest* why Prospero must renounce his magic after putting it to such effective use. Here, too, there is room for complementary insights. Like many others, Alvin Kernan points to Shakespeare's conflicted relation to his own art:

> The greatest of the world's playwrights was apparently unable to shake off his knowledge that the theater even at its best was only greasepaint trumpery, magic in its most trifling sense of prestidigitation, a few words, some stock jokes, a couple of costumes, a prop or two, music, and a dance. Here for an illusory moment, then gone forever.[23]

This is a good account of the dreamlike transience of Shakespeare's fiction, but as we have seen, the biggest problem with Prospero's art may not be its crudeness but its harshness. Scholars who have focused specifically on the play's magic in a less metaphorical sense have noted how Prospero pursues morally problematic ends by theurgic means; how his very concern with magic has underfed his humanity; and how his real-life creator needed to defuse contemporary qualms about conjurers and enchanters.[24] Hermione's statue in *The Winter's Tale* has no sooner sprung to life than Leontes attempts to exonerate this theatrical miracle indirectly to the audience: 'If this be magic, let it be an art / Lawful as eating' (5.3.110–11).

Fiction and magic are similar in that they can both suspend the ordinary laws of nature and make the impossible possible, but in *The Tempest* Shakespeare moves well beyond such vague thematic analogies. The inclusion of magic in his play as a central plot device allows him to change his own dramatic ground rules by having his protagonist transcend the otherwise immutable distinction between soliloquy, aside, and ordinary dialogue. This divergence from standard practice infuses Prospero with almost unthinkable power – not only over the elements or over his fellow human beings, but over the very dramatic medium to which he owes his existence, producing wish-fulfilling satisfactions to which no ordinary mortal could (or should) aspire. When Prospero 'works his ends upon the senses' of the other characters, he manages to orchestrate their perceptions, silence their mouths, and even decode their secretive speech as if it were ordinary dialogue.[25]

Such power – such rough magic, which threatens to reduce his fellow characters to mere puppets – is incompatible with the play's redemptive structure. Its moral dubiousness points squarely in the direction of artistic nihilism, since a character cannot assume complete control of his fictional environment without also emptying the fiction of its meaning. A brief comparison with a more recent novelistic masterpiece seems called for here, given the close parallel between the character-dramatist Prospero and the author-character Briony in Ian McEwan's *Atonement*:

> The problem these fifty-nine years has been this: how can a novelist achieve atonement when, with her absolute power of deciding outcomes, she is also God? There is no one, no entity or higher form that she can appeal to, or be reconciled with, or that can forgive her. There is nothing outside her. In her imagination she has set the limits and the terms.[26]

It has often been claimed that Prospero's failure to reconcile all characters is a failure of his magic, but there is an obvious reason why Shakespeare cannot give him the power to transform the will or the conscience of his fellow beings permanently. It is problematic enough to give Prospero the powers of a witch and a necromancer, but that would be a truly godlike power; one that was not even enjoyed by all versions of the Christian God, but found only in the most rigidly deterministic formulations of Calvinist theology.

In *The Tempest*, Shakespeare seems to cleave to the 'fundamental inaccessibility' of the human mind. He probably never grants Prospero the capacity to read minds or to change their content permanently, but he does come very close to such a transgression, and he does allow his protagonist to transcend the basic principles governing dramatic speech, shoring up a power over friends and foes that no ordinary person or Shakespearean character could possibly hope for. To the extent that Prospero was a thinly veiled self-portrait, this must have made for a very questionable satisfaction on Shakespeare's part, making the self-effacing Epilogue with its powerless and humbled theatrical servant absolutely essential. At the same time, however, Prospero's artless expression of frailty and dependency may mask another sense in which his transcendent power remains unabated. After having transcended the conventions of speech on the internal level of the fiction, he now performs another act of transcendence, becoming conscious of his own status as a fictional creation and straddling the divide between art and actuality.

Richard II: The King's Speech

Here is a simple quantitative fact about Shakespeare's *Richard II*: the King does not deliver a single soliloquy or solo aside until act 5, scene 5, when he has been imprisoned at Pomfret and discourses imaginatively with his own thoughts to make up for the lack of company. One does not need any special scientific software to notice this dramatic imbalance, and many readers will have done so in the past. But one of the many virtues of a mixed-methods approach is that the properties of a single play, scene, or character can be compared systematically to Shakespeare's other works, allowing for a more precise understanding of how it compares with his general dramatic practice.

A word count in the SID demonstrates that Richard's soliloquy generates 91 per cent of the play's insides, with the additional 9 per cent supplied by Salisbury's fearful soliloquy prophesying the King's imminent fall (2.4.18–24).[27] All private speech in the play, even that spoken by Salisbury,[28] is thus directly concerned with Richard's person, and almost all of it is delivered by Richard himself in the final act. Such an uneven concentration of a play's insides is very unusual in Shakespeare.[29] The only other plays that come close are *Much Ado about Nothing* (81 per cent spoken in act 2) and the apocryphal *Edward III*, where, as we shall see in Chapter 3, Shakespeare appears to have written almost every single inside. Such unevenness will naturally be most frequent in plays that have few soliloquies and asides, such as *Much Ado about Nothing*. Only one play in the Shakespeare canon (*Coriolanus*) rivals *Richard II*'s scarcity of insides (one inside and one ambiguous speech), and only four plays (*Henry IV, part 2, The Merchant of Venice, As You Like It,* and *Coriolanus*) have a more asymmetrical ratio between insides and dialogue.

We can conclude, then, that Shakespeare does something quite unusual when he squeezes over 90 per cent of *Richard II*'s insides into the fifth act. The most obvious consequence, at least from the perspective of the present study, is that we have to wait until act 5 for the protagonist to speak without being heard by other characters on the stage. This is a notable gap: as we have seen, insides are important dramatic devices for the construction of the inward character because the content of the private speech has not been modulated to suit the hearing of other characters. This does not mean, however, that Richard's mind remains a black box in acts 1 to 4. Although he only begins truly to *soliloquise* shortly before his violent death in act 5, he still supplies the audience with generous information about his tortured inward state along the way. More problematically, he also supplies the same information to his fellow characters on the internal level of the dramatic fiction.

Since Richard does not soliloquise or speak in asides, he expresses his secret thoughts as well as his growing desperation openly in the company of other characters. This is, presumably, what led the editors of the RSC edition to confuse his long, tortured speeches with soliloquies and conclude, erroneously, that he 'soliloquises frequently and at length'.[30] On more than one occasion, Richard realises what he is doing and quickly asks his followers to excuse or disregard his vain talk (e.g. 3.2.23, 3.170–1). This behaviour stands in powerful dramatic contrast to Bolingbroke, who, in Charles Forker's formulation, 'never soliloquizes', which means that 'we have no access to his private thoughts and must judge him almost exclusively by his actions'.[31] Partly for this reason, Bolingbroke comes across as guarded, aloof, inscrutable, and a powerful dramatic contrast to Richard.

The next question must be why Richard talks in this way. As I hope to show, the tendency of Richard's speech to undermine the conventional distinction between dialogue and inside on the level of content is more than a vital aspect of his characterisation. It also contributes more broadly to the play's interrogation of the nature of kingship, and particularly its potential moral and psychological effects on the individual holding the office. What I am after here, in other words, is the analytical nexus between character, theme, sociocultural context, and dramatic form.

Since our principal subject is the speech of a monarch it will be useful to compare Richard to two other illustrious royal figures, Cleopatra and Lear, with whom he shares a number of central characteristics. For all their differences, Lear and Cleopatra have one thing in common that cannot fail to remind us of Richard: they never deliver any speeches in private, unattended by other characters on the stage. To my knowledge, the first modern critic to point out Cleopatra's lack of soliloquies was A. C. Sprague, who argued that this 'want of soliloquy leaves her enigmatic and, it may be, all the more fascinating'.[32] The same thing has been said about Lear. According to Oliver Ford Davies, for example, Lear

> has no soliloquies. He confides nothing *directly* to the audience ... One reason for this absence of soliloquy must be that Shakespeare conceived his Lear as fatally lacking in self-awareness. Lear doesn't tell us who he is, not because he won't, but because he can't. His discovery of self comes only through madness. Bloom goes further: 'His lack of self-knowledge, blended with his awesome authority, makes him unknowable by us.'[33]

Lear's famous speeches on the heath (3.2.1–9, 3.2.14–24, 3.4.28–36) are not technically soliloquies since they are delivered in the immediate presence of other characters (the Fool and Kent). In act 3, scene 2, Lear enters the storm-ridden stage with the Fool, who attempts to reason with him: 'O, nuncle, court holy water' (10–13), but the King continues his verbal assault on the elements without even acknowledging his jester's presence (14–24). The Fool once more tries to bring him to his senses, but to no avail. When Lear has composed himself somewhat, deciding to be 'the pattern of all patience' and to 'say nothing' (36–7), Kent enters the stage and addresses the other two: 'Who's there?' (39). When Kent addresses Lear individually with a description of the storm, the latter immediately jettisons his resolve to be patient and quiet, launching yet another apostrophised speech: 'Let the great gods' (49–60). There is still no indication in either Folio or Quarto that Lear has even detected Kent, even if he must clearly be aware of his presence by now.

Lear's third speech on the heath is even more ambiguous since he switches from addressing the storm to addressing a human being, in a speech that could just as well be addressed to Everyman as to the newly arrived Kent (who will soon take the full brunt of Lear's indignation). The thematic force of the speech undermines the distinction between speaking to oneself and speaking to others; it is equally about Lear himself, about his suffering subjects, and about mankind in general. S. S. Hussey gets it just right: 'we follow laboriously the progress of Lear's self-discovery. Technically there are no soliloquies; often it is difficult to be sure whether or not the other characters are meant to overhear him.'[34] This divergence from Shakespeare's standard practice – neither soliloquy nor solo aside – has some interesting implications for my argument here.

According to James Hirsh, *King Lear* contains many speeches where a character speaks without guarding his words from the hearing of other characters. Hirsh sees this as a 'major recurring element in the play, one that emphasizes the poignant isolation of characters in their suffering'.[35] But is this really the most apposite explanation? Lear and Gloucester have many things in common, but the latter also has moments where he detaches himself from his surroundings and reflects on his experience in private speech (1.2.23–6, 4.6.273–8). In fact, most of the other characters in *King Lear* (Edmund, Edgar, the Fool, Kent, Gloucester, Cordelia, and Goneril, with Regan as the only exception) deliver more than one genuine soliloquy or aside where they reflect privately on their experience. Lear never does. Is it a coincidence that the one character who does not soliloquise in this play is also the King? Could we plausibly imagine a reversal of roles on the heath, so that the King waited patiently as the Fool vented his anger and desperation into the wind?

The fact that Shakespeare gives Lear, Cleopatra, and Richard so few soliloquies must have something to do with their royal status. The simplest explanation might be that they are typically seen in the presence of servants; to be King is to be attended, as Lear makes so eminently clear to his daughters, and to be stripped of your retinue is to be a *regius emeritus* in name but not in practice. To advance this as a *sufficient* explanation for their lack of soliloquy is, however, to formulate the problem on the wrong level. A SID search reveals that Shakespeare almost always gave his royal characters private time on the stage,[36] so the explanation must be more specific to these particular plays and the royal characters that populate them.

A second common denominator between Lear, Cleopatra, and Richard is their striking lack of self-restraint. They are driven by emotion, and their noticeable tendency to kill the messenger betrays an almost childish inability to draw the line between their own feelings, their interlocutor, and the conversational content. Cleopatra spends most of act 2, scene 3, abusing a messenger from Rome on account of the bad news he is bringing, alternately hauling him around by his hair and threatening him with a knife. In act 3, scene 3, the messenger has clearly learned his lesson and only tells the Queen what she wants to hear, at which point she concurs with Charmian that their newborn flatterer is a 'proper man' (3.3.37). Lear's 'hideous rashness' (1.1.152) is even more legendary, causing him to explode with rage as soon as others fail to say the required thing, and his susceptibility to flattery is thematised almost as actively as in *Richard II*.

King Richard's rashness, finally, was stressed by several of his early commentators. Coleridge found a character dominated by 'the most rapid transitions – from the highest insolence to the lowest humility',[37] while Dowden found him 'at the mercy of every chance impulse and transitory mood'.[38] Along similar lines, Hazlitt found his behaviour arbitrary and lacking in resolution in the first act of the play.[39] In act 1, scene 3, for example, Richard first breaks off the duel between Bolingbroke and Mowbray; then banishes the two combatants with highly unequal sentences; and then gratuitously strikes away four years from Bolingbroke's sentence because the latter's father is looking distraught. Shakespeare's portrait of the Queen is strikingly similar: she too kills the messenger (3.4.100–1), never soliloquises, and frequently unburdens her heart in the company of her followers (e.g. 2.2, 3.4).

These royal figures share a fundamental boundary issue, a basic incapacity to regulate the relationship between self and world. It is mirrored in their lack of soliloquies, in their intense emotionality, in their susceptibility to flattery, and in their lack of self-restraint. At least in the case of Richard and Lear, the rashness is matched by insensitivity to other people's needs and interests. Although Lear's moral conversion on the heath seems both genuine and moving, his newfound pathos is still best described as a great big pathetic fallacy. It is not so much a discovery of other people's radically different conditions of life as the imaginative inclusion of these lives into his own tortured mental universe. Philip Collington formulates it nicely: 'Lear's particular form of empathy does not entail placing himself in another's shoes, but merely finding another whose shoes are as uncomfortable as his own.'[40] The fact that Lear *sees* only what he himself *feels* is brought home very subtly at times:

> Come on, my boy. How dost my boy? Art cold?'
> I am cold myself.
>
> (3.2.67–8)[41]

The distinctive nature of these monarchs can be clarified even further by contrasting them with Coriolanus, who, as we saw above, is like them in that he speaks only one soliloquy and forms part of an unusually soliloquy-free play. He too has a profound boundary issue, but of a very different kind. As A. D. Nuttall has observed perceptively, Caius Martius (later dubbed Coriolanus) 'has no inside. All he has was given him by his mother and confirmed in him in the physical stress of battle.'[42] His singularly unsentimental mother Volumnia even explains that she packed her son off to war when he was so young that no mother should 'sell him an hour from her beholding' (*Coriolanus*, 1.3.5). It is not surprising, therefore, that Caius Martius, brought up on a diet of hardship and violence, comes to loathe dependence on the Roman populace more than anything else. At least until act 5 he defines himself in negative terms, as someone who maintains his integrity by standing aloof from the perceptions or expectations of the social world.

The pampered Lear and Cleopatra have the opposite problem: they cannot draw this very line between their passionate selves and the surrounding world. They paint the world with their feelings. They have no genuine inside because they recognise no genuine outside, and it is to their camp that *Richard II* belongs. (The word 'hollow' is used five times in *Richard II*, which is more than in any other Shakespeare play.)[43]

We saw above that royal status cannot be a *sufficient* explanation for the dearth of insides in these plays, since we would then expect most Shakespearean Kings and Queens to speak in this manner. It would, however, be hard to imagine a stronger historical impetus for such amorphous selfhood than the combination of great power and gross idealisation that pervaded the official discourse of late Tudor and early Stuart monarchy, to which I will now turn.

His Majesty the Baby

In 1989, Peter Hammond Schwartz drew heavily on the Tudors, the Stuarts, and Shakespeare's *Richard II* in an interesting historical meditation on 'narcissism [as] a defining feature of royal authority and, more generally, of all concentrated and consecrated forms of political authority'. In his view, the 'identification of the royal figure with an image of perfection in the orthodox psychoanalytic and mythological account does not differ greatly from formulations of the divine right of Kings emanating from the royal court in Tudor-Stuart England'.[44] Schwartz saw *Richard II* as a particularly graphic example of this phenomenon.

Is it anachronistic to describe the fictional Richard and his real-life counterparts as early modern narcissists? Schwartz himself raises the question in his article and deems it unanswerable: a commendable stance which seems even more relevant now, nearly thirty years later, when narcissism appears to be on its way out as a clinical diagnosis.[45] Soon after the publication of his article he was also taken to task for having joined a 'well-established Freudian tradition of extrapolation from the psychogenesis of the individual to the psychogenesis of a nation'.[46] My own position is that one need not be a true believer in the trans-historical validity or explanatory force of Freudian theory to grant Schwartz his central points. After all, very similar claims are made explicitly by Shakespeare's characters in *King Lear*. They tell us directly that flattery can distort a monarch's self-image to the point where he thinks himself ague-proof (4.6.104), or that bad habits that go unchecked can gradually harden into an endemic aspect of one's personality (1.1.298).

Historical explanation is a crucial part of the literary-critical toolkit, but when it hardens into historicism it paradoxically runs the risk of not being sufficiently historical, of narrowing the focus too much and advancing particularistic explanations of phenomena that require a wider historical lens. Ultimately, that history is the history of our species. While hunter-gatherer societies tend towards relatively egalitarian social structures, the tendencies described by Schwartz have almost certainly been at work in other highly stratified and complex societies with a highly unequal distribution of wealth and glory. We are also likely to find them among the metaphorical Kings and Queens of the modern media landscape.[47] In a modern study of American college athletes, Patricia and Peter Adler found that young basketball players were profoundly affected by a glorified public image that gradually ate its way into their private lives, leading to a process of 'self-aggrandizement', an inflation of their own sense of self-importance. Celebrity allowed this 'gloried self' to rise to prominence in a way that was 'detrimental to other aspects of the self, even to the point of detachment from personal identity outside athletics'.[48] There is more than a fleeting resemblance here to Richard, who has become King at such an early age and who identifies so completely with this role.

How does such a reading compare with received opinion about *Richard II*? Can we use it to explain the play's divergent handling of soliloquies, asides, and dialogue? The most widespread historical interpretation of *Richard II* relates the play to the medieval political theory, still influential in Tudor times, that a King had two bodies: a mortal body natural (signifying his physical body) and a mystical body politic (embodying the kingdom). In his classic study, Ernst Kantorowicz included a short discussion of *Richard II*, arguing that the frail body natural and ideal body politic are gradually teased apart in the play, evincing a tragic process of decomposition of divine kingship into the naked misery of the individual man. In 1996, David Norbrook noted that the two-bodies concept was now 'so familiar that it [had] been absorbed into productions of *Richard II* and [had] become the common currency of literary criticism'.[49] In 2011, Laura Estill observed that 'Kantorowicz's notions of the king's two bodies' were still often 'taken as axiomatic in early modern literary studies'.[50]

More recent Shakespeare criticism, including Norbrook's and Estill's, has modified two aspects of Kantorowicz's critical legacy: his account of early modern political theory (which is too selective) and his account of Richard (which is too sympathetic and sentimental). In the third Arden edition of the play, Charles Forker grants Kantorowicz much of his argument but sees the play's politics as a classic case of Shakespearean perspectivism: the author does not side with any political stance but actively complicates our view of absolutist and constitutional monarchy.[51] Similar ideas are expressed by David Norbrook:

> Over-emphasis on mystical bodies has given a quite misleading account of Parliamentary agency as a tragic fissuring of an organic body politic. And that distortion has also affected understanding of the political connotations of Shakespeare's play ... In his much-praised reading of Shakespeare's *Richard II*, Kantorowicz's sympathies are one-sidedly with Richard ... The whole orientation of the reading assumes that Richard is a 'unified' figure in the first part of the play and that his descent into disunity is wholly tragic.[52]

Norbrook's criticism of Kantorowicz's dominance is justified on both counts, but it also seems to smuggle in a familiar new historicist dichotomy between *authoritarian unity* and *subversive difference*. A similar dichotomy is at work when the editors of the Oxford Shakespeare edition sum up a central fault line in the criticism on the play: *Richard II* has been seen either to endorse 'an idea of sacral kingship by telling the tragic story of the sundering of Richard's unified duplex body', or to advance an 'oppositional' perspective 'where the ruler is supposed to be the servant of the commonwealth and where his rule is assured by common law and the consent of the people'.[53]

The main problem with such dichotomies is that they conflate two different questions: (1) whether or not Richard can meaningfully be said to be 'unified' as a person in the first acts of the play, and, if so, (2) whether or not that unity would have been considered 'ideal' from the perspective of early modern political theory. The alternative reading that disappears from view is that Richard's self might be 'unified' in a way that was quite unacceptable to most early modern political theorists (including exponents of the mystical two-bodies doctrine). Even a brief consideration of Edward Plowden's *Commentaries, or Reports* shows that the distinction between body natural and body politic was frequently employed by jurists to *distinguish* between the King's different capacities, and that the King could be expected to negotiate flexibly between the two.[54] *Richard II* cannot be hijacked for either politically conservative or radical purposes because the phenomenon Shakespeare explores – a monarch who loses touch with reality and drastically oversteps the limitations of his office – would have been unacceptable to most people in Shakespeare's time (with the possible exception of monarchs who dreamed of a world without parliaments).

In other words, I believe it can be argued on both historical and textual grounds that Richard's tragedy results from too much harmony between his royal office and his nature as an ordinary, fallible mortal. James Phillips gets it just right in a 2012 essay:

> Richard is deposed for abuse of office. In the eyes of his enemies, he has not conducted himself in a moderate manner and has demonstrated his unfitness for the title of King. But Richard long resists the idea that a distinction can be drawn between the office of King and the man who holds it.[55]

More than anything else, *Richard II* is a play about the disastrous consequences when the individual desire to be whole, to avoid feeling self-divided, is allowed to swallow up an entire kingdom.

It is therefore significant that Shakespeare adds not one, but *two* characters to his play that differ markedly from Richard in their astounding ability to separate their private from their public lives. Both Gaunt and York will rather sacrifice the most precious thing they have, their own flesh and blood, than scant their public duty. Gaunt even concurs with the banishment of his own son because he has been consulted as a councillor and not as a father (1.3.230), while York does not hesitate to reveal his son's high treason to the King: 'Were he twenty times my son, I would appeach him' (5.2.101–2). Shakespeare is not holding up either Gaunt or York as some sort of dramatic role model here, since their rigidity comes to be lamented either by themselves (Gaunt) or by their spouse (York). Their central function is rather to accentuate Richard's inability to distance himself from his own desires in a similar fashion. It is this failure to respect and uphold the duality of his own regal person that is the source of his tragedy: he has only one amorphous, emotion-driven, voracious body where there should have been two.

The same incapacity to grasp the fundamental duality of his regal person is at work in the deposition scene. If body politic and body natural cannot really coexist for Richard, with all the inescapable tense-ness and tenuousness that this entails, then the loss of the crown will be the death of self:

BOLINGBROKE
    Are you contented to resign the crown?
RICHARD
    Ay, no. No, ay; for I must nothing be.

(4.1.200–1)

The same wording will return in the prison soliloquy, where Richard must be either 'king' or 'nothing' (5.5.35, 38).

We can now return better armed to the question of the King's divergent speech. Richard's amorphous royal self is mirrored stylistically in more ways than his lack of soliloquy or his direct statements about his own person. We also find it in the tendency of his dialogical speech to suspend the distinction between the private and public realms.

In act 1, scene 4, when Richard decides to confiscate Gaunt's property and debar Bolingbroke from his inheritance, the audience gets to see directly what Richard is like when he is not under immediate pressure. In the absence of soliloquy, this is as close as we ever get to seeing him in a relaxed state. It is also a situation where even the most hardened of criminals might describe their own actions euphemistically – if not to themselves, then certainly to others. Moral rationalisation can be defined as 'the cognitive process that individuals use to convince themselves that their behavior does not violate their moral standards',[56] but Richard lets it all hang out without the slightest hesitation or moral compunction:

> KING RICHARD
> Now put it, God, in the physician's mind
> To help him to his grave immediately!
> The lining of his coffers shall make coats
> To deck our soldiers for these Irish wars.
> Come, gentlemen, let's all go visit him.
> Pray God we may make haste and come too late!
> ALL
> Amen!
>
> (1.4.59–65)

In most Shakespeare plays, this would have been an exit speech, delivered as an inside where the character reveals his unspeakable intentions to the audience. But surrounded by flatterers, Richard sees no important difference between talking to his entourage and talking to himself; he has nothing to hide because he has no one to hide from. The deeply sacrilegious nature of his final line – so easily lost on modern, secularised audiences, and exacerbated by a collective 'Amen' in the Folio version of the play – even betrays a boundary issue of cosmological proportions. God's anointed representative on earth is urging heaven to further his immoral ends.

What Shakespeare does in this scene, formally speaking, is to graft the expected content of an inside onto the dramatic form of dialogue, producing a queasy parallelism between suspended moral, psychological, and formal boundaries. The general amorphousness that permeates the scene stands in massive contrast to Bolingbroke's later use of innuendo and indirection when he orders Richard's death in act 5, scene 4 ('Have I no friend?'). Since Bolingbroke is a *zoon politikon*, armed with a strong sense of tact and considerable self-restraint, he knows all too well that there are things that must not be spelled out or stated openly, not even when everyone understands what is really being said. He is the early modern equivalent of the modern media-trained politician. It is an important aspect of his characterisation that he never soliloquises about his guilt but admits it in dialogue, and that he only does so at the precise point when the discovery is unlikely to have any serious repercussions.

In his excellent Arden edition of the play, Charles Forker dubs Richard the 'master of self-dramatization'.[57] This claim can perhaps be made more precise: Richard's rhetorical self-display is both copious and richly elaborated, but it is hardly masterful in the sense of *controlled*. Especially in the climactic speeches of act 3, scenes 2 and 3, when he is gradually exposed to the full extent of his powerlessness, his outbursts are beautiful, even elegant, but their rhetorical pathos is ultimately pathetic. Shakespeare never lets us forget that Richard's words mainly serve to humiliate him in the eyes of his followers, underscoring his rapidly dwindling status before the advancing Bolingbroke. What is sometimes seen as Richard's 'humility' is better described as an acute awareness of being ridiculous:

> [RICHARD]
> Mock not my senseless conjuration, lords.
>
> (3.2.23)

> CARLISLE
> My lord, wise men ne'er sit and wail their woes,
> But presently prevent the ways to wail.
>
> (3.2.178–9)

> [RICHARD]
>   Well, well I see
> I talk but idly, and you laugh at me.
>
> (3.3.170–1)

To read such passages as instances of a newfound Christ-like humil-ity on Richard's part is to miss the point made hard upon this by Northumberland:

> BOLINGBROKE
> What says his majesty?
> NORTHUMBERLAND   Sorrow and grief of heart
> Makes him speak fondly like a frantic man.
>
> (3.3.184–5)

What makes these speeches so senseless, idle, and frantic? It can hardly be their content since Richard's desperation at having the royal rug pulled from under his feet is all too human. It is what most humans could be expected to feel if faced with the imminent loss of extraordinary privileges, enormous power, a glorious public image, and quite possibly their lives. Richard's speech strikes Northumberland and others as frantic because he does not keep this inner anguish to himself, because he demeans himself and his office by failing to separate the inward from the outward man. His desperate outburst on the palace walls, spoken in the presence of Carlisle, Aumerle, Scroope, and Salisbury, is a case in point in its almost complete approximation of the language of soliloquy:

> O God! O God! That e'er this tongue of mine,
> That laid the sentence of dread banishment
> On yon proud man, should take it off again
> With words of sooth! O that I were as great
> As is my grief, or lesser than my name!
> Or that I could forget what I have been!
> Or not remember what I must be now!
> Swell'st thou, proud heart? I'll give thee scope to beat,
> Since foes have scope to beat both thee and me.

> (3.3.133–41)

Richard sounds frantic and fond precisely because he does not soliloquise, because he shares things with other characters that should normally be reserved for himself (and, directly or indirectly, the audience).

Throughout the play, Richard's references to his own person slide back and forth between the magnificent 'royal we' and the unassuming 'I'. These pronouns become a dependable index of his level of confidence – either real or projected – in his own identity as King, and his oscillation between them picks up speed in act 3 when he feels that the crown is slipping between his fingers. The word 'we' also comes with special complications that are rooted in Richard's amorphous self-image. He begins the speech on the hollow crown by instructing his followers that all their discourse must mirror his own despair, thus dismantling any potential tensions between self and world:

> Of comfort no man speak!
> Let's talk of graves, of worms and epitaphs,
> Make dust our paper and with rainy eyes
> Write sorrow on the bosom of the earth.
> Let's choose executors and talk of wills.
> And yet not so, for what can we bequeath
> Save our deposed bodies to the ground?
> Our lands, our lives and all are Bolingbroke's,

And nothing can we call our own but death
And that small model of the barren earth
Which serves as paste and cover to our bones.

(3.2.144–54)

This is another example of Shakespeare's stylistic blurring of Richard's dialogue. It could easily be taken for another instance of the 'royal we' if it were not for the presence of a plural noun ('lives') and two imperatives ('Let's'). Richard has merely replaced his hollowed-out *royal we* with a *loyal we*, a group of individuals whose interests are so tightly associated with his own that they seem to have little external substance.[58] Once this *loyal we* is in place, he gradually shifts his attention to a genuinely plural *royal we* that allows him to project his own misery on a grand historic scale. This 'we' is first composed of former Kings who suffered similar misfortunes –

For God's sake let us sit upon the ground
And tell sad stories of the death of kings –

(155–6)

– and then turned into a pure abstraction of Royalty: 'For within the hollow crown / That rounds the mortal temples of a king / Keeps Death his court' (160–2). The final part of Richard's speech is still focused entirely on himself, but this time in the role of ordinary mortal. He knows by now that exaggerated 'pomp' has filled him with the 'vain conceit' that he was 'brass impregnable' (3.2.168). But since he still does not recognise any substantive social boundaries – between himself and his followers, or between body natural and body politic – he once again arrives at a simple either/or where he is either a king or a person of flesh and blood:

Throw away respect,
Tradition, form and ceremonious duty,
For you have but mistook me all this while.
I live with bread like you, feel want,
Taste grief, need friends.

(172–6)

In act 4, scene 1, when Richard has finally been deposed and proceeds to smash the mirror that was supposed to show him 'what a face I have, / Since it is bankrupt of his majesty' (4.1.266–7), Bolingbroke picks up on his inability to separate essence from semblance, inside from outside, self from surroundings:

[RICHARD]
Mark, silent King, the moral of this sport,
How soon my sorrow hath destroyed my face.

BOLINGBROKE
> The shadow of your sorrow hath destroyed
> The shadow of your face.

(4.1.290–3)

Richard still finds it difficult to imagine himself as a private *and* a public person, as a body natural *and* a body politic, as someone who exists for others as well as for himself, and who must therefore negotiate conflicting demands. Hence his only retort to Bolingbroke's challenge must be to deny categorically the reality of the outward person:

KING RICHARD   say that again!
> The shadow of my sorrow? Ha, let's see.
> 'Tis very true, my grief lies all within;
> And these external manners of laments
> Are merely shadows to the unseen grief
> That swells with silence in the tortured soul.
> There lies the substance.

(293–9)

Richard may be speaking in dialogue here, but his words mark an important new development in the play by cordoning off a space of private feeling that cannot be fully shared. As such, they lead us directly to his final soliloquy in act 5, scene 5.

Soliloquy at Last

So far Shakespeare has given us a King who cannot imagine any identity for himself beyond his public role; who never enters the stage alone or engages in private speech; and who finds it impossible to keep his innermost feelings and thoughts to himself. As a consequence of this inability to detach himself from his own desires, to exist for others and not just for himself, he comes to be perceived as fond, idle, and foolish. In act 5, scene 5, this very same character is suddenly placed in solitary confinement.

The fact that the soliloquising Richard now finds himself in a situation that is sometimes defined as a form of torture is rarely touched upon in the literature on the play. Many decades of psychological research have shown that being denied human intercourse for an extended period of time can have drastic psychological and physiological consequences, from insomnia to confusion or even insanity.[59] The individual effects naturally depend greatly on the length of confinement as well as the personal characteristics of the inmate, and the same is true of the strategies people use to cope with their imposed isolation.

Many prisoners find survival in physical exercise, prayer, or plans for escape. Many carry out elaborate mental exercises, building entire houses in their heads, board by board, nail by nail, from the ground up, or memorizing team rosters for a baseball season.[60]

The authors of a study of coping strategies among captured American aviators in Vietnam found that these 'aggressive, assertive, energetic, action-oriented men' had become highly focused on controlling their environment and anticipating the moves of their captors. At least in their own self-report, they were not particularly given to internal dialogue of the kind that we find in Richard's soliloquy: 'Talking to Self was rated as only somewhat more useful than Thinking About Suicide.'[61]

Seen from the perspective I have sketched here, Richard's forcible removal from human contact looks almost like a psychosocial experiment. What will happen when this person, of all people, suddenly finds himself without an audience on the internal level of the dramatic fiction, faced with a binary choice between soliloquy and silence? To see the character from this perspective hopefully captures some of his humanity as well as his individuality. It can also help us see his soliloquy less as the final stage in some abstract developmental trajectory and more as a contingent response to an intensely stressful situation. More than anything else, it will give us a lucid example of the connection made in Chapter 1 between audience address and the speaker's *structural* and *mental* detachment from the rest of the action.

There is a fairly widespread agreement among Shakespeare scholars that Richard's soliloquy reveals a man who has learned little from his experience, and that its chief function is to inspire audience sympathy in preparation for his tragic death. Coleridge in his time found Richard's inconsistency to be a singularly consistent trait: 'what he was at first, he is at last, excepting as far as he yields to circumstances'.[62] A similarly unchanging view of Richard is put forward by a central authority on Shakespearean soliloquy, Wolfgang Clemen: '[W]ith its mixture of narcissism, metaphorical embellishment of the situation, brooding reflection and theatricality, the soliloquy is in keeping with the character of the King as we have come to know it during the five Acts of the play.'[63]

Other scholars grant Richard at least a fleeting measure of insight. Rolf Soellner thinks he 'grows toward a limited self-awareness ... The particular charm of *Richard II*, as John Middleton Murry has said, lies in the "nascent self-awareness" with which it is pervaded.'[64] According to Charles Forker, finally, Richard may have 'shed enough of his egoism to be capable of gratitude', but his private 'attempt to come to terms with his own tragedy seems flawed and incomplete, too deeply mired in pain, regret and frustration to allow for full moral self-recognition or access to the larger, more metaphysical significances of his experience'.[65]

Those who claim that Richard does not change very much are right about one thing: the final soliloquy is the ultimate proof of his endemically self-centred nature. His mind is still firmly fixed upon his own person. There are no worries about the Queen, about Aumerle, or about the future of his subjects under Bolingbroke. For all its elaborate and imaginative rhetoric, the content of the soliloquy boils down to a set of simple propositions: *All my thoughts are discontented. All humans are discontented until they die. Everyone hates me.* His mind still oscillates between two Lear-like poles of suffering – his own microcosmic grief, mirrored narcissistically by a grieving macrocosmic humanity – while everything else is thrown to the wind.

In Richard's soliloquy, the studied rhetorical artifice that has characterised his discourse takes on a slightly new direction. When he now calmly taps into the *contemptus mundi* tradition, he mainly seems to be playing with words, engaging in a rhetorical exercise, keeping his mind busy, as one might expect from an expert rhetorician who desperately needs to occupy his mind with just about anything. One part of his speech deserves particular attention here for three related reasons: because it constitutes Richard's only act of explicit self-criticism, because it is directly concerned with his boundary issue, and because the previous criticism on the play has not done justice to its significance and complexity.

When Richard hears music coming from behind the prison wall, the musician's failure to keep time reminds him of his analogous failure as King:

> And here have I the daintiness of ear
> To check time broke in a disordered string;
> But for the concord of my state and time,
> Had not an ear to hear my true time broke:
> I wasted time, and now doth time waste me.

> (5.5.45–9)

The third line, 'for the concord of my state and time', seems crucial, but it is not without interpretative cruces. How, for example, are we to read the preposition 'for'? It can be read plausibly as *for the sake of*, or *with regard to*, so that the entire passage reads something like this: 'I can hear that this music is out of beat, but I was deaf when the same thing happened to my kingdom.' One cannot, however, rule out *for* in the sense of 'because of, on account of' (*OED* 21), which is what the word means when that other vain Shakespearean King is told that he will have 'as many dolours for thy daughters as thou canst tell in a year' (*Lear*, 2.2.229). Even more poignantly, 'for' could mean '[b]y reason of, under the influence of (a feeling or subjective condition)' (*OED* 20). In this reading, which picks up on the explicit contrast with Richard's 'time' and his 'true time' in the next line, the concord between his state and time is not a desired end but the underlying problem. The line constitutes a direct admission on Richard's part that the (unhealthy and ultimately illusory) concord between his 'state' and 'time' was to blame for his overthrow.

The plot thickens when we proceed to examine the words 'state' and 'time'. The rich complexity of the word 'state', first of all, can be explored usefully in relation to Sonnet 29, where Shakespeare appears to play deliberately on its polysemic nature. The poet first 'alone beweep[s] my outcast state' (his social situation), but then remembers his beloved patron and 'scorn[s] to change my state with kings'. In the second usage, 'state' takes on one or more of these additional meanings: 'high rank or exalted position; a (specified) office of power or importance' (*OED* 15.a); the 'costly and imposing display associated with monarchs and other persons of high rank', perhaps even be an ironic reference to the King's 'throne' (*OED* 16, 17.a); or 'a person's private means or income' (*OED* 31). Since Shakespeare's Richard III famously offered to trade an entire kingdom for a horse, we cannot rule out the possibility that the poet is turning down the hypothetical offer of 'a commonwealth, a nation' (*OED* 25).

These meanings are all potentially at work when Richard says 'my state', and the phrase 'my time' is almost equally indeterminate. Charles Forker wilfully glosses the phrase as 'my time on earth', discounting two highly relevant senses out of three in the *OED*:

> 3.a. Usu. with possessive. The period during which a person or thing lives, occupies a particular position, is active in a particular sphere, exercises influence or dominance, etc.; (sometimes) *spec.* the lifetime of a person or animal. Also: one's lifetime up to the present (esp. in *in one's time*).
>
> 4. Usu. with possessive or *of*. The period which is contemporary with the life, rule, activity, dominance, etc., of a specified person or group of people; (a person's) age, era, or generation.
>
> 5.a. A particular period in history, or in the existence of the world, the universe, etc.; an era, an epoch, an age.

When Richard says 'my time', he can plausibly be taken to mean three different things: my life as an individual, my reign, or, even more abstractly, the historical period or epoch associated with my reign (i.e. something analogous to the 'Elizabethan period').

It could well be objected here that someone with the right frame of mind and the *OED* in hand can make a single Shakespearean word mean almost anything. But that is true only so long as we disregard the nature of the speaker and the verbal context. If Richard were an ordinary Englishman, the inclusion of a possessive pronoun in the phrase '*my* state and time' would have acted as a powerful semantic constraint. It would do what possessives normally do; it would separate that which pertains to the individual from that which is clearly not his own. When a recently deposed King says 'my state', however, he may be referring to his personal situation, his royal office, his throne, his courtly splendour, his property, his country, his eponymous historical epoch, or perhaps to all of these at the same time. They were all recently *his* in a formal sense, which means that the play's formal and thematic boundary issue reproduces itself semantically on the lexical level. As we have seen, something similar happens to the word 'time', whose meaning ranges from the short lifespan of a single puny mortal to the epoch that bears Richard's name.

This semantic boundary issue, which is causally connected to the larger boundary issue we have been exploring, is one reason why Richard's conceit on music and time becomes difficult to follow. Consider, as a choice example, his highly condensed observation that

> my time
> Runs posting on in Bolingbroke's proud joy,
> While I stand fooling here, his jack o'the clock.

> (58–60)

The 'time' referred to here is not, as the Arden 3 once again has it, Richard's 'life on earth', but the epoch that corresponds to his reign as King of England. The point that is being made here – with reference to the Elizabethan postal system, where a colossal number of horses formed an intricate system of relays across the country – is that the world goes on as before, that the individual horse/King becomes unimportant as soon as it has submitted its legwork in the service of the postal/regal system. *My time* has quickly become *Bolingbroke's time*. The one thing that sets Richard apart from most other Kings, and which forces him to 'stand fooling here' in the dungeon, is that he has outlived his own reign and must confront the full relativity of his transient glory.

In the passage above, the 'I' that Richard uses to identify himself as a person has finally become firmly detached from his regal identity. This leads us directly to the most novel thing about his soliloquy, which sets it apart even from Hamlet's introspective brooding: its deeply metacognitive nature. The speech is the product of a mind that detaches itself from itself, observes itself, and discovers a multitude of internal voices. This widened gap between a contemplative self and an experiencing self marks a new development not only in Richard's career, but also in Shakespeare's. Earlier Shakespearean soliloquists certainly testify to their mental confusion, characterise themselves in some detail, think up stratagems, and give eloquent, extended expression to particular passions. One of them, Antipholus of Syracuse, even stands back and interrogates the reality of his sense experience. But as far as I can tell, no soliloquy written in Shakespeare's hand before this time contains anything like Richard's proto-Cartesianism.

This difference is most apparent when we compare this speech to its most similar-sounding predecessor: the King's final soliloquy in *3 Henry VI*, where another powerless monarch expounds on the weight of his princely cares and winds an elaborate literary conceit around the passing of time (2.5.1–54). In that play, Henry dreams of death and conjures up a pastoral fantasy that might rid him of his princely troubles. He is, simply put, one person who wishes he were someone else. Richard, by contrast, detaches himself from his own experience; he stands back to describe a sequence of shifting thoughts and passions as if they were separate from himself.

It is the same old self-centred Richard, but a version of that Richard whom solitary confinement has taught a measure of emotional and cognitive distance from his beloved self. This detachment is nothing less than the necessary foundation for those abilities that he has so far lacked: to adapt one's behaviour to shifting circumstances, to imagine oneself in more roles than one, and to speak prudently when in the presence of other people. In this way, *Richard II* gives us the necessary counterpoint to Edgar's flat insistence in *Lear* that we should '[s]peak what we feel, not what we ought to say' (5.3.323).

The most important result of Richard's newfound self-detachment is a nascent capacity to see himself for what he is:

> Thoughts tending to content flatter themselves
> That they are not the first of fortune's slaves,
> Nor shall not be the last – like silly beggars
> Who, sitting in the stocks, refuge their shame,
> That many have and others must sit there;
> And in this thought they find a kind of ease,
> Bearing their own misfortunes on the back
> Of such as have before indur'd the like.

(5.5.23–30)

Here Richard conjures up several mental habits that contributed directly to his own downfall: his complacency, his vulnerability to flattery, and his attempt to evade shame or guilt by mentally collapsing his misfortune into that of former Kings. The interesting paradox is that he is really diagnosing his own disastrous incapacity to tolerate negative emotion – his tendency simply to look away from it, to cover it in a thick layer of flattery, or to explain it away – and yet manages to remain philosophically aloof from the pain that such recognition ought to bring. Engaging in a fictive conversation with his own personified thoughts creates the impression that he is not really talking about himself.

To whom is Richard's soliloquy addressed? In Chapter 1, I argued that Shakespeare's tendency to write speeches designed for direct audience address was closely correlated with the character's degree of detachment. His soliloquists are more prone to replace self-address with audience address if they are *structurally* separated from the rest of the action or *mentally* detached from their environment. These criteria come together in Richard's soliloquy, and they are also combined with a familiar relational marker:

> Now sir, the sound that tells what hour it is
> Are clamorous groans which strike upon my heart.

> (55–6)

The expression 'Now sir' is employed only twice in Shakespeare's complete insides. It is used in Richard's final soliloquy and in the one speech that practically all scholars (including James Hirsh) consider to be audience-addressed: Launce's leave-taking speech in *Two Gentlemen of Verona*. This is an excellent example of the close connection between characterisation and dramatic form. Forcibly detached from his fellow characters, and even mentally detached from himself, Richard quickly finds himself a new audience in the *actual* audience.

One of Richard's chief vehicles for this detached view of himself is the rhetorical figure of speech known as **prosopopoeia**, or 'personation', defined by the early modern rhetorician Abraham Fraunce as 'feigning the speech of another'. It is one of several techniques that allowed Shakespeare to infuse the private speech of his characters with a dialogical quality. When he applies this technique to his own scrupulous thoughts, Richard turns them into dialogical counterparts, allowing him to externalise and examine his own shortcomings at one remove from his own person. In the next chapter we will look more closely at such dialogical elements in the Shakespearean inside.

Notes

1. Bradbrook, *Themes and Conventions of Elizabethan Tragedy*, 118.
2. McConachie, *Engaging Audiences*, 66.

3. Michael Bristol, 'Introduction: Is Shakespeare a Moral Philosopher?', in *Shakespeare and Moral Agency*, ed. Michael Bristol (London and New York: Continuum, 2010), 1–12, 2.

4. Irving Goffman, *The Presentation of Self in Everyday Life*, 1959 (London: Penguin, 1990), 9.

5. Goffman, *Presentation of Self*, 187.

6. Hirsh, *History of Soliloquies*, 156.

7. Hirsh, *History of Soliloquies*, 43.

8. Patrick Grant, 'The Magic of Charity: A Background to Prospero', *Review of English Studies*, n.s. 27: 105 (1976): 1–16, 10.

9. Alvin B. Kernan, *Shakespeare, the King's Playwright: Theater in the Stuart Court 1603–1613* (New Haven: Yale University Press, 1995), 160. 'It was Thomas Campbell in 1838 who first found in Prospero a piece of Shakespearean autobiography, a claim developing out of the assumption that the play was Shakespeare's farewell to the stage.' Stephen Orgel, 'Introduction', in William Shakespeare, *The Tempest*, Oxford Shakespeare edition (Oxford: Oxford University Press, 1987), 1–89,10.

10. Katherine Duncan-Jones, *Ungentle Shakespeare: Scenes from his Life* (London: Arden Shakespeare, 2001), 238.

11. Brian Sutton has explored how Prospero's plight echoes the Biblical story of Joseph in the Book of Genesis: both are ostracised victims of jealous siblings who make new lives for themselves in a faraway land and eventually take similar action when the tables are finally turned: 'Joseph and Prospero eventually achieve positions of power over their former betrayers. Both can choose from a variety of actions: seek revenge, test for signs of repentance, or offer forgiveness. Both men eventually choose all three, in the aforementioned order.' Brian Sutton, '"Virtue rather than vengeance": Genesis and Shakespeare's *The Tempest*' *Explicator* 66:4 (2008): 224–9, 226.

12. Duncan-Jones, *Ungentle Shakespeare*, 239.

13. Frank Kermode, *Shakespeare's Language* (London: Penguin, 2000), 291.

14. Jonathan Bate, 'Introduction', in William Shakespeare, *The Tempest*, RSC edition, ed. Jonathan Bate and Eric Rasmussen (Houndmills: Macmillan, 2008), 1–19, 8. For a negative appraisal of Prospero's actions compared to early modern standards of good parenting, see Hiewon Shin, 'Single Parenting, Homeschooling: Prospero, Caliban, Miranda', *SEL* 48: 2 (2008): 373–93.

15. Patrick Colm Hogan, 'Narrative Universals, Heroic Tragi-Comedy, and Shakespeare's Political Ambivalence', *College Literature* 33:1 (2006): 34–67, 56. Hogan identifies a general Shakespearean tendency to infuse the vindication of a slighted hero with considerable ambivalence. Although we rarely doubt whom we should root for, 'Shakespeare's use of familiarization, his intensification of the suffering of the usurper figure (through the death of his/her beloved and his/her own suicidal tendencies), and his association of the deposed ruler with the invading enemy, all tend to make the heroic plot much more ethically and emotionally ambivalent' (40).

16. 'rough, adj. (and int.)'. *Oxford English Dictionary Online* (Oxford: Oxford University Press, 2010–15), accessed 13 February 2014.

17. See, for example, Rose Abdelnour Zimbardo, 'Form and Disorder in *The Tempest*', *Shakespeare Quarterly* 14: 1 (1963): 49–56.

18. Full-text search for keyword='rough' and author='Shakespeare', in *Literature Online*. Cosmo Corfield sees Prospero as 'an irritable old man unable to control his emotions' and 'a powerful mage, but his powers are going in the wrong direction. Far from being holy and impassively just, they have become impurely applied to mean and personal ends. And Prospero's use of the phrase "rough magic" recognizes this.' 'Since Prospero has failed his magic, and his magic has failed his humanity, he will abjure it.' Cosmo Corfield, 'Why Does Prospero Abjure His Rough Magic?', *Shakespeare Quarterly* 36: 1 (Spring, 1985): 31–48, 36, 42, 47.
19. Shakespeare, *The Tempest*, RSC edition, 98, italics mine.
20. It is telling that *Understanding Shakespeare*, the experimental service linking selected Shakespeare plays to scholarly citations in the JSTOR archive, lists up to eleven citations for every single line in Prospero's speech except this one. *Understanding Shakespeare* <http://labs.jstor.org/shakespeare/the_tempest>, accessed 9 April 2015.
21. Bertram Evans, *Shakespeare's Comedies* (Oxford: Clarendon, 1960).
22. Corfield, 'Why Does Prospero Abjure', 45.
23. Kernan, *Shakespeare, the King's Playwright*, 167.
24. See, for example, Corfield, 'Why Does Prospero Abjure'; Grant, 'Magic of Charity'.
25. Reginald Scot, one of Shakespeare's acknowledged sources, attributes the 'invocation, binding, and dismissal of spirits' to the category of 'preternatural' magic. Scot's section on the supposed powers of witches is often reminiscent of Prospero: witches can, for example, 'alter the minds of judges, that they can have no power to hurt them ... procure to themselves and to others, taciturnity and insensibilitie in their torments ... strike terror into the minds of them that apprehend them ... manifest unto others, things hidden and lost, and foreshow things to come; and see them as though they were present ... alter mens minds to inordinate love or hate'. Philip C. Almond, *England's First Demonologist: Reginald Scot and the 'Discoverie of Witchcraft'* (London and New York: I. B. Tauris, 2011), 146, 33–4.
26. Ian McEwan, *Atonement* (London: Vintage, 2001), 371.
27. All references to *Richard II* in this chapter have been taken from William Shakespeare, *King Richard II,* Arden 3, ed. Charles Forker (London: Methuen, 2002).
28. Only the F version of *Richard II* has the Captain exit before Salisbury, which means that Q could conceivably conceive the final speech as dialogue, but this is a very unlikely interpretation since Salisbury's speech passes moral judgement on people who do what the Captain says he will do (jump ship).
29. SID, matrix query for **play** and **act**.
30. Jonathan Bate, 'Introduction', in William Shakespeare, *Richard II*, RSC edition, ed. Jonathan Bate and Eric Rasmussen (Basingstoke: Macmillan, 2010), 1–22, 11.
31. Charles Forker, 'Introduction', in William Shakespeare, *King Richard II*, Arden 3, 1–169, 23.
32. Sprague, *Shakespeare and the Audience*, 76.
33. Oliver Ford Davies, *Playing Lear* (London: Nick Hern, 2003), 59.
34. S. S. Hussey, *The Literary Language of Shakespeare*, 2nd edn (London: Longman, 1992), 189.

35. Hirsh, *History of Soliloquies*, 156.
36. SID coding query (**class** > Royal). Kings and Queens speak insides in no fewer than twenty-three Shakespeare plays (as explained in Appendix 3, Emperors are regarded as synonymous with royalty for the purposes of coding). Of the remaining plays, most have no royal insides for the prosaic reason that they have no royal characters (they typically have Dukes at the apex of the dramatis personae). Only three plays contain Kings (or in one case, a 'Prince') who do not soliloquise, two of whom are minor characters (*All's Well* and *Much Ado*): a fate also shared by the Queen in *Richard II*. In only one play, the highly collaborative work *1 Henry VI*, do we find a King with a substantial role who delivers no insides: Henry enters the stage in act 3, scene 1, and never utters a single line where he does not either address another character directly by means of a title or personal pronoun or ask a direct question that is answered.
37. Samuel Taylor Coleridge, *Shakespearean Criticism*, ed. Thomas Middleton Raysor (London: J. M. Dent, 1961), 223–4.
38. Edward Dowden, *Shakespeare: A Critical Study of His Mind and Art*, 1875 (London: Routledge & Kegan Paul, 1967), 193–202.
39. William Hazlitt, *The Collected Works of William Hazlitt*, ed. W. E. Henley (London: J. M. Dent, 1903), vol. 8, 278–84.
40. Philip D. Collington, 'Self-Discovery in Montaigne's "Of Solitarinesse" and *King Lear*', *Comparative Drama* 35 (2002): 247–69, 260.
41. Compare Walter Pater's brilliant observation that Shakespeare's kings are ordinary mortals who have been 'thrust upon greatness, with those pathetic results, the natural self-pity of the weak heightened in them into irresistible appeal to others as the net result of their royal prerogative' ('Shakespeare's English Kings', in *Appreciations: With an Essay on Style* (London: Macmillan, 1910), 185–204, 199.
42. A. D. Nuttall, *The New Mimesis: Shakespeare and the Representation of Reality* (London: Methuen, 1983), 116.
43. See *Shakespeare's Words* <shakespeareswords.com> accessed 10 November 2015.
44. Peter Hammond Schwartz, '"His majesty the baby": Narcissism and Royal Authority', *Political Theory* 17:2 (1989): 266–90, 266–7, 275–6.
45. On the theoretical problems involved in applying a term like narcissism to Shakespeare, see the introduction to Eric Langley's *Narcissism and Suicide in Shakespeare and His Contemporaries* (Oxford: Oxford University Press, 2009). In a review of Langley's book, Heather Hirschfield notes that the diagnosis 'narcissistic personality disorder' was dropped from the 2013 version of the *Diagnostic and Statistical Manual of Mental Disorder* in favour of a more complex diagnostic approach: see *Shakespeare Quarterly* 63:2 (2012): 265–70. In *The Tears of Narcissus: Melancholia and Masculinity in Early Modern Writing* (Stanford: Stanford University Press, 1995), finally, Lynn Enterline integrates early modern and psychoanalytic perspectives on narcissism.
46. Patricia Springborg, '"His majesty is a baby?": A Critical Response to Peter Hammond Schwartz', *Political Theory* 18:4 (1990): 673–85, 674.
47. The widespread suspicion that 'celebrities are a highly narcissistic group' may have something to it; see S. Mark Young and Drew Pinsky, 'Narcissism

and Celebrity', *Journal of Research in Personality* 40: 5 (2006): 463–71, 463.

48. Patricia A. Adler and Peter Adler, 'The Glorified Self: The Aggrandizement and the Constriction of Self.', *Social Psychology Quarterly* 52:4 (1989): 299–310 (abstract).

49. David Norbrook, 'The Emperor's New Body? *Richard II*, Ernst Kantorowicz, and the Politics of Shakespeare Criticism', *Textual Practice* 10:2 (1996): 329–57, 329.

50. Laura Estill, '*Richard II* and the Book of Life', *SEL* 51:2 (2011): 283–303, 287.

51. Forker, 'Introduction', 18–23.

52. Norbrook, 'Emperor's New Body', 348.

53. Anthony B. Dawson and Paul Yachnin, 'Introduction', in William Shakespeare, *Richard II*, Oxford edition (Oxford: Oxford University Press, 2011), 7–46, 17.

54. Kantorowicz stresses that the 'difficulties of defining the effects as exercised by the body politic – active in the individual king like *a deus absconditus* – on the royal body natural are obvious … It was anything but a simple task [for the Tudor jurists] to remain consistent when one had to defend at once the perfect union of the King's Two Bodies and the very distinct capacities of each body alone.' Ernst H. Kantorowicz, *The King's Two Bodies: A Study in Medieval Political Theology* (Princeton: Princeton University Press, 1957), 12. Consider these brief passages from Plowden's *Commentaries, or Reports* (London: S. Brooke, 1816): '[I]f land descends to the king from his common ancestor, he shall have it by reason of his body natural, for this body is privy to the descent, but the body politic is not privy to this descent' (213). 'The king has a double capacity, and that both remain in him at one same time, and that he may take in the one or in the other, according as the gift is made to him … And if the body politic is more large than the body natural, then it is more beneficial for king *Henry* 7 to take it in that than in the other capacity' (237–8). In other words, a prudent king had to know in what role he was currently acting: am I receiving this particular gift, or holding this particular property, in the capacity of body natural or body politic?

55. James Philips, 'Practicalities of the Absolute: Justice and Kingship in *Richard II*', *ELH* 79:1 (2012): 161–77, 169.

56. Jo-Ann Tsang, 'Moral Rationalization and the Integration of Situational Factors and Psychological Processes in Immoral Behavior', *Review of General Psychology*, 6:1 (2002): 25–50, 26.

57. Forker, 'Introduction', 34.

58. The same is true of his parting words to the newly exiled Queen, which could conceivably be spent trying to cheer her up. But Richard urges his wife to tell the Frenchmen 'the lamentable tale of me' (5.1.44) and to join him in sorrow's union: 'So two together, weeping, make one woe' (86–7).

59. Peter Scharff Smith, 'The Effects of Solitary Confinement on Prison Inmates: A Brief History and Review of the Literature', *Crime and Justice* 34:1 (2006):441–528.

60. Atul Gawande, 'Hellhole', *The New Yorker*, 30 March 2009), accessed 14 January 2014.

61. John E. Deaton, et al. 'Coping Activities in Solitary Confinement of U.S. Navy POWs in Vietnam', *Journal of Applied Social Psychology* 7:3 (1977): 239–57, 249.
62. Coleridge, *Shakespearean Criticism*, 72.
63. Clemen, *Shakespeare's Soliloquies*, 25–6.
64. Rolf Soellner, *Shakespeare's Patterns of Self-Knowledge* (Columbus: Ohio State University Press, 1972), ch. 6, 97–122, 110.
65. Forker, 'Introduction', 46.

Chapter 3

Dialogue

After years and years of battering their soldiers' heads against the walls of Troy, the Greek commanders in Shakespeare's *Troilus and Cressida* finally admit to themselves that they cannot do without their proudest and most pre-eminent warrior, Achilles. The situation has quickly grown intolerable since he not only refuses to lift his sword but is actively lowering the morale of the Greek troops by poking fun at their superiors. The task of bringing Achilles back into the fold is assigned to the sly fox Ulysses, who understands that the best way to conquer an ego of such galactic proportions is to rob it of its fuel. On his advice, the Greek commanders systematically deny Achilles his wonted attention, producing a rapid identity crisis in the Thetan lord that makes him easy prey for a cunning rhetorician:

ULYSSES   Now, great Thetis' son.
ACHILLES What are you reading?
ULYSSES   A strange fellow here
    Writes me, that man, how dearly ever parted,
    How much in having, or without or in,
    Cannot make boast to have that which he hath,
    Nor feels not what he owes, but by reflection,
    As when his virtues shining upon others
    Heat them, and they retort that heat again
    To the first giver.

ACHILLES   This is not strange, Ulysses.
    The beauty that is borne here in the face
    The bearer knows not, but commends itself
    To others' eyes; nor doth the eye itself,
    That most pure spirit of sense, behold itself,
    Not going from itself; but eye to eye oppos'd
    Salutes each other with each other's form;
    For speculation turns not to itself
    Till it hath travell'd and is mirror'd there
    Where it may see itself. This is not strange at all.

                                                    (3.3.94–111)

When Achilles takes the bait, smugly informing Ulysses that he is merely spouting commonplaces, the latter quickly turns an *epistemological* argument (that we know ourselves through other people) into a *moral-political* argument (about our rights and obligations), and perhaps even an *ontological* one (that other people make us who we are):

> ULYSSES I do not strain at the position –
>   It is familiar – but at the author's drift,
>   Who in his circumstance expressly proves
>   That no man is the lord of anything,
>   Though in and of him there be much consisting,
>   Till he communicate his parts to others;
>   Nor doth he of himself know them for aught,
>   Till he behold them form'd in the applause
>   Where they're extended; who, like an arch, reverb'rate
>   The voice again; or, like a gate of steel
>   Fronting the sun, receives and renders back
>   His figure and his heat.

(112–23)

As Nancy Selleck observes in *The Interpersonal Idiom*, the

> overall problem Ulysses speaks to is the impossibility of knowing oneself immediately: not only can one not see what one is, but one cannot even feel 'what one owes' except through the mediation of others. In this conception, if the self can be said to have form or substance, it is only via the reflected appraisals of others ('applause', for instance), in which one's 'parts' find their only reality, or extension.[1]

Such words must be both appealing and frightening for a child of Narcissus, but the element of appeal evaporates quickly when Ulysses denies Achilles the expected account of his brilliance. Instead he passes it on to Ajax:

>   I was much wrapt in this,
>   And apprehended here immediately
>   The unknown Ajax. Heavens, what a man is there!
>   A very horse, that has he knows not what!

(123–6)

The success of this rhetorical stratagem is brought home lucidly in the closing lines of the scene, where a botched attempt at introspective mirroring on the part of Achilles is ridiculed by the spiteful Thersites:

> ACHILLES My mind is troubled, like a fountain stirr'd,
>   And I myself see not the bottom of it.
>   *Exeunt Achilles and Patroclus.*

THERSITES Would the fountain of your mind were clear again, that I might water an ass at it: I had rather be a tick in a sheep than such a valiant ignorance. *Exit.*

(306–10)

In its concern with rhetoric and the dialogical structure of self-knowledge, this scene from *Troilus and Cressida* weaves together two analytical strands in this third chapter on the Shakespearean inside: that self-knowledge is a dialogical process, and that a dialogical self is, by extension, also a rhetorical self. How are we to understand the psychological and rhetorical mechanisms in this Shakespearean scene, and what happens to these mechanisms when a character switches from dialogue to soliloquy? I will begin with a brief exploration of human selfhood and self-talk which integrates perspectives from philosophy, psychology, and neuroscience. This introductory section will be followed by a systematic overview of dialogical elements in Shakespeare's insides, with a particular focus on selected rhetorical figures of speech that endow these speeches with a dialogical quality. My main focus here will lie on **apostrophe**, Shakespeare's dialogical device par excellence, but we will see that attention to less frequent dialogical traits can also be instructive. The chapter ends with an analysis of *Hamlet* that seeks to demonstrate how a new type of literary data can underpin new insights into one of the most famous works in world literature.

The Dialogical Self

Let us leave both drama and rhetoric aside for a moment and concentrate on the dialogical underpinnings of human selfhood. Since Nancy Selleck is interested in how early modern culture talked about the self, her analysis of Shakespeare and his contemporaries gravitates towards historical specificity on the linguistic level. What she finds in the early modern period is a 'radically interpersonal' idiom which stands in contrast to more atomistic accounts of the self in later centuries. The question is, however, whether the dialogical self was really so specific to Shakespeare's historical period, given that similarly far-reaching claims have been made in more recent times.

The dialogical self has been a favourite concern among humanistic and social-scientific theorists from George Herbert Mead to Mikhail Bakhtin. According to the influential moral philosopher Charles Taylor, the self

can never be described without reference to those who surround it ... My self-definition is understood as an answer to the question Who I am. And this question finds its original sense in the interchange of speakers. I define who I am by defining where I speak from, in the family tree, in social space, in the geography of social statuses and functions, in my intimate relations to the ones I love, and also crucially in the space of moral and spiritual orientation within which my most important defining relations are lived out ... This is the sense in which one cannot be a self on one's own. I am a self only in relation to certain interlocutors: in one way in relation to those conversation partners who were essential to my achieving self-definition; in another in relation to those who are now crucial to my continuing grasp of languages of self-understanding – and, of course, these classes may overlap. A self exists only within what I call 'webs of interlocution'.[2]

It can be objected here that Taylor's sweeping formulations run the risk of collapsing *Homo sapiens* into *Homo sociologicus*. The absolutes in his formulations – where the self *can never* be described, *one cannot be* a self on one's own, I am a self *only* in relation to interlocutors, a self exists *only* in webs of interlocution, and so forth – seem to imply that human beings have no innate nature and are constructed only through the appraisals and demands of the social group. As Kenneth Baynes points out in an otherwise favourable assessment of Taylor's philosophy, it has been a frequent complaint against him that a self capable of *conversing*, *defining* itself, or asking *questions* cannot constitute itself out of thin air. Somewhere deep down there has to be an antecedent self that does the constituting.[3]

As Baynes notes, Taylor's socially constructed self needs to be anchored in deeper and more evolutionarily ancient processes of the kind that are currently being explored in neuroscience and related fields.[4] Human identity is profoundly shaped by language and culture, as modern-day literary theorists have stressed so fervently, but the nature and extent of this shaping force cannot be properly understood in isolation from the evolved circuitry upon which it operates. From the perspective of Jaak Panksepp's affective neuroscience, even cognitive theorists – those self-proclaimed champions of universality and nature–nurture interactionism – have focused too much on higher-order mental structures that are massively dependent on environmental input as they develop. They have done so at the expense of more fundamental evolved processes that we share with other mammals and that help us orchestrate our sensory experience and motor skills into a coherent sense of who we are.[5] Among other useful things, these ancient processes inform me or my cat that it is *my* hand or paw that is fiddling with the toy mouse, so if I sink my teeth into this particular appendage then it's going to *hurt*.

These neuroscientific perspectives constitute a useful reminder of the common humanity that suffuses our cultural being,[6] offering a partial corrective to inflated claims about radical paradigm shifts on the level

of culture or society. The primal dialogue that makes us human begins
in early infancy, with the rhythmic give-and-take between infant and
caretaker,[7] and it continues even when our original conversational partners are no longer with us. It does so because we have internalised their
voices and made them our own – even when this means reacting forcefully against them, perhaps even in a lifelong argument or quarrel. Over
time, it is complemented with new dialogical relations that may well
exert an even more powerful effect on our personalities, values, and
beliefs. The aggregate sum of these voices becomes the internal yard-
stick by which we measure and define ourselves, for good and for bad.

As it matures, the human self-interpreting animal asks ever more
complicated questions about its own nature: *What am I like? What
can I become? Who or what made me who I am? How important am
I? What is my purpose in life?* Most, if not all, of these questions must
be answered with reference to other people, and they are processed in
parts of the brain that are highly susceptible to environmental influences. We can therefore expect them to be answered quite differently
in different social, cultural, and historical contexts. It is also likely that
they will become more pressing in complex or fast-changing environ-
ments with high demands on individuals to adapt their behaviour (as
opposed to collectivist societies characterised by low social mobility
and high mutual dependence).[8] One of the hallmarks of Shakespearean
drama is its engagement with this historical transition from collectivism
to individualism.[9]

When we read or watch a Shakespeare play, his fictional approximations of human beings will therefore confront us with a mixture of same-
ness and difference. If real human beings have always been inveterately
dialogical by nature, and if Shakespeare's fictional characters are mod-
elled mimetically upon real human beings, then some of this dialogical
disposition may persist even when his characters find themselves alone.
There is now a sizeable corpus of research suggesting that private self-
talk – the real-life equivalent of the self-addressed speech – performs a
number of important functions for humans and that it persists well into
adulthood.[10] As John Freeman notes, with reference to an eclectic mix of
sociology, cognitive theory, and discourse analysis, 'soliloquizing is not
as far removed from ordinary speech situations as some would portray
it' because our private speech never loses its intersubjective dimension.[11]

In a 2012 article on the topic of dialogical soliloquies, James Hirsh
notes that

> Shakespeare often turns what would seem to be the most monologic type
> of utterance possible into one of the most acutely dialogic ... [so that] a
> character might experience a multiplicity of emotions that do not coexist

in a stable hierarchy, that a character might have profound emotions that are unvoiced but clearly implied, that a character might express an emotion ironically or facetiously for his own amusement, and that a character might engage in the process of talking himself into an emotion.[12]

Shakespeare's insides are indeed riddled with concrete dialogical elements, some of which are amenable to systematic analysis. His characters will, for example, simulate the speech or presence of others, either as imagined counterparts or as internalised others, or they will act as their own externalised sounding boards or argumentative adversaries. They will address characters or entities that either are absent or have no powers of hearing; they will address themselves in the second person, refer to themselves in the third person, or ask themselves questions that either are in earnest or have predetermined answers. They will adopt the hypothetical perspective or mimic the speech of an absent or imaginary counterpart, or respond to things that others have said either offstage or onstage.

Many of these dialogical elements can be explained as a mimetic component in Shakespeare's art, as an indirect reflection of the human psyche as mediated through his dramatic fictions. That is to say, on the *internal* level of dramatic communication, Shakespeare pays intuitive tribute to the dialogical nature of human beings. We come into this world predisposed for social dialogue, our selfhood is gradually built up in relation to other people, and such habits die hard when we talk only to ourselves (especially when we are emotionally upset or self-divided).

Such dialogical elements must also have reflected another exigency on the external dramatic level for Shakespeare and his contemporaries. In Chapter 1, I embraced a modified version of Hirsh's argument that Shakespeare's soliloquies and solo asides were typically self-addressed in the form of actual speech. Now if the late Elizabethans and Jacobeans were quite sparing in their use of audience address, usually preferring a more self-contained mode of stage delivery that distanced itself from the practices of the medieval stage, then long soliloquies would have been particularly risky when it came to holding the audience's attention. Characters prating at length to themselves do not necessarily produce engaging, lively, dynamic drama. So on the *external* level of dramatic communication, the dramatist's need to avoid boring his audience with long, introverted, self-addressed speeches would have created another strong dialogical impetus. In the words of Simon Palfrey and Tiffany Stern, it is 'obvious enough why soliloquies might be so liberal with short speech units and brisk prosodic shifts. In the absence of other characters to respond to or react against, the discrete speech has to produce its own "dialogue".'[13]

I will now turn to a systematic overview of selected figures of speech and other techniques that imbue Shakespeare's insides with much of their dialogical qualities: **apostrophe** (addressing absent or abstract entities), **reported words, prosopopoeia** (adopting the role of an external speaker), **illeism** (speaking of oneself in the third person), and **tuism** (addressing oneself in the second person). In this discussion the mixed-methods component will become increasingly pronounced as I combine descriptive statistics on these selected tropes with brief close readings, culminating in a reading of *Hamlet* which integrates detailed attention to Shakespeare's text with meso-level quantitative patterns. This reading will focus on Shakespeare's usage of different types of **apostrophe** and the complex interplay between **erotema** (the rhetorical question) and ordinary questions.

Apostrophe

The figure of speech known as **apostrophe** was Shakespeare's single most important device for infusing his insides with the energy and dynamism of dialogue, and it will therefore receive considerable attention in this chapter.[14] In his rhetorical manual entitled *Directions of Speech and Style*, written in 1599, John Hoskins observed that it is 'most convenient sometimes for the bringing in of life and luster to represent some unexpected strains beside the tenor of your tale, and act, as it were, your meaning'. One way that this can be accomplished, according to Hoskins, is by apostrophe, or 'feigning' the 'presence' of an interlocutor.[15]

That sounds neat enough, but as Margaret McKay has shown in a useful dissertation on the subject,[16] the brief definitions of apostrophe offered by Tudor rhetoricians such as Puttenham or Peacham were typically disappointing and vague. In fact, they sometimes failed to include the one criterion that both Hoskins and modern literature professors deem absolutely central: that the addressee must either not be present or not be able to hear. After closely considering the definitions together with the concrete examples in the rhetorical handbooks, McKay concludes that early modern apostrophe is 'a direct address of unusual mental or emotional intensity to a person, object, or abstract quality which in the most effective examples is almost invariably absent or incapable of hearing. It may be marked by an emphatic turning.'[17]

The hedging in McKay's revised definition opens the door to so many borderline cases and exceptions that the concept becomes unworkable from a quantitative perspective. The criterion of emotional intensity is a case in point, since, as McKay herself points out, '[m]ost of the asides [in Shakespeare] which are conventionally spoken to a person who does not hear have none of the intensity necessary to qualify as apostrophes', and it is therefore sometimes 'difficult to make a clear distinction'.[18] Since the speaker's degree of emotional involvement in a particular passage cannot be quantified, it cannot be used as a criterion that isolates **apostrophe** from ordinary dramatic speech. The problem is compounded by the fact that some of the most emotionally intense passages in Shakespeare's insides are *invectives* that cannot safely be categorised as direct address to an absent person. Who can say for certain if Hamlet is speaking in the second or third grammatical person when he calls Claudius a 'villain, villain, smiling damned villain!' (1.5.106)?

When we remove the unworkable criterion of emotional intensity, **apostrophe** can be defined more broadly in terms of its central characteristic: it is speech addressed to someone or something that the speaker knows cannot hear. As with the basic definition of the inside, a negative definition becomes even more precise: an **apostrophe** is a speech or part of a speech that is not addressed to a character who is physically present on the stage and can be expected to hear what is said.

Perhaps controversially, this negative criterion includes those situations where characters address spiritual beings or deities that are never visible on the stage but whose relationship to the speaker may still be conceived as both direct and intimate. Alan Richardson puts it nicely: 'Whether prayers to God – who, as Wordsworth's Goody Blake puts it, is "never out of hearing" – can be considered "proper" apostrophes may be a question for theological debate as much as for literary theory to decide.'[19] The coding in the SID controls partly for this problem by applying a separate code for apostrophes addressed to deities, allowing for easy separation from other types.

Defined by means of this inclusive negation – not addressed to another character on the stage who can be expected to hear – **apostrophe** is at work in one-fifth of the insides in the complete plays (or 20 per cent). It also appears to be a Shakespearean trademark. A comparison with the most widely accepted attributions to collaborators in the Shakespeare canon shows that Shakespeare always uses more apostrophe in his insides than do his colleagues. On average, he writes more than twice as much (Table 3.1). The difference is substantial in *Timon of Athens*, *Titus Andronicus*, and *Two Noble Kinsmen*; moderate in *Pericles*; and negligible in the unusually **apostrophe**-free *Henry VIII*. In *Edward III*, finally, Shakespeare appears to have written almost all of the play's insides, or 92 per cent. Table 3.2 lists the number of words spoken as

Table 3.1 Shakespeare's usage of **apostrophe** in insides compared to that of his co-authors.

Play	CO-AUTHOR			SHAKESPEARE		
	Insides	Apostr.	% apostr.	Insides	Apostr.	% apostr.
Titus Andronicus	262	16	6%	546	184	34%
Timon of Athens	899	231	26%	1107	870	79%
Pericles	1204	387	32%	218	94	43%
Henry VIII	515	16	3%	415	17	4%
Two Noble Kinsmen	2446	213	9%	871	251	29%
Total	5326	863	16%	3157	1416	45%

Table 3.2 Shakespeare's contributions to the insides of *Edward III*.

Scene	Word count, insides
1.1	
1.2	296
2.1	781
2.2	363
3.1	
3.2	
3.3	
3.4	
4.1	50
4.2	72
4.3	
4.4	
4.5	
4.6	
4.7	
5.1	
Total	1562

insides in each scene of *Edward III*, with the most frequent attributions to Shakespeare shaded grey.

As we shall see in the final section of this chapter, which will concern itself with the dearth of dialogue in *Hamlet*'s insides, Shakespeare's use of **apostrophe** also varied over time according to a distinctive pattern.

Some types of Shakespearean **apostrophe** are naturally more common than others. The most frequent one is, unsurprisingly, address to an offstage character, which makes up almost half (190) of the total number of apostrophes in the complete insides (410). Shakespeare's characters also frequently deliver apostrophes to abstractions (45), to the dead (36), to nature or natural phenomena (24), and to deities or spiritual beings (47). Beyond these basic categories, the diversity of individual objects is truly astounding. Shakespeare's characters address apostrophes to bullets, their tongues, mythical ancestors, windows, verses they have written, the world, a sheet of paper, a country, a piece of cloth, a bracelet, a book, their hearts, their souls, their sinews, their bosoms, their knees, swords, rapiers, drums, daggers, crowns, diseases, their eyes, naked wretches, the air, wax seals, their thoughts, their pens, their imagination, leaves, their ears, blood, bloodstains, candles, their powers, medicine, another person's breath, the time of day, a grave, elves, or a house. Other objects of Shakespearean apostrophe include gold, the speaker's own hands, a name, a jest, a dog, a portrait, a garden, sailors, a hallucination, and an infant.

We are not done yet. In *Timon of Athens*, the most **apostrophe**-laden play in the Shakespeare canon, the relative word count for **apostrophe** rises to a staggering 53 per cent of the total word count for insides, and Shakespeare also subjects this figure of speech to an interesting formal experiment. When Timon has left Athens he produces a long, nested apostrophe (4.1.1–40) that first addresses the hated city and its walls and then moves inside for an extended reckoning with its inhabitants. In the course of this remarkable volley of apostrophes he addresses a number of *stock citizens* (matrons, slaves, fools, bankrupts, servants, maids, sons); abstracted *moral virtues* (piety, fear, religion, peace, justice, truth, domestic awe, night-rest); *moral vices* (lust, liberty); various *diseases* (plagues, sciatica, itches, and blains); and, finally, the gods.

Timon of Athens is, by Shakespearean standards, an unusually univocal cry of outrage against how some people exploit their fellow men while others allow themselves to be abused. It has very little of the moral and characteriological perspectivism and complexity that we normally expect from Shakespeare's mature art. This furious one-dimensionality is reflected in the monotony of the play's insides, whose almost exclusive function is to bring home the corrupt nature of Timon's suitors and his own recklessness in allowing himself to be used by them. Of the play's 23 insides, no fewer than 22 contain comments on Timon's imprudence or the immorality of his suitors. The only speech that departs from this pattern is a brief aside spoken by the greedy suitor Lucullus, who speculates about the nature of his next gift from Timon's hand (3.1.5–7). It may be tempting here to posit a general causal connection between moral outrage and a propensity for **apostrophe** – on the assumption that strongly emotional speech would veer naturally towards the grammatical second person – but as we will see in the reading of *Hamlet* below, the mechanisms involved are far more complex and more interesting.

Given the ubiquity of **apostrophe** in Shakespeare's soliloquies and asides, it is all the more striking to find a single play – *The Comedy of Errors* – where the **apostrophe** count suddenly drops to zero. The play is in fact unique in a more fundamental sense since its insides do not contain a *single* dialogical device of the kind explored in this chapter. Based on Plautus's *Menaechmi* and *Amphitruo*, it tells the farcical story of how Antipholus of Syracuse is repeatedly mistaken for his wealthy twin. As a result, he finds himself in a series of absurd situations where complete strangers take him for their old acquaintance, their business associate, or even their husband. The cognitive dissonance produced by his mistaken identity forces Antipholus to disengage mentally from a world that makes no sense to him, to the point where he repeatedly questions the reality of his experience: Is this real? Is it magic or witchcraft? Am I dreaming? *The Comedy of Errors* has four instances of such literal 'reality checks', which is more than any other Shakespeare play. Only *The Tempest* has as many, and *Macbeth* has three, and these are both plays where the illusory nature of reality and the relative trustworthiness of one's senses are important motifs.

Since Antipholus of Syracuse speaks ten insides that add up to 74 per cent of the private speech in *Comedy of Errors*, his verbal dominance of the play's private speech is an important reason for its scarcity of dialogical elements. As he withdraws further and further into the recesses of his own mind, his semi-Cartesian detachment is mirrored in his basic vocabulary. A word frequency search in the SID[20] reveals that the second-person pronouns 'thy' and 'thou' rank as the fifteenth and eighteenth most frequent words in Shakespeare's complete insides, and that the insides of the average Shakespeare play yield sixteen instances of these pronouns. The insides in *Comedy of Errors*, by contrast, slip consistently into the first and third person: there is not a single instance of a second-person pronoun in their total of 706 words! The only other play where something similar happens is *King John*, whose principal soliloquist, the Bastard, exhibits a similar detachment and dominates the private speech with a similar percentage (78 per cent).

A related stylistic and narratological trait that sets *Comedy of Errors* apart from most other Shakespeare plays is that more than half of the words spoken as insides (54 per cent) are devoted to the **reporting** of onstage and offstage events, which we will examine more closely in the next section. This is the highest score for this narrative speech act in any Shakespeare play, and more than twice as high as the Shakespearean mean (24 per cent). This intensified **reporting** has a double rationale on the internal and external levels of dramatic communication. Antipholus the character needs to recount and process his strange experiences in

Table 3.3 The five highest percentages for **reporting** in Shakespeare's complete insides.

	Words	Reporting	% reporting
Comedy of Errors	713	381	53%
King Richard III	1923	916	48%
Two Gentlemen of Verona	3160	1272	40%
The Tempest	1768	710	40%
King Richard II	601	234	39%

order to make sense of them, just as Shakespeare needs to control a convoluted plot where the same actor probably plays two different characters who look the same. It is worth mentioning here that the other four plays with the highest **reporting** counts for insides all have a character that (1) speaks a dominant share of the play's insides (Antipholus 74 per cent, King John 78 per cent, Richard III 72 per cent), and/or (2) dominates the play by some other means, such as Prospero's control of the plot and the choric status of Launce's soliloquies (Table 3.3.).

In *The Comedy of Errors*, Shakespeare intensifies Antipholus of Syracuse's mental isolation stylistically by giving him the majority of the play's insides; by withholding **apostrophe** or any other dialogical tropes from his speeches; by eradicating any second-person pronouns from his speech; and by having him engage in an extended commentary on his experience. I would now like to consider how the same basic phenomenon, the inverse relation between *character isolation* and **apostrophe**, plays out in a much later, collaborative work.

The Two Noble Kinsmen (c. 1614) offers a second example of how Shakespeare's selective deployment of **apostrophe** subserves the construction of character and theme. This late play – a reworking of Chaucer's *The Knight's Tale*,[21] written in collaboration with John Fletcher – tells the story of two virtuous cousins, Palamon and Arcite, whose bond of eternal friendship and loyalty is compromised when they are taken prisoners of war by Duke Theseus and fall head over heels in love with the Duke's sister-in-law, the beautiful and chaste Amazon Emilia. In a subplot without precedent in Chaucer, Fletcher and Shakespeare describe how the Jailor's Daughter's unrequited passion for Palamon leads to her social isolation, madness, and eventual reabsorption into society by means of marriage to another man.

It is a critical commonplace that Fletcher and Shakespeare extended the pessimism in their literary source by painting a dismal picture of the amorous passions: 'Where Chaucer is concerned with the subtle workings of Fortune, *The Two Noble Kinsmen* lays its emphasis on the destructive power of love.'[22] Some, like Eugene Waith, have seen

Kinsmen as a play where love 'does not score very high',[23] while others have studied it in terms of a conflict between love and reason,[24] between sexual and non-sexual love, between love and friendship,[25] or between friendship and marriage.[26] Many, if not most, critics have noted its indebtedness to classical models of ideal friendship, including Montaigne's rather forceful distinction between friendship and marriage (the former an idealised merger and the latter an amalgam of socially prescribed duties and intemperate biological necessities).[27]

Throughout their play, Shakespeare and Fletcher remind us of love's tendency, not only to join people together, but also to divide them from each other as well as from themselves. The play also explores how human beings conceptualise or experience love in quasi-mathematical terms as something that can be divided up, counted, or measured. What unites these two strands of dramatic inquiry (like two sides of a single coin) is a fearful suspicion that love might not be the synergetic life force we would like it to be but a desperate zero-sum game based on limited resources. Such a love will sunder in the very act of joining together; it will produce misery in the very act of producing happiness, and even getting what you want will make you self-divided through the act of forgoing something else.[28]

The subplot constructed around the Jailor's Daughter deserves special attention here for three reasons. She is the play's most salient example of love's divisiveness; her soliloquies constitute an unusual structural and rhetorical experiment on Fletcher's and Shakespeare's part; and she holds a special place in the play's deployment of **apostrophe** by means of insides.

When the Daughter breaks Palamon out of prison she knows that this amounts to a death sentence for her unknowing father, but her unreciprocated desire is frustrated when Palamon does not meet her at the designated place. In an uncommon move, quite unheard of in the rest of the Shakespeare canon, Fletcher and Shakespeare separate the Daughter from the rest of the action by means of four soliloquies (scenes 2.4, 2.6, 3.2, and 3.4) that run parallel to the main action as they chart her intensifying depression and eventual loss of sanity. This cordoning off of a character in quasi-choric fashion from the rest of the action is an effective formal correlate of the play's thematic concerns. Unrequited and unsanctioned love has driven the Daughter into the wilderness, into a loneliness so profound that she finally loses her mind, and even into a parallel theatrical space that is not occupied by another fictional soul. Even the fearful Prologue and Epilogue, who are similarly separated from the rest of the action, have someone to talk to (the audience).

The special nature of the Daughter's soliloquies can be illuminated by the play's general deployment of insides as well as its specific distribution of **apostrophe** in these speeches. *Kinsmen* ranks among the most 'inward' plays in the Shakespeare canon, quantitatively speaking, in that its percentage of insides (14 per cent) is twice that of the average Shakespeare play (7 per cent). It is outstripped only by *Cymbeline* (17 per cent) and *The Two Gentlemen of Verona* (16 per cent), and rivalled only by two other plays (*Macbeth* and *3 Henry V*). This formal aspect of the play's inwardness can be described more precisely. *The Two Noble Kinsmen* is one of only eight Shakespeare plays that have no unmistakeable solo asides. We can therefore conclude that the stage characters in *The Two Noble Kinsmen* are more solitary – in the literal, objective sense that the actors who play them deliver more of their lines alone on the stage – than their counterparts in most other Shakespeare plays.

In her acutely isolated state, separated from the rest of the action, the Jailor's Daughter has strong psychological reasons to speak in apostrophes. She does use this rhetorical device occasionally, addressing her absent father as well as abstractions like Love, the State of Nature, her own life, and finally a hallucinatory vision of a shipwreck. What sets her speeches apart from the dramatic discourse of love in this period, however, is the complete absence of any apostrophes addressed to Palamon, her love object, who is consistently referred to in the third person. As a result, she comes to speak 50 per cent of the play's total insides but only 17 per cent of its apostrophes.

This stylistic anomaly can be expected to intensify the audience's sense of her isolation as she gradually unravels in her loveless theatrical space. It sets her soliloquies apart from those of the other characters, such as Arcite's long soliloquy where he apostrophises both his beloved Emilia and his newfound enemy Palamon (3.1.1–30); Palamon's returning the favour by apostrophising Arcite (3.6.7–10); and Emilia's apostrophes to both kinsmen in her long self-divided soliloquy (4.2.1–54). The Daughter's dearth of **apostrophe** and gradual descent into insanity are also reminiscent of the pattern we found in *The Comedy of Errors*, where the cognitively estranged Antipholus questions his own sanity, forgoes **apostrophe**, and replaces the latter with speech elements that suggest psychological distance (the grammatical third person, reality checks, reported words).

The Daughter's failure to apostrophise her beloved even causes the overall **apostrophe** count for *Kinsmen* to depart markedly from Shakespeare's habitual practices. As Table 3.4 illustrates, Shakespeare's percentage of **apostrophe** was surprisingly consistent in the romances,[29] with the noticeable exception of this particular play.

Table 3.4 **Apostrophe** in Shakespeare's romances.

Play	Words	Apostrophe	% apostrophe
Cymbeline	4542	1370	30%
Pericles	1422	481	34%
The Tempest	1768	465	26%
Two Noble Kinsmen	3317	468	14%
Winter's Tale	2473	713	29%
Total	13522	3497	26%

If we exclude the Daughter's insides, the figure for *Kinsmen* rises to 23 per cent, which is much closer to the elevated apostrophe count for Shakespeare's romances in general. Was the low **apostrophe** count perhaps John Fletcher's doing, given that he co-authored a major part of *Kinsmen*? The answer is simply no. Shakespeare did write more apostrophe in *Kinsmen* than did Fletcher (26 per cent versus 9 per cent), as he always seems to have done when collaborating with another dramatist, but in the one soliloquy he wrote for the Jailor's Daughter (3.2.1–38) the percentage dwindles to 10 per cent (almost exactly the same as Fletcher's average). This is not the only area in *The Two Noble Kinsmen* where Shakespeare and Fletcher have synchronised their dramatic practice in unexpected ways; as we shall see in Chapter 4, they also make the same striking departure from Shakespeare's typical distribution of insides according to gender.

When the Daughter finally returns to society in act 4, the audience finds her speaking into thin air, wrapped up in an imaginary dialogue about hellfire that is her horrible substitute for real human intercourse. It takes a stratagem involving the Wooer – whom her clouded mind already takes for Palamon, so that the standard bed-trick becomes quite unnecessary – to bring her back into the social fold. Strictly in terms of plot, the Daughter's trajectory is therefore that of separation from the community through unlawful desire and reintegration by means of marriage. But by 1613, Shakespeare had long since outgrown the formulaic requirements of the romantic comedies, whose endings were rarely completely harmonious anyway, and whose structure proved woefully incapable of containing the complexity and tonal dissonance of his mature vision. The ordinary protocols of dialogue are once again distorted painfully as the Daughter addresses the man she takes to be Palamon:

DAUGHTER   But you shall not hurt me.
WOOER   I will not, sweet.
DAUGHTER   If you do, love, I'll cry.   *Exeunt.*

(5.2.111–12)

If '[g]ood comedy is tragedy narrowly averted', as Jonathan Bate puts it succinctly,[30] then Shakespearean tragicomedy can perhaps be defined as tragedy averted too late. *The Two Noble Kinsmen* is an unnerving play because it sinks its teeth relentlessly into all the unfulfilled and conflicting desires that human flesh is heir to. Shakespeare and Fletcher conjure up a cluster of generally admirable individuals who strive very hard to live in accordance with their idea of the good, even as they buckle under incompatible or unacceptable desires and negotiate impossible dilemmas. It is a world where people do not know what they want; where they want too many incompatible things at the same time; where they do not get what they want; or where they pay so dearly for what they actually get that the victory leaves a bitter aftertaste.

Reported Words

An **apostrophe** simulates a dialogue with someone or something that cannot hear. I would now like to turn to those situations where the onstage or offstage speech of one character is reported inside another character's soliloquy or inside. Such **reported words** are, in other words, a subset of the larger category of **reporting**, a frequent means for Shakespeare's characters to process their own experience (internal level) and keep the audience or reader abreast of plot developments (external level). Puttenham calls it *dialogismus* when it's about fitting the speech to the person: 'We are sometimes occasioned in our tale to report some speech from another man's mouth, as what a king said to his Privy Council or subject, a captain to his soldier.'[31] If we count those passages where characters import the actual statements of onstage or offstage characters as direct quotations or indirect paraphrases into their own private speech, then such **reported words** make up 3.7 per cent of the total insides in the average Shakespeare play. There is also a marked dominance by the comic subgenre (Table 3.5).

At first sight, it seems logical that comedy should score higher than other subgenres for reported words given its intensive concern with

Table 3.5 **Reported words** in insides according to subgenre.

	Total words	Reported words	% reported words
Comedy	17706	1184	6.7%
History	17408	568	3.3%
Tragedy	16589	380	2.3%
Romance	13522	255	1.9%
Total	65225	2387	3.7%

social information and gossip. On closer inspection, however, the over-representation of the comic genre is produced by extreme scores in three individual comedies: *Love's Labour's Lost* (23.6 per cent), *Twelfth Night* (16.4 per cent), and *The Comedy of Errors* (16.1 per cent).

Shakespeare's characters report the words of others in two basic ways: by citing or paraphrasing them, or by reading a letter out loud. From the perspective of coding and quantification, therefore, **letters** are a subset of **reported words**, and they will be my main concern in what follows. As Alan Stewart has shown in the book-length study *Shakespeare's Letters*, the author had a rich and multifarious tradition of letter writing to fall back on, ranging from Erasmian grammar-school templates via Plutarchan and Euripidean models to the stock letters of the sixteenth-century stage. It is a constant source of chagrin to Shakespeare scholars worldwide, and sometimes also a source of conspiracy theories, that the author did not leave any private letters behind for posterity. He made up for this amply in the production of stage letters, however, since there are almost as many of these as there are Shakespeare plays. As Stewart notes, letters are 'the most common stage property in Shakespeare's plays, appearing more frequently than any other object except costumes and "prosthetic" props such as swords, crowns, handkerchiefs, beards, and hairpieces'.[32]

Stewart also makes a specific observation of immediate interest to this chapter. When Shakespeare's characters read stage letters out loud while commenting on them, the words of an offstage character become nested inside the speech of an onstage character:

> Of the thirty-one letters read out on the Shakespearean stage, eleven are interrupted by commentary and interjections, sometimes from the speaker (who is, of course, not the 'writer' of the letter), sometimes from other characters. Some of the most memorable moments in Shakespearean drama arise from a character reading, and responding to a letter alone (or believing himself alone): Hotspur's angry rejection of Worcester's[33] urging him to caution (1H4 2.3.1–15); Brutus' betraying of his secret ambition in interpreting and completing the letter sent anonymously from Cassius (JC2.1.46–58); 'Ganymede's perverse reading of Phoebe's letter to 'him' (AYL,4.3.40–63); and the most sustained example, Malvolio's willful self-delusion as he reads the letter dropped in his path by Maria (TN2.5.82–179). In these instances, a letter, supposedly the voice of its sender, becomes instead a dialogue between sender and recipient.[34]

Let us look more closely at one of these passages, Hotspur's angry reading of the letter in *Henry IV, part 1*, where Shakespeare constructs an elaborate dialogical structure around this simple stage prop. I examined this passage briefly in Chapter 1 as a likely instance of direct address to the audience, but I would now like to explore how the ostensibly monological speech of the solitary Hotspur also becomes an intricate web of perspectives and points of view, making this speech one of the most richly dialogical insides in the Shakespeare canon.

Hotspur's name symbolises his hot temper and inveterate ambition, qualities that feed an irrepressible urge to speak his mind irrespective of the consequences. Shakespeare establishes this emphatically when the character makes his first appearance with his father and uncle in act 1, scene 3, secretly expressing a desire for self-expression so strong that it even outweighs his instinct for self-preservation: 'I will ease my heart, / Albeit I make a hazard of my head' (1.3.126–7).[35] As they talk, Hotspur's uncle finds it hard to get a word in edgewise:

[HOTSPUR] Therefore, I say –
WORCESTER   Peace, cousin, say no more.

(1.3. 186)

[WORCESTER]
[*to Hotspur*] Good cousin, give me audience for a while.

(210)

WORCESTER Hear you, cousin, a word.

(255)

The young Hotspur only seems to open his ears after being roundly criticised by his father Northumberland for having failed to listen, '[t]ying thine ear to no tongue but thine own!' (236).

When the audience next encounters Hotspur, at the beginning of act 2, he enters the stage alone. This would seem like an excellent opportunity to speak without being contradicted, but what happens is something quite different. Since he enters reading a letter that punches large holes in his plot against the King, he is already in a state of dialogue with the offstage character who wrote it:

HOTSPUR *But, for mine own part, my lord, I could be well contented to be there, in respect of the love I bear your house.* He could be contented: why is he not then? In respect of the love he bears our house: he shows in this, he loves his own barn better than he loves our house. Let me see some more. *The purpose you undertake is dangerous* – Why, that's certain; 'tis dangerous to take a cold, to sleep, to drink; but I tell you, my lord fool, out of this nettle, danger, we pluck this flower, safety. *The purpose you undertake is dangerous, the friends you have named uncertain, the time itself unsorted, and your whole plot too light for the counterpoise of so great an opposition.* Say you so, say you so? I say unto you again, you are a shallow cowardly hind, and you lie: what a lack-brain is this! By the Lord, our plot is a good plot, as ever was laid, our friends true and constant: a good plot, good friends, and full of expectation: an excellent plot, very good friends; what a frosty-spirited rogue is this! Why, my Lord of York commends the plot, and the general course of the action. 'Zounds, an I were now by this rascal I could brain him with his lady's fan. Is there not my father, my uncle, and myself? Lord Edmund Mortimer, My Lord of York and Owen Glendower? Is there not besides the Douglas? Have I not all their letters to meet me in arms by the ninth of the next month, and are they not some of them set forward already? What a pagan rascal is this, an infidel! Ha! You shall see now in very sincerity of fear and cold heart will he to the King, and lay open all our proceedings! O, I could divide myself, and go to buffets, for moving such a dish of skim milk with so honourable an action! Hang him, let him tell the King, we are prepared: I will set forward tonight.

(2.3.1–34)

This speech shows how a single Shakespearean stage letter may serve numerous dramatic functions. It allows Shakespeare to incorporate an external point of view into the character's solitary speech, raising doubts about the felicity of the plot that is under way, while also giving the onstage character an opportunity to affirm the integrity of his own vision. Hotspur's characterisation is consistent from act 1, scene 3, since his desire to affirm his own convictions is unabated even in the absence of a real interlocutor. If anything, his extended talking back to a person who can neither hear nor respond seems quite similar to Prospero's confrontation with his spellbound enemies in *The Tempest*. From the character's perspective, on the internal level of the dramatic fiction, there are real psychological benefits to be had from simulating the intensity of a real exchange.

In the first half of his speech, Hotspur see-saws between second- and third-person address, alternately saying deprecating things *about* the anonymous letter writer and confronting him head on by means of **apostrophe**. Although Hotspur is using prose, his apostrophic address combines effectively with other figures of speech with a dialogical quality, especially **asteismus** (the brief, witty retort that plays upon an element in another person's formulation, defined by Puttenham as the 'figure of reply').[36] The second part contains a string of rhetorical questions (**erotema**), that, like most rhetorical questions, have the chief function of bolstering his personal convictions. *Henry IV, part 1* has the third highest **erotema** percentage in the complete plays, 8 per cent, which is twice as high as the Shakespearean mean. As we shall see towards the end of this chapter, however, it is *Hamlet* that reigns supreme in this particular area.

As we saw briefly in Chapter 1, rhetorical questions are interesting from the perspective of early modern performance because they lend themselves equally well to self-address or direct address to the audience – as exemplified by Iago's 'And what's he then that says I play the villain?' (2.3.325–51). I also suggested that audience address is more likely to be at work in speeches involving mental detachment and that either begin or end a scene (because they are not delivered 'in the midst of the action'). These criteria are clearly met in Hotspur's soliloquised dialogue with the letter writer, and he soon adds a third criterion in the form of second-person address:

> Ha! You shall see now in very sincerity of fear and cold heart will he to the King, and lay open all our proceedings!
>
> (30–2)

Who is being addressed here? Hotspur's first words are certainly very similar to those used by Falstaff in another passage that we have mined for audience address:

> O, you shall see him laugh till his face be like a wet cloak ill laid up!
>
> (*Henry IV, part 2*, 5.1.85)

I personally find it hard to see Hotspur engaging in some sort of elliptically self-addressed speech when a direct appeal for the audience's attention and complicity seems so much more plausible. If this reading is correct, then Hotspur's private moment on the stage becomes a very complex triangulation of three dialogical partners, two of whom are not present on the stage: his own person, the absent letter writer, and the semi-absent audience.

Prosopopoeia

Among the many ambiguous terms strewn across the history of literary criticism, **prosopopoeia** is surely one of the most annoying. It can be understood either as a synonym for *personification* – 'the godlike capacity to breathe life into dead things'[37] – or as an act of *personation* where the speaker adopts a role and pretends to speak in the capacity of another person. Only the latter of these widely divergent meanings, personation, will be relevant here, in keeping with the explicit pronouncements of several early modern rhetoricians. When John Hoskins defined apostrophe as 'feigning the presence' of other persons, for example, he added in the same breath that **prosopopoeia** was about feigning their 'discourse'.[38]

Another contemporary authority on the subject, Abraham Fraunce, gave a fuller definition: '*Prosopopoia* is a fayning of any person, when in our speech we represent the person of anie, and make it speake as though he were there present: an excellent figure, much used of Poets.'[39] If Shakespeare did attend New School in Stratford, as seems likely, then he would have received systematic training in this crucial skill for a literary dramatist:

> In the higher forms of grammar schools, students were sometimes told to write a speech in the persona of a particular character in a particular set of circumstances, known as a 'prosopopoeia'. They might write speeches in the persona of Helen of Troy, or of Queen Hecuba after the sack of Troy.[40]

Since literary personation creates a gap between the speaking self and an adopted persona, the relationship between the two typically becomes uncertain and open to interpretation. According to Gavin Alexander, the roots of Shakespearean personation in classical rhetoric prescribe particular interpretative caution:

> The theory of rhetoric that taught authors the persuasive value of compelling characterisation also taught that any character created in words was a performance of a persona – the creation and adoption of a mask, a *prosopopoeia*. That mask could be realistic, but it was still a mask. Where we might think of literary characters as believable individuals (as later Shakespeare criticism encouraged us to do), the Renaissance rhetorical tradition helps us think about them as convincing and persuasive personae. This creates interesting conundrums in drama – to what extent is the Hamlet we see a performance, and whose performance is it (Shakespeare's? Hamlet's? the actor's?)? In lyric we have the additional problem of looking at the mask and not being sure whom it represents. It might be a representation of the author or it might be a piece of fiction. And even if it is self-representation, that is still a fictive activity (the author is *auctor personae meae*).[41]

What Alexander describes as a 'conundrum' –'whose performance is it?' – is perhaps really a question of multiple analytical levels in the dramatic fiction. As soon as an actor opens his or her mouth on the stage, we are treated to three simultaneous performances: one by the author, one by the character, and one by the actor. On the level of character, Alexander's analysis of personation has considerable common ground with Hirsh's analysis of self-addressed speech, where, as we have seen, a Shakespearean soliloquy cannot be interpreted unambiguously as a record of the speaker's actual thoughts or actual self. Speakers may try and talk themselves into a particular emotion as often as they express their deepest feelings or convictions. The complexity increases when we consider that personation is sometimes at work on two levels of dramatic communication. Shakespeare's characters are not only personated by their author but sometimes personate other characters, pretending to speak on their behalf. At times they even personate themselves in an imagined future role, as Malvolio does so memorably in *Twelfth Night*, or they combine personation with personification in poetic blazon.

In the discussion of letter writing above, I noted how Hotspur's indefatigable dialogical impulse generates some interesting complexities in *Henry IV, part 1*. His angry response to the letter writer, ostensibly a speech spoken in solitude, appears to become a triangular dialogue with the letter writer and the audience. In fact, Hotspur's dialogical predisposition is so strong that he even continues to speak – albeit indirectly, through another's voice – when he is either offstage or has departed from the world of the living. In both cases the feat is accomplished by Prince Hal by means of personation.

The first, 'offstage' instance is a fairly straightforward case of satire, spoken in conversation with Poins. Hal pushes Hotspur's valour into ridiculous hyperbole:

> PRINCE That ever this fellow should have fewer words than a parrot, and yet the son of a woman! His industry is up-stairs and down-stairs, his eloquence the parcel of a reckoning. I am not yet of Percy's mind, the Hotspur of the north; he that kills me some six or seven dozen of Scots at a breakfast, washes his hands, and says to his wife 'Fie upon this quiet life! I want work.' 'O my sweet Harry,' says she, 'how many hast thou killed today?' 'Give my roan horse a drench,' says he, and answers, 'Some fourteen,' an hour after; 'a trifle, a trifle.' I prithee, call in Falstaff; I'll play Percy, and that damned brawn shall play Dame Mortimer his wife. *Rivo!* says the drunkard: call in Ribs, call in Tallow.
>
> (2.4.97–110)

In the second example from *Henry IV, part 1*, the dying Hotspur gives up his breath in mid-sentence and Prince Hal takes it upon himself to finish his line by means of soliloquy:

> [HOTSPUR]   O, I could prophesy,
>   But that the earthy and cold hand of death
>   Lies on my tongue: no, Percy, thou art dust,
>   And food for – [Dies.]
> PRINCE For worms, brave Percy.
>
> (5.4.82–6)

Prince Hal next delivers a lengthy apostrophic speech addressed to the dead Hotspur, keeping him alive as a figurative counterpart to be engaged in dialogue:[42]

>   Fare thee well, great heart!
>   Ill-weav'd ambition, how much art thou shrunk!
>   When that this body did contain a spirit,
>   A kingdom for it was too small a bound;
>   But now two paces of the vilest earth
>   Is room enough. This earth that bears thee dead
>   Bears not alive so stout a gentleman.
>   If thou wert sensible of courtesy

I should not make so dear a show of zeal;
But let my favours hide thy mangled face,
And, even in thy behalf I'll thank myself
For doing these fair rites of tenderness.
Adieu, and take thy praise with thee to heaven!
Thy ignominy sleep with thee in the grave,
But not remember'd in thy epitaph!

(86–100)

Interestingly, Hal admits that he would never have said these things to Hotspur if the latter were 'sensible of courtesy', suggesting, ironically, that he can have a deeper and more meaningful conversation with the dead Hotspur than with the creature who lived and breathed only a moment ago. This is, in one respect, a testament to one of the chief functions of soliloquy: to provide inside information about the character's internal state of mind. Towards the middle of the speech, however, the tender tone is complicated by an unusual action on Hal's part. Presumably because it takes two to tango in a proper reconciliation scene, he decides to not only *speak to* but also to *speak on behalf of* his dead enemy, thanking himself on Hotspur's behalf for doing these 'rites of tenderness'. This is, presumably, his way of ensuring that the conversation keeps going even beyond the grave. The audience is not given any time to let this strange act sink in before Hal strikes up yet another apostrophic conference with the dead:

[He spieth FALSTAFF on the ground.]
What, old acquaintance, could not all this flesh
Keep in a little life? Poor Jack, farewell!
I could have better spar'd a better man:
O, I should have a heavy miss of thee
If I were much in love with vanity:
Death hath not struck so fat a deer to-day,
Though many dearer, in this bloody fray.
Embowell'd will I see thee by and by,
Till then in blood by noble Percy lie.

Exit.
(101–9)

Since Falstaff is merely playing dead and easily overhears Hal's apostrophic address, a soliloquy that mimics ordinary dialogue is transformed into actual dialogue by the interlocutor's discrepant awareness.

Illeism and Tuism

We saw above that Shakespeare seems to have loved writing apostrophes, since he always wrote more of them than did his co-authors. The same thing cannot be said about two other dialogical figures of speech that make only sparse appearances in the complete plays: **illeism** (reference to oneself in the grammatical third person singular) and **tuism** (self-address in the second person singular). The common denominator between **illeism** and **tuism** is the creation of a cognitive and linguistic space by which characters distance themselves from their own person, albeit for very different purposes. **Illeism** allows speakers to *detach* themselves from their own person or from other people. With **tuism**, by contrast, the act of mental distancing is only a necessary stepping-stone for a *confrontation* with one's own person. These tropes make only rare appearances in Shakespeare's plays and are often entirely absent, but such infrequent phenomena may still have an interesting story to tell precisely because of their relative rarity. As we shall see, Shakespeare's use of **illeism** and **tuism** is culturally specific, functionally restricted, and may even help us distinguish his work from that of his co-authors.

Illeism and **tuism** seem to have met the same fate as **erotema**, the rhetorical question, when we consider Shakespeare's complete plays. They were used more frequently in the first phase (3 per cent in 1590–4) and then trailed off before disappearing almost completely in the last phase (0 per cent in 1610–14). It may be tempting to see Shakespeare moving away from overtly rhetorical speech to more natural-sounding formulations, but these are risky conclusions for two different reasons. The first is that the infrequent nature of the trope renders such statistical generalisations tenuous at best. Another interesting complication is that a large quantity of the illeistic and tuistic passages in the early works may not actually have been written by Shakespeare. As we shall see, the distribution of **tuism** in a co-authored play like *Titus Andronicus* reveals major differences between the passages typically attributed to Shakespeare and to his co-author, George Peele.

Let us begin with **illeism**. Focusing primarily on the internal level of dramatic communication, S. Viswanatham calls it 'an effective way … of making the character momentarily detach himself from himself, achieve a measure of dramatic (and philosophical) de-personalization, and create a kind of aesthetic distance from which he can contemplate himself'.[43] It is thus primarily a *distancing* device whereby speakers momentarily place themselves at one mental remove from their own persons, but the 'de-personalization' it offers is really quite paradoxical. To stand back from one's own person and grant it a quasi-objective status is typically to endow it with considerable importance and status (as witnessed, for example, by the annoying tendency of twenty-first-century celebrities and politicians to talk about themselves

Table 3.6 **Illeism** and **tuism** according to class in Shakespeare's complete insides (%).

	Royalty	Aristocracy	Gentry	Commoner
Illeism	27	52	15	8
Tuism	17	55	25	3
Insides	21	36	29	14

in the third person). It is therefore not surprising that the usage of **illeism** and **tuism** in the complete plays is heavily inflected by class (Table 3.6).[44]

Commoners speak 14 per cent of Shakespeare's total insides but a much smaller slice of the illeistic passages. Aristocrats, by contrast, speak 36 per cent of Shakespeare's insides but deliver more than half of his illeistic and tuistic passages (52 per cent **illeism**, 55 per cent **tuism**). Royal figures are hardly over-represented at all in their use of **illeism**, and even seriously under-represented when it comes to **tuism** (17 per cent, where one would expect 21 per cent on statistical grounds), but this is not strange since they have recourse to an even more formidable device for rhetorical self-elevation: the royal we. Shakespeare's gentry complete the picture by falling predictably between aristocrats and commoners, being slightly under-represented on both fronts. We can, in other words, deduce with some confidence that there is a strong link between these rhetorical figures and the social class of the speaker. The tropes in question are also inflected by gender. The male characters in the Shakespeare canon are twice as prone as the women to objectify themselves linguistically in this way (**illeism** 1.1 vs. 0.4 per cent, **tuism** 1.3 vs. 0.6 per cent), a fact that may reflect men and women's perceived – and internalised – status in a patriarchal society.[45]

Can we also say something more specific about the objects of **illeism**, that is, the phenomena from which Shakespeare's characters typically distance themselves? A scrutiny of all instances reveals that the aesthetic distance Viswanatham points to is invariably connected with *moral* distance in Shakespeare's insides. It can be broken down to the expression of four basic affects: *guilt, shame, disgust, and glee*.[46] The first two, guilt and shame, involve an *internal* act of distancing from a self that is seen as morally problematic. Guilt, for example, is at work when Enobarbus regrets his treachery in *Antony and Cleopatra*, when the guilt-ridden Brutus vows to strike at Julius Caesar, and when *Richard III*'s actions have finally caught up with him. *Disgust* and *glee*, by contrast, involve an *external* distancing from the world through the affirmation of a controversial feeling. **Illeism** is thus used gleefully when

Aaron the Moor in *Titus Andronicus* delights in his own evil and when Hume plans to 'make merry' with the Duchess's gold in *2 Henry VI*. It is used to express disgust by characters as diverse as the Queen Mother in *Richard III*, Timon of Athens, Lucius in *Titus Andronicus*, and Julia in *The Two Gentlemen of Verona*.

Scholars have so far failed to agree about the origins of Shakespearean **illeism**. According to Viswanatham, the technique was

> handed down to Shakespeare from the medieval theater, by which a character has perforce to announce himself and reveal his identity tritely enough as an elementary trick of the stage. It is part of the primitive stage convention of self-revelation, of 'direct self-explanation', which is born of an inevitable theatrical exigency, going back farther still than the Herod of the medieval Miracle cycle but extending even into the latest drama.[47]

John Velz,[48] by contrast, extends the roots of Shakespearean **illeism** back to the author's classical forebears. He argues that Shakespeare saw **illeism** primarily as a Roman phenomenon, even if he also extended it to non-Roman plays such as *Troilus* and *Timon*.

Since **illeism** is easily quantified, Velz's claim for a Roman connection can be tested by means of a search in the SID. It turns out that Shakespeare's Roman plays contain seven times as much **illeism** as his other dramatic works (Table 3.7).

These are quite striking figures, even if a closer consideration of the individual word counts for the Roman plays show that the pattern is not perfectly consistent (Table 3.8).

Once again we must bear in mind that *Coriolanus* constitutes a special case given its unusual dearth of insides. It has only a few scattered speeches of this kind that make up 1 per cent of the complete text, placing the play on the quantitative bottom rung alongside *Much*

Table 3.7 **Illeism** in Shakespeare's Roman and non-Roman plays.

	Words	Illeism	% illeism
Insides in Roman plays	3393	171	5.0%
Complete insides excl. Roman plays	61832	450	0.7%

Table 3.8 **Illeism** in Shakespeare's Roman plays.

Play	Insides	Illeism	% illeism
Antony and Cleopatra	1060	42	4.0%
Coriolanus	257	0	0.0%
Julius Caesar	1268	60	4.7%
Titus Andronicus	808	69	8.5%
Average	3393	171	5.0%

Ado about Nothing. Such low figures may, of course, easily skew the figures on the level of the individual play. Even if we do not factor in this complication, the figures above strongly support Velz's view that Shakespeare saw **illeism** as a distinctively Roman phenomenon.

Another complication, which leads us to the problem of uncertain authorship, is that the Shakespeare canon contains two plays whose uniquely high scores for **illeism** combine with strong evidence of multiple authorship. One of these is the Roman play *Titus Andronicus* (8.5 per cent), co-written with George Peele, where we now have a fairly good sense of Shakespeare's contribution (he probably wrote everything except act 1 and scenes 2.1, 2.2, and 4.1). In this play Shakespeare intensifies his Roman pattern by writing 10 per cent **illeism** while Peele produces 5 per cent. But the highest internal percentage for **illeism** in the Shakespeare canon is found in the collaborative history play *1 Henry VI* (10 per cent), a text where Shakespeare's share is much more uncertain. The four illeistic passages in *1 Henry VI* are spoken by Plantagenet (3.1.61–4), Exeter (3.1.200–1), Winchester (5.1.56–62), and Suffolk (5.5.103–6) in speeches that attribution scholars typically consider to be of doubtful provenance. It seems possible, therefore, that the illeistic passages in *1 Henry VI* were co-authored by a fellow dramatist who either did not consider this figure of speech to be a specifically Roman trait (as Shakespeare seems to have done), or was still content to place it in the mouths of medieval Englishmen.

If **illeism** is an instrument for mental detachment (from oneself, from one's surroundings, or both), then **tuism** is its opposite: a rhetorical means for self-confrontation. It is used by characters when they seek to regulate their behaviour or handle conflicting impulses (to rouse themselves, or, indeed, to refrain from a desired action). Like **illeism**, **tuism** is a fairly infrequent phenomenon in the complete insides, making up a single per cent of the total word count. Once again it is the aforementioned plays, *1 Henry VI* and *Titus Andronicus*, that steal the show with elevated scores of 10 per cent and 11 per cent. The real fun begins, however, when we compare the percentage of tuism in Shakespeare's and Peele's sections of *Titus Andronicus*. The difference between the two authors is really quite extraordinary: while Shakespeare's soliloquies and solo asides in *Titus* do not contain a single tuistic formulation, those in scenes written by Peele (1, 2.1, 2.2, 4.1) contain no less than 40 per cent **tuism**. This is *forty* times the average score for **tuism** in the complete insides.[49]

This striking stylistic difference tallies well with Brian Vickers's argument in *Shakespeare, Co-Author* that Peele has a much higher incidence of *vocatives* in his sections of the play.[50] Vocatives are a closely related type of stylised, formal-sounding second-person address: Peele uses them once every 6.2 lines, while Shakespeare has only one instance per 16.2 lines. Stefan Daniel Keller also notes that Peele uses his vocatives indiscriminately, with little consideration of the dramatic context, even 'where they are clearly unnecessary or even dysfunctional ... It seems that he was less capable than Shakespeare of varying utterance according to character or context.'[51]

There may, however, be some mechanical method to Peele's vocative madness. Drawing on modern conversation analysis, Keller notes that vocatives typically function in highly stylised exchanges as 'turn allocation techniques' whereby a speaker hands over the word to the next speaker. Though Keller does not make this point explicitly, one surmises that a barrage of turn-allocating vocatives would have greatly reduced the risk that actors would address their speeches to the wrong character. It would, after all, require gross incompetence for an actor to address the following speech to the wrong colleague: 'Titus Andronicus, thy favours done'.

According to Keller, 'Shakespeare's mercurial mind must have become dissatisfied quickly with the endless iteration of (often polysyllabic) names in ongoing conversation, in the way Peele used *vocative* in *Titus*.'[52] Shakespeare does, however, appear to use **tuism** for quite similar ends, as self-directed cues for the individual actor. In his single-authored plays, tuistic formulations function simultaneously as self-addressed exhortations on the level of *character* and as instructions for the *actor* to move upstage or make a swift transition from inside to dialogue. Consider the following examples from different subgenres:

Soft you now!

(*Hamlet*, 3.1.88)

Withdraw thee, wretched Margaret: who comes here?

(*Richard III*, 4.4.8)

Withdraw thee, Valentine; who's this comes here?
(*The Two Gentlemen of Verona*, 5.4.18)

Aside, aside; here is more matter for a hot brain.
(*The Winter's Tale*, 4.4.683)

Such lines can be delivered in character and still function effectively as stage cues. This would, no doubt, have made them particularly useful in a demanding, intense repertory system with limited time and opportunities for group rehearsal.

This is not to say that Shakespeare did not explore the literary or aesthetic potentials of **tuism**. One of the most memorable instances is

Angelo's tortured reckoning with his own moral corruption in *Measure for Measure*:

> What dost thou, or what art thou, Angelo?
> Dost thou desire her foully for those things
> That make her good? O, let her brother live!
> Thieves for their robbery have authority,
> When judges steal themselves.

> (2.2.173–7)

This passage is particularly interesting because Angelo's **tuism** is formulated as a question that chafes painfully at the boundary between a rhetorical question and an ordinary question. As a result, his speech seems to fall halfway between a bitter indictment of his own moral corruption and a genuine expression of ignorance about his own nature: what sort of person am I, since I am capable of such things? This tense relation between rhetorical questions and genuine questions is an important stylistic trait in *Hamlet*, to which we will now turn for a final consideration of the interplay between dramatic characterisation and dialogical elements of speech.

Hamlet: Dialogue and Depression in Denmark

Think inwardness, introversion, interiority, introspection, soliloquies, and Shakespeare: which play springs to mind? Few questions in literary criticism tend to generate a complete consensus, of course, but most people will surely answer '*Hamlet*'.[53] It may come as a small surprise, therefore, that the play's ratio of soliloquies and solo asides is not particularly high. If we count lines in the SID – whose Arden 2 source conflates passages from the First Folio and the Second Quarto and therefore includes the soliloquy 'How all occasions do inform against me' – *Hamlet* contains 8 per cent insides. This puts the play just above the Shakespearean mean of 7 per cent and well below plays like *Cymbeline* (17 per cent) or *Macbeth* (13.5 per cent). From a quantitative point of view, *Hamlet*'s insides are more remarkable for the intensity of their moral commentary. A staggering 64 per cent of the words spoken as insides in this play are devoted explicitly to moral judgement,[54] around three times as much as in the average Shakespeare play.

This pervasive moral commentary is one of several similarities between *Hamlet* and *Timon of Athens*, where another protagonist recoils from his corrupt environment and is overcome by misanthropic feelings. As we saw earlier in this chapter, almost every single inside in *Timon* is concerned with the protagonist's foolishness or the despicable nature of his suitors. We also saw that more than every other word in *Timon* (53 per cent) forms part of an **apostrophe**, a speech addressed to an absent person or to an entity that cannot reasonably hear. The play's **apostrophe** count soars far above the already substantial Shakespearean average of 20 per cent, and if we remove the passages normally attributed to revision by Thomas Middleton, the percentage even rises to a staggering 65 per cent.

One might well expect *Hamlet* to exhibit a comparable **apostrophe** count in view of its pent-up emotions and solitary outbursts, but as Margaret McKay notes in her full-length study of Shakespearean apostrophe, the play actually has fewer apostrophes than any other tragedy except *Coriolanus* (which, as we have seen, is a statistical problem child). McKay deems it 'impossible' to account for this dearth of apostrophe in *Hamlet*, likening herself to 'an anthropologist trying to reconstruct a temple dome from a mere handful of mosaic fragments'.[55] A SID search confirms that the same dearth of **apostrophe** can be found in the play's insides: *Hamlet*'s precise percentage is 13 per cent, compared to the 20 per cent Shakespearean mean for soliloquies and asides.

One way to make sense of the difference between *Hamlet* and *Timon* is to consider their approximate dating. Shakespeare's usage of **apostrophe** varied, not only from play to play, but also over time (Figure 3.1).

Timon was most likely written between 1605 and 1608, and thus it forms part of a five-year phase when Shakespeare's use of **apostrophe** peaked dramatically. The mean for the plays written between 1605 and

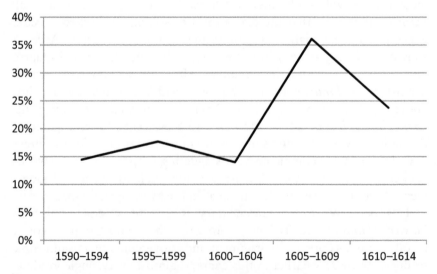

Figure 3.1 Shakespeare's usage of **apostrophe** over time.

1609 is 36 per cent **apostrophe**, almost twice the (already substantial) count of 20 per cent for the complete plays.[56] *Hamlet*, in turn, is just as representative of the preceding phase. The plays written in the first five years of the seventeenth century were marked by a minor *slump* in the use of **apostrophe**, and *Hamlet* mirrors the 14 per cent average almost exactly.

Could these be misleading results based on uncertain dating? Although the exact years for many Shakespeare plays are highly contentious, their assignation to discrete five-year phases is supported by a broad editorial consensus. Would the pattern disappear if we removed extreme scores for individual plays? Not really. There is not a *single play* written between 1605 and 1609, except the statistical outlier *Coriolanus*, that scores lower than the highest score for 1600–4. This throws some doubt upon McKay's contention that 'the number of apostrophes in a specific play is not governed primarily by the year in which the play is written'.[57]

The spike in apostrophes between 1605 and 1609 can be understood more precisely if we factor in the dramatic speech act **requesting**, where a character reaches out and asks for something from someone who cannot hear. This dramatic speech act exhibits a very similar spike in this period (Figure 3.2).

Since it contains only 7 per cent **requesting**, *Hamlet* once again mirrors the mean for the phase 1600–4 almost exactly.

To say that *Hamlet*'s low **apostrophe** count is typical of the time

Figure 3.2 Shakespeare's usage of **requesting** over time.

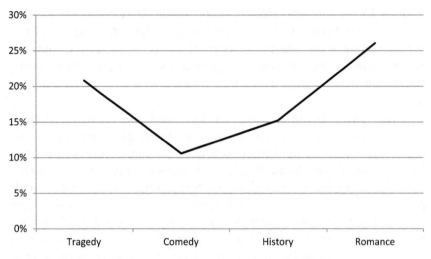

Figure 3.3 Shakespeare's usage of **apostrophe** according to subgenre.

when it was written does not preclude other explanations. Theoretically speaking, at least, there can be many causes for the temporal pattern we have uncovered, from deep psychological mechanisms or conscious artistic design to random events resulting in a temporary authorial habit. One benefit of a mixed-methods approach involving multiple research variables is that we can test an indefinite number of rival hypotheses based on different textual attributes. This can help us do battle against the tyranny of our self-confirming bias, including the temptation to content ourselves with the first explanation that seems to make sense.

One factor that clearly affects the figures for **apostrophe** is Shakespeare's employment of different subgenres over time. Figure 3.3 shows that **apostrophe** is much less frequent in the insides of comedies than in other subgenres.

The 1605–9 phase, which scores so very high for apostrophe, contains no comedies whatsoever. If we factor in its elevated word counts for both **apostrophe** and **requesting**, it is tempting to posit an unusual preponderance of tragic protagonists who are pushed to their wits' end and reach out to a universe that cannot hear them. The previous phase, to which *Hamlet* belongs, is unusually comedy-rich, with four comedies out of a total of six plays.

Alas, to say that the tragedy of *Hamlet* has few apostrophes because it belongs to a distinctively comic phase in Shakespeare's career is hardly a satisfying conclusion.[58] If anything, it prompts a search for explanations that are more firmly rooted in the play itself.

Table 3.9 **Apostrophe** in insides per tragic protagonist.

	Apostrophe	Words	% apostrophe
Lear	207	221	94%
Timon	867	952	91%
Titus	58	81	72%
Mark Antony	190	428	44%
Juliet	329	1087	30%
Othello	171	570	30%
Brutus	181	606	30%
Romeo	295	1101	27%
Macbeth	258	1233	21%
Hamlet	191	1784	11%
Coriolanus	5	333	2%
Julius Caesar	0	24	0%
Cleopatra	0	20	0%

Like certain other Shakespearean protagonists, Hamlet dominates the private speech of his play by speaking between 65 and 71 per cent of its insides, depending on the edition used and the original publication(s) on which it is based.[59] Such over-representation on the level of the individual character may of course have a powerful impact on the play's total inside count. Thanks to the SID, the general **apostrophe** figures for *Hamlet* can be broken down easily on the level of individual **character** and restricted to the subgenre of **tragedy**. A comparison of all eponymous tragic protagonists in Shakespeare's complete plays yields some striking figures (Table 3.9).

As soon as Timon and Lear open their mouths to speak an inside, they immediately start spouting apostrophes, while Julius Caesar and Cleopatra hardly deliver any private speech at all. Coriolanus is a more complicated case – partly because he speaks so few insides, and partly because of a conservative methodological principle applied in the coding process.[60] The most important thing here, however, is that Hamlet delivers very little **apostrophe** compared to most other tragic protagonists. If we run a new SID search for **apostrophe** in *Hamlet* and exclude the protagonist, the play's word count comes very close to the Shakespearean norm of 20 per cent. It still makes sense to say that the play's low **apostrophe** count is representative of a larger trend in Shakespeare's writing, but we can now identify a more precise cause for this scarcity on the level of the individual character.

It may be tempting to explain Hamlet-the-character's low score for **apostrophe** by means of a sweeping combination of statistics and stylistics: since he speaks more lines than any other tragic protagonist, we might expect his language to be more varied than, say, Lear's or Mark Antony's.[61] In that case, however, we would surely expect it to gravitate towards the *mean* for Shakespeare's complete plays rather than fall so far below it. As we shall see more clearly in a moment, a broad statistical argument of this kind does a poor job of explaining Hamlet's stylistic idiosyncrasies, at least in the case of **apostrophe**.

A more fruitful approach to the difference between Hamlet and the top-ranking tragic *apostrophes* is to consider differences in character and tone. Timon is simply furious with treacherous humanity, and a similar sense of outrage is voiced more temperately by his loyal Steward. In his speeches on the heath, Lear is so beside himself with fury that he seems oblivious to his surroundings. Neither Timon nor Lear exhibits any real capacity to separate the inward from the outward person: an incapacity that we explored with special reference to *Richard II* in Chapter 2, and that contributes directly to their downfall. Hamlet, by contrast, is not only angry: he is also subject to a sharp mental isolation from his surroundings.

It can be argued plausibly that the depth of Hamlet's social isolation constitutes his most important difference from Shakespeare's other tragic protagonists. Macbeth has his Lady and partner in crime for the better part of the play; Lear has his Fool for the first part of the action, until the latter disappears mysteriously and Lear himself goes mad; Coriolanus has his mother and Cominius; Othello certainly *thinks* he has a dear friend in Iago; Timon first has his loyal Steward and then turns to Alcibiades and Apemantus for some Gestalt therapy in the wilderness; Antony has recourse to Eros when he is cross with Cleopatra, while Cleopatra has constant access to Charmian and her maids; Titus has Lucius and Marcus; and Romeo and Juliet have each other. Hamlet, by contrast, is in what Alex Newell calls the 'confusing and stifling situation' of not being able to say anything to anyone – not even his close confidante, Horatio – about his situation.[62]

As Joseph Carroll notes in a reading that vindicates and updates some of A. C. Bradley's hundred-year-old insights, there are also important human continuities between what Shakespeare or Bradley called *melancholy* and what we moderns call *depression*. Hamlet's depression is mirrored both in his powerful fits of rage and guilt and in his spells of *anhedonia*, the lack of positive affect leading to indifference and apathy.[63] Could it be that Hamlet's catastrophic loss of genuine dialogue with other people – which is part and parcel of *anhedonia*, as well as his paranoid, claustrophobic situation at court, especially after his meeting with the Ghost – has something to do with his dearth of **apostrophe**?

This suspicion is confirmed when we examine the more specific nature of the play's apostrophes. *Hamlet* may be low on **apostrophe** in general, but it is also extraordinarily *rich* in a particular type of **apostrophe**: the kind that is addressed reflexively to one's own bodily or mental faculties. There are nineteen of these in Shakespeare's complete insides, of which no fewer than seven (or 35 per cent) are to be found in *Hamlet*. When he is left to his own devices, Hamlet addresses parts of himself – his soul, his conscience, his sinews, or his heart – much more often (seven times) than he addresses absent characters (twice, or three times if we include the Ghost). This makes him unique among Shakespeare's protagonists. When he does make reference to other people it is typically in the form of rapid, distancing invectives ('Villain!') that cannot be safely defined as either second- or third-person address, or through statements that are clearly in the grammatical third person.

Let us now consider these findings in the larger context of Shakespearean scholarship. Over a hundred and sixty years ago, Matthew Arnold remarked poignantly that the soliloquies in Hamlet evince 'the dialogue of the soul with itself'.[64] In the 1990s, Alex Newell used Arnold's remark as his springboard for an extended analysis of the play's structural design in relation to its larger themes and issues. Newell's overriding argument deserves to be quoted at length:

> The strongest impression the soliloquies in Hamlet make collectively is that of an intense dramatization of the human mind as the innermost realm of consciousness, where the reality of the private self is distinguished from the public self, and where the reasoning faculty, looking before and after, finds and parses the terms of consciousness. The revelation of what is going in the mind (and feelings) of a characters is, of course, one of the basic functions of a soliloquy as a dramatic device, but Shakespeare, taking this function one step further in Hamlet, has used soliloquies with remarkable consistency to bring attention to the mind itself, especially to the mind as a uniquely human instrument of reflection and ratiocination. Using the soliloquies to project forceful images of the mind, Shakespeare makes the mind itself and what happens to it a major focus of the tragedy.[65]

What I have shown here is that Arnold's 'dialogue of the mind with itself' and Newell's 'dramatization of the human mind' are reflected measurably in Hamlet's special use of **apostrophe**. His inward language closely mirrors his depressive oscillation between self-absorbed weariness and objectifying hatred, both of which involve a radical estrangement of the self from the surrounding world. His introverted, self-addressed apostrophes are thus a striking stylistic token of the 'radical reflexivity' that John Lee has attributed to him.[66] This is a wonderful example of Shakespeare's capacity to suit the rhetorical word to the speaker and the action.

A Play Full of Questions

In *Everybody's Shakespeare*, Maynard Mack observes that 'Hamlet's world is pre-eminently in the interrogative mood. It reverberates with questions.'[67] This claim will ring true for many readers, not least since the play's most famous soliloquy comes in the form of a question. To some extent, this interrogative aspect is probably a matter of rhetorical conventions. According to a more recent argument by J. K. Harmer, Hamlet's 'self-debate' is

> entirely consonant with the kinds of rhetorical framework one would expect Renaissance dramatists to work with when representing a character in a revenge tragedy: generally speaking, the psychomachic conflict between reason and passion; more specifically, argumentation *in utrumque partem*; at a still more local level, the dialectical *quaestio*.[68]

But Mack clearly seems to be suggesting something more in the citation above: that *Hamlet* is unusually question-ridden compared to Shakespeare's other works. This will remain only an intuitive impression based on anecdotal evidence until we compare the play systematically to the rest of the Shakespeare canon.

While this project has no data for *Hamlet* in its entirety, a SID search for all grammatical questions in the complete insides places the play's uniquely interrogative nature on a firm statistical footing.[69] Almost a fifth (19 per cent) of Hamlet's insides take the form of a **question**, which is more than twice as much as the Shakespearean mean of 8 per cent. The closest contenders are *Romeo and Juliet* and *1 Henry VI*, with 16 per cent and 15 per cent respectively. This unique prevalence of questions is another instance of *Hamlet*'s 'internal dialogue', and we can also narrow it down further to the figure of speech known as **erotema** (the rhetorical question).

Rhetorical questions are very similar to **prosopopoeia** (personation) in that speakers momentarily consider a hypothetical standpoint that is different from their actual stance. Where the personating speech presupposes the explicit adoption of another person's identity, vantage point, or perspective, speakers of rhetorical questions formulate their words in their own capacity in order to bring home an implicit premise. The recursive, circular structure of the rhetorical question naturally bespeaks a mind that revolves around itself, setting out only to return to its point of departure, even when it tackles issues of great philosophical magnitude.

Erotema is, admittedly, one of the most treacherous codes in this study since it sometimes requires substantial inferences on the part of the coder: is this meant to be a genuine question, or is the speaker simply trying to prove a point? It is a relatively frequent phenomenon in Shakespeare's insides, making up around 4 per cent of the total word count, but it also trails off quite noticeably in the last years of his career. It is tempting to connect this with the parallel decline in illeistic and tuistic speech, both of which are associated with a formal style that differs markedly from the late Shakespearean approximation of the natural rhythms and processes of normal speech. Consider, as a lucid example of the early style, the 'subtle orator' (3.1.6) Warwick's dying speech in *3 Henry VI*:

> WARWICK Ah, who is nigh? Come to me, friend or foe,
> And tell me who is victor, York or Warwick?
> Why ask I that my mangled body shows? –
> My blood, my want of strength, my sick heart shows? –
> That I must yield my body to the earth,
> And, by my fall, the conquest to my foe.
> Thus yields the cedar to the axe's edge,
> Whose arms gave shelter to the princely eagle,
> Under whose shade the ramping lion slept,
> Whose top branch overpeer'd Jove's spreading tree
> And kept low shrubs from winter's powerful wind.
> These eyes, that now are dimm'd with death's black veil,
> Have been as piercing as the mid-day sun,
> To search the secret treasons of the world;
> The wrinkles in my brows, now fill'd with blood,
> Were liken'd oft to kingly sepulchres;
> For who liv'd king, but I could dig his grave?
> And who durst smile when Warwick bent his brow?
> Lo, now my glory smear'd in dust and blood!
> My parks, my walks, my manors that I had,
> Even now forsake me; and of all my lands
> Is nothing left me but my body's length.
> Why, what is pomp, rule, reign, but earth and dust?
> And live we how we can, yet die we must.

(5.2.5–28)

This is a beautifully crafted speech, and one that is eminently suited to the speaker. Warwick dies the way he lived, as an expert rhetorician, equipped with a style and diction that seem more suited to a courtier on official business than a mangled soldier who helplessly watches his last drops of blood trickle into the mud. *3 Henry VI* contains more rhetorical questions than any other Shakespeare play if we count the number of individual codings, but the word count still offers slender pickings compared to *Hamlet*, where every sixth or seventh word spoken as an inside forms part of a rhetorical question.[70] An extended word count produces fairly dramatic results: *Hamlet* is responsible for no less than 16 per cent of all rhetorical questions in Shakespeare's complete insides, while *3 Henry VI* scrapes together 'only' 8 per cent.

This intense concentration of **erotema**, a fundamentally recursive rhetorical technique, seems to be another stylistic token of *Hamlet*'s ruptured social dialogue. I would now like to end this analysis of the play – and the larger chapter on dialogical insides – by briefly examining how the play's unusually high incidence of rhetorical questions feeds into a tightly patterned interplay between *rhetorical* questions and *genuine* questions in speeches by Hamlet and Claudius as they waver between the attempt to control their world and a naked desire for absolution. It is almost as if Shakespeare had found a cognitive and stylistic recipe for the construction of guilt-ridden internal conflicts.

Shakespeare begins the speeches of Hamlet and Claudius by having them assert a clear moral stance by means of a string of rhetorical questions. The character then unsettles this position by confronting a genuine, searching question that is almost impossible to answer by deductive means. This interplay between rhetorical question and counter-question may be repeated one more time if necessary. Once the character's inner conviction has been eroded, he reaches desperately for an 'outside perspective' and considers his situation in relation to hypothetical observers or larger patterns in human experience. This shift to an external or intersubjective viewpoint, this attempt to see himself and his feelings from outside, does not, however, offer him any satisfaction. Now that the quest for inner as well as outward certainty has been frustrated, the inner pressure cooker boils over, leading to a cognitive breakdown where the ponderous blank verse gives way to raw emotion in the form of a string of unstructured exclamatives.

I will pass over Hamlet's first soliloquies, which do not follow this tortured pattern, as well as the extended, undisturbed rhetorical question that is 'To be or not to be', turning directly to one of the play's most conflict-ridden speeches, the soliloquy 'O what a rogue and peasant slave am I'. This speech begins with Hamlet's straightforward assertion of his guilty state, leading up to three rhetorical questions that elaborate further on his problematic moral position and whose implicit answer is quite straightforward:

> Is it not monstrous that this player here … ?   [Yes.]
> What's Hecuba to him … ?   [Nothing.]
> What would he do … ?   [Act.]

So far the powerful emotion is controlled and kept within firm bounds, as Hamlet assesses his own moral status: it is simply despicable of him to *do* nothing and *say* nothing. But then he suddenly unsettles himself with a genuine question: 'Am I a coward?' This is a question that goes straight to the heart of the honour code that underpins his aristocratic identity. It is followed immediately by a second question with a decisively rhetorical import, where Hamlet asserts to himself, prosopoietically, that nobody is in fact calling him a coward. As we have seen, personation is an important means for Shakespeare's characters to detach themselves from their own vantage point in order to orient themselves in moral space.

The only problem is that Hamlet is the last character on earth to be reassured by judgements based on external appearances. It is one thing to be *perceived* as a bad person, and quite another to *be* one, as the speaker notes so bitterly in Sonnet 121. The emphatic answer to the first question about outward appearances has done nothing to assuage Hamlet's fears of ignobility and cowardice; it has only widened the painful gap between self and world that was foregrounded earlier in the play ('Seems, madam?').

Faced with this mismatch between the inward conscience and the outward persona, this inability to find his bearings in an external world, Hamlet reverses the process, moving from the inward perception of his own cowardice to its outward correlative by means of a purely hypothetical argument. He arrives at this conclusion not by searching his feelings (as one might expect) but by inferring his own moral status from outside, judging himself only by his actions: since I act the way I do, I must not only be *perceived* as a coward, I must *be* a coward too. This is a choice example of how Shakespeare, in Brian Boyd's wording, takes the 'intense process of social monitoring' in the source play 'to new levels by making Hamlet not only a riddle to others in the story, but also to a riddle to himself and to us'.[71]

This piling of question upon question is destined to convince no one, and least of all Hamlet himself, and so all that is left to him is a powerful volley of hatred and self-disgust. At this point the centripetal motion in his mind – a mind revolving around itself, faster and faster, in ever smaller circles – becomes so intense that he even ends up cursing his own curses: 'This is most brave ... that I ... fall a-cursing like a very drab, / A scullion! Fie upon't! Foh!' The verse breaks down completely before Hamlet finally manages to collect himself: 'About, my brains. Hum – I have heard'. At this point the inward spiral is finally broken, giving way to the last segment where he thinks up the Mousetrap and can once more achieve a sense of purpose and determination.

Let us now consider how closely Claudius's guilt-ridden soliloquy 'O my offence is rank' (3.4.36–72) matches the interrogative dialogi-

cal structure we found in 'O what a rogue and peasant slave am I'.
Like Hamlet, Claudius begins with a straightforward moral indictment of his own person. Like Hamlet, he then poses three rhetorical questions, with the important difference that these questions do
not underscore his previous point but rather hold up the opposite
promise of salvation. The important thing for my purposes here is that
Claudius's rhetorical questions, like Hamlet's, are used to establish a
moral framework:

> Is there not rain enough in the sweet heavens ... ?   [Yes.]
> Whereto serves mercy but to confront ... ?   [Nothing.]
> What's in prayer but this twofold force ... ?   [Nothing.]

These self-bolstering rhetorical questions allow Claudius to posit a
providential grace so all-encompassing that even the worst culprit can
be forgiven. As in Hamlet's 'O what a rogue' speech, however, this
tenuous rhetorical certainty is quickly eroded by a disruptive counterpoint in the form of an embarrassingly concrete and genuine query:

> – but O, what form of prayer
> Can serve my turn?

This is not an easy question to answer, and Claudius responds much
in the same way that Hamlet responded to his painful question about
cowardice. Claudius immediately reverts to a rhetorical stance with the
following counter-question:

> 'Forgive me my foul murder'?

This ironic question, formulated in personated form as a hypothetical
quotation, endows Claudius with a measure of psychological distance.
It introduces the next new phase in the soliloquy where he reflects thematically on the impossibility of fooling God in the way that one fools
other people, anchoring his own experience in a broader human perspective. This section of the soliloquy is thus comparable to Hamlet's
unconvincing attempt to gauge his own moral status by personating an
outside perspective ('Who calls me villain?') and inferring his own inner
state from his external actions ('it cannot be / But I am pigeon-livered').
In both cases, the incapacity of the individual self to harness its own
guilt generates a deep need for the kind of external point of view that
no soliloquy could ever offer in genuine form.

So far Claudius's soliloquy has followed the structure of Hamlet's
soliloquy quite faithfully. An initial admission of guilt leads to three
rhetorical questions, followed by a counterpoint in the form of a
genuine question, which in turn provokes an act of personation

and a concomitant search for an external vantage point where the speaker might see himself 'from outside'. Claudius now makes a subtle departure from Hamlet's pattern by taking the technique of question and counter-question for another spin, raising two short, genuine questions that are followed by rhetorical ones:

> What then? What rests?
> Try what repentance can. What can it not? [Nothing].
> Yet what can it, when one cannot repent? [Nothing.]

At this point the rhetorical word is turned against the rhetorical word. Claudius's renewed attempt to reassure himself by means of one rhetorical question ('What can it not?') is immediately undercut by another question that works in the opposite direction, bringing home the sheer hopelessness of his moral situation. After this detour which builds up additional psychological pressure, Claudius arrives at Hamlet's final destination, namely, the collapse of structured and meditative thought in a burst of exclamatives that unleash raw desperation:

> O wretched state! O bosom black as death!
> O limed soul, that struggling to be free,
> Art more engag'd! Help, angels!

Claudius's final bulwark against the inward/downward spiral is, suitably enough, an appeal to his own steely heart and stubborn knees; a good example of the inward-looking, self-addressed apostrophes that characterise this play.

As the play unfolds there is a direct correlation between Hamlet's increasing success in dispelling his own doubt and the force of his rhetorical questions. His next soliloquy, 'Now might I do it pat'(3.4.73–96), also draws heavily on rhetorical questions, but this time only two:

> How his audit stands who knows save heaven? [No one.]
> Am I then revenged ... ? No! [Spelled out.]

This time Hamlet's **erotema** is not compromised by any genuine questions that might upset the self-assurance he seeks: in fact, it even receives an emphatic answer ('No!'). This allows him to brush aside his doubt and quickly devise a plan that lies well in the future but that still gives him a satisfying sense of agency. In the next soliloquy, 'How all occasions do inform against me'(4.4.32–66), he appears to have fully mastered the use of the rhetorical question as an instrument for self-assurance and composure. He begins by drawing a contrast between humans and animals, confessing ignorance as to whether his own procrastination is a sign of thinking too little (which would be bestial oblivion) or too much (which would be a distinctly human activity). We now reach the by now familiar *thematic* turn, as Hamlet, who is already standing at one remove from himself and speculating about his own motivation, seeks an objective reference point for his own moral status:

> Examples gross as earth exhort me,
> Witness this army of such mass and charge,
> Led by a delicate and tender prince,
> Whose spirit, with divine ambition puff'd,
> Makes mouths at the invisible event,
> Exposing what is mortal and unsure
> To all that fortune, death, and danger dare,
> Even for an eggshell. Rightly to be great
> Is not to stir without great argument,
> But greatly to find quarrel in a straw
> When honour's at the stake.

(46–56)

Once this moral map is in place, the scene has been set for a new rhetorical question that brings home his moral situation in the starkest terms:

> How stand I then ...   [Badly.]

Once again, no genuine questions intervene to disrupt the systematic progress of his thought, allowing Hamlet to embrace the idea of revenge fully: 'O from this time forth / My thoughts be bloody or be nothing worth.' Doubt has finally been dispelled, and from this point onwards no further questions will be asked, rhetorical or otherwise.

There will also be very little private speech in the rest of play, so with respect to Hamlet's introspective dialogue, the rest is indeed silence. While the average Shakespeare play packs 14 per cent of its insides into the final act, with *Richard II* as the extreme outlier (91 per cent), *Hamlet* belongs to the mere handful of plays that spread less than 1 per cent of their insides across act 5.[72] This is, as we shall see more clearly towards the end of Chapter 4, another quasi-comic aspect of this play, in that the social integration of forlorn protagonists in the comedies naturally works towards minimising the tension between the inward self and the community. The final chapter of this study will look more closely at how Shakespeare guides our response to his plays through the selective distribution of insides across individual plays and characters.

Notes

1. Nancy Selleck, *The Interpersonal Idiom in Shakespeare, Donne, and Early Modern Culture* (Basingstoke: Palgrave Macmillan, 2008), 94.

2. Charles Taylor, *Sources of the Self: The Making of the Modern Identity* (Cambridge: Cambridge University Press, 1989), 35, 36. For a fine application of Taylor's theory to Shakespeare, see Mustapha Fahmi, 'Quoting the Enemy: Character, Self-Interpretation, and the Question of Perspective in Shakespeare', in *Shakespeare and Moral Agency*, ed. Michael Bristol (London and New York: Continuum, 2010), 129–41.

3. Kenneth Baynes, 'Self, Narrative and Self-Constitution: Revisiting Taylor's "Self-Interpreting Animals"', *Philosophical Forum* 41:4 (2010): 441–57, esp. 443–4.

4. Baynes, 'Self, Narrative and Self-Constitution', 444.

5. Jaak Panksepp et al., 'The Philosophical Implications of Affective Neuroscience', *Journal of Consciousness Studies* 19:3–4 (2012): 6–48.

6. Indeed, Harry Harlow's gruesome experiments in the 1960s on socially deprived rhesus macaques seemed to indicate just how necessary this primal dialogue may be for normal development in humans and related mammals: infant monkeys that were denied a primary caretaker would become subject to horrible behavioural aberrations. The story is described vividly and accessibly by the science journalist Deborah Blum in *Love at Goon Park: Harry Harlow and the Science of Affection* (Chichester: Wiley, 2003).

7. See Ellen Dissanayake, *Art and Intimacy: How the Arts Began* (Seattle: University of Washington Press, 2000).

8. A classic analysis of the differences between collectivist and individualist societies is offered by Harry C. Triandis in *Individualism and Collectivism: New Directions in Social Psychology* (Boulder: Westview Press, 1995). For an illuminating account of social systems based on communal sharing, equality, authority, or market thinking, see Alan Page Fiske, *Structures of Social Life: The Four Elementary Forms of Human Relations* (New York: Free Press, 1991). For early modern perspectives on collectivism and individualism, see Paul Delany, *British Autobiography in the Seventeenth Century* (London: Routledge and Kegan Paul, 1969).

9. On the latter aspect, see especially Peter Holbrook, *Shakespeare's Individualism* (Cambridge: Cambridge University Press, 2010).

10. Children are natural-born soliloquists. It is a cornerstone of Vygotsky's developmental psychology that their overtly verbalised thoughts serve as an instrument for problem-solving and self-regulation by helping them detach themselves from the environment. Modern research has shown that self-talk continues into adolescence (Carol Marie Kronk, 'Private Speech in Adolescents.' *Adolescence* 29:116 (1994), EBSCOHOST, web) and adulthood (Robert M. Duncan and J. Allan Cheyne, 'Incidence and Functions of Self-Reported Private Speech in Young Adults: A Self-Verbalization Questionnaire', *Canadian Journal of Behavioural Science* 31:2 (1999): 133–6). Self-talk also appears to be positively correlated with emotional intelligence (Anne-Marie DePape et al., 'Self-Talk and Emotional Intelligence in University Students', *Canadian Journal of Behavioural Science* 38:3 (2006): 250–60). For the most authoritative text on private speech to date, see Adam Winsler et al., *Private Speech, Executive Functioning, and the Development of Verbal Self-Regulation* (Cambridge: Cambridge University Press, 2009).

11. John C. Freeman, 'Interrogating the Soliloquist: Does it Really Go without Saying?' *symplokē* 18, nos. 1–2 (2010): 131–54, 135. Unfortunately, Freeman partly bases his argument on a 180–degree misreading of Hirsh, confusing the latter's position with the one he is criticising. Hirsh is said to '[separate] speech from thought in claiming, "The words spoken by the actor do not represent words spoken by the character but words merely passing through the mind of the character" (2003 [*History of Soliloquies*], 13)' (132). As we have seen, one of Hirsh's central contributions to Shakespeare studies and the history of soliloquies more generally has been to challenge this view of soliloquy as interior monologue.

12. James Hirsh, 'Dialogic Self-Address in Shakespeare's Plays', *Shakespeare* 8:3 (2012): 312–27, 317, 324.

13. Palfrey and Stern, *Shakespeare in Parts*, 356.

14. As Bernard Beckerman notes, 'Shakespeare depends a great deal upon apostrophe to sustain the soliloquy … instead of directing the soliloquy inward, the apostrophe enabled the actor to direct it outward.' *Shakespeare at the Globe*, 184.

15. John Hoskins, *Directions for Speech and Style*, ed. and intro. Hoyt H. Hudson, Princeton Studies in English 12 (Princeton: Princeton University Press, 1935), 47–8.

16. Margaret Rachael McKay, 'Shakespeare's Use of the Apostrophe, Popular Rhetorical Device of the Renaissance', PhD dissertation, University of Colorado, 1969.

17. McKay, 'Shakespeare's Use of the Apostrophe', 20–1.

18. McKay, 'Shakespeare's Use of the Apostrophe', 24.

19. Richardson, 'Point of View in Drama', 76. The difference between this type of spiritual address and other insides may not always be so significant given the general dialogical tendencies in Shakespeare's insides. (I am grateful to Ewan Fernie for this point – personal communication, The Shakespeare Institute, Stratford-upon-Avon, 19 March 2015.)

20. Stop words: articles, conjunctions, proper names, stage references, numerals.

21. For a comparison between Chaucer's and Shakespeare/Fletcher's version of the story, see E. Talbot Donaldson, *The Swan at the Well: Shakespeare Reading Chaucer* (New Haven and London: Yale University Press, 1985), ch. 3, 50–73.

22. G. R. Proudfoot, 'Introduction', in John Fletcher and William Shakespeare, *The Two Noble Kinsmen* (London: Edward Arnold, 1970), xi–xxvi, xxi.

23. Eugene M. Waith, 'Shakespeare and Fletcher on Love and Friendship', *Shakespeare Studies* 18 (1986), 235–50, 248.

24. Proudfoot, 'Introduction', xxii.

25. Mary Beth Rose, *The Expense of Spirit: Love and Sexuality in English Renaissance Drama* (Ithaca: Cornell University Press, 1998).

26. Barry Weller, 'The Two Noble Kinsmen, the Friendship Tradition, and the Flight from Eros', in *Shakespeare, Fletcher, and The Two Noble Kinsmen*, ed. Charles H. Frey (Columbia: University of Missouri Press, 1989), 93–108. Compare Laurie J. Shannon's forceful, if slightly overstated, rejoinder to previous accounts of the play as a journey towards the maturity of marriage: that these scholars 'fail to grapple with the astonishingly

negative conception of marriage the drama involves' ('Emilia's Argument: Friendship and Human Title in *The Two Noble Kinsmen*', *ELH* 64:3 (1997): 657–82, 662). See also Shannon's *Sovereign Amity: Figures of Friendship in Shakespearean Contexts* (Chicago: Chicago University Press, 2002).

27. See Michel de Montaigne, *The Essays of Montaigne, Done into English by John Florio,* 3 vols., ed. W. E. Henley (New York: AMS Press, 1967), esp. vol. 1, ch. 27, and vol. 3, ch. 5. For a view of early modern and Shakespearean friendship as the chief 'arena' where men 'make themselves meaningful', see Tom MacFaul, *Male Friendship in Shakespeare and His Contemporaries* (Cambridge: Cambridge University Press, 2007).

28. For a fuller interpretation of *The Two Noble Kinsmen,* see Marcus Nordlund, 'Divisive Desires in *The Two Noble Kinsmen*', in *Pangs of Love and Longing: Configurations of Desire in Premodern Literature,* ed. Anders Cullhed et al. (Newcastle upon Tyne: Cambridge Scholars, 2013), 130–43.

29. The standard deviation for apostrophe in the romances (including *The Two Noble Kinsmen*) is 8 percentage points, a figure that is comparable to the comedies (8) and the problem plays (7) but substantially lower than the corresponding figures for the tragedies (13) and histories (13). If we exclude *Kinsmen*, however, the remaining four plays exhibit an extremely low standard variation of 3 percentage points.

30. Jonathan Bate, 'Introduction', in William Shakespeare, *A Midsummer Night's Dream*, RSC edition, ed. Jonathan Bate and Eric Rasmussen (Houndmills: Macmillan, 2008), 4.

31. George Puttenham, *The Art of English Poesy: A Critical Edition,* ed. Frank Whigham and Wayne Rebhorn (Ithaca: Cornell University Press, 2007), 320.

32. Alan Stewart, *Shakespeare's Letters* (Oxford: Oxford University Press, 2008), 21.

33. It is by no means evident, and perhaps even unlikely, that Worcester is the writer behind this letter, and we cannot even say if Hotspur himself knows the identity of the sender. I will therefore refer to it as 'anonymous' in the discussion below.

34. Stewart, *Shakespeare's Letters*, 31–2.

35. In fact, even death – the natural end-all of human speech – seems strangely incapable of fully closing Hotspur's mouth, since we will see later in this chapter that Prince Hal responds to his death by addressing himself on Hotspur's behalf (5.4.96–7).

36. Puttenham, *Art of English Poesy*, book 3 ('Of Ornament Poeticall').

37. I am citing Sylvia Adamson's 'The Grand Style', in *Reading Shakespeare's Dramatic Language: A Guide,* ed. Sylvia Adamson et al. (London: Arden Shakespeare, 2001), 31–50, 38. Adamson defines prosopopoeia as 'the form of metaphor that attributes human characteristics to animals or inanimate objects' and finds that it is 'always implicit in the use of apostrophe since whatever is addressed (whether skylarks, urns or thunderbolts) is by the very fact of being addressed made equivalent to a human interlocutor'. This is of course a much more restrictive conception of apostrophe than the one employed in this study since it clearly excludes address to absent characters.

38. Cited in McKay, 'Shakespeare's Use of the Apostrophe', 20.

39. From the Arcadian Rhetorike (1588), cited in Gavin Alexander, '*Prosopopoeia*: The Speaking Figure', in *Renaissance Figures of Speech*, ed. Sylvia Adamson et al. (Cambridge: Cambridge University Press, 2007), 97–112, 103.
40. Colin Burrow, *Shakespeare and Classical Antiquity*, Oxford Shakespeare Topics (Oxford: Oxford University Press, 2013), 42.
41. Alexander, '*Prosopopoeia*', 111.
42. Such apostrophic address to a dead person is quite frequent in Shakespeare. A SID search for **apostrophe** to the **dead** yields almost as many instances (thirty-six) as there are plays, and one play (*3 Henry VI*) contains no fewer than eight speeches of this kind.
43. S. Viswanatham, '"Illeism with a Difference" in Certain Middle Plays of Shakespeare', *Shakespeare Quarterly* 20:4 (1969): 407–15, 409.
44. SID matrix query, **class** and **illeism/tuism**.
45. SID matrix query for the nodes **illeism** and **tuism** and the attributes **male, female**.
46. Qualitative analysis of SID coding query for **illeism** (complete plays).
47. Viswanatham, '"Illeism with a Difference"', 408. He distinguishes between 'illeism proper' (reference to oneself in the third person singular) and 'illeism with a difference' (using one's proper name). I have not heeded this distinction here since 'illeism with a difference' clearly involves an implicit third-person perspective that distances speakers from their own person.
48. John W. Velz, 'The Ancient World in Shakespeare: Authenticity or Anachronism? A Retrospect', *Shakespeare Studies* 31 (1979): 1–12.
49. The corresponding figures for **illeism** are not so dramatic. Peele writes 5 per cent **illeism** in his sections of the play while Shakespeare doubles his normal percentage for Roman plays (10 per cent).
50. Brian Vickers, *Shakespeare, Co-Author: A Historical Study of Five Collaborative Plays* (Oxford: Oxford University Press, 2002), 226–30.
51. Stefan Daniel Keller, *The Development of Shakespeare's Rhetoric: A Study of Nine Plays*, Swiss Studies in English (Tübingen: Franke, 2009), 81.
52. Keller, *Development of Shakespeare's Rhetoric*, 80.
53. As J. K. Harmer observed in 2011, '[m]uch recent criticism has focused on the material conditions of Hamlet's world, and concomitantly on ways in which a characterisation of Hamlet as brooding and introspective might be jettisoned as a post-Romantic critical imposition' ('Hamlet's Introspection', *Essays in Criticism* 61:1 (2011): 31–53, 35). Such readings clearly constitute an extreme swing of the critical pendulum. It is one thing to say that there is more to Hamlet or *Hamlet* than inwardness (true) or that modern literary scholarship is still influenced by Romantic notions (true), but it is quite another to argue that Hamlet the character is not particularly introspective (false).
54. SID matrix query for **Hamlet (play)** and **assessing morality**, divided by total word count for **Hamlet (play)**.
55. McKay, 'Shakespeare's Use of the Apostrophe', 146.
56. The figure has been computed as a percentage of the total word count for each phase. Interestingly, the *high* average for **apostrophe** in the 1605–9 phase is paralleled by consistently *low* scores for another dialogical

element, **prosopopoeia** (1 per cent mean vs. 4 per cent for the complete plays).

57. McKay, 'Shakespeare's Use of the Apostrophe', 29.
58. It is certainly tempting to explain *Hamlet*'s 'comic' tendencies in the area of apostrophe with reference to tonal and thematic similarities between this play and the 'problem comedies' written around the turn of the century, but this promising avenue of inquiry lies beyond the scope of the present study.
59. In a conflated edition such as the Complete Arden Shakespeare that combines the Quarto 2 and Folio versions of the play, Hamlet speaks 71 per cent of the play's insides. In a strictly Folio-based version that adds a soliloquy for Claudius in act 4, scene 3, and removes Hamlet's soliloquy in act 4, scene 4, among other things, Hamlet's portion drops to a still substantial 65 per cent.
60. It is at least possible to argue that Coriolanus's entire speech 'O world, thy slippery turns!' constitutes a long apostrophe to the World (in which case the apostrophe percentage for this play rises to 35 per cent due to its general scarcity of insides). My methodological principle in the coding process has been to code an entire passage of this kind as apostrophe only if the rest of the speech contains additional relational markers that are consonant with second-person address. Since there are no such signals in the rest of the speech, only the first five words, 'O world, thy slippery turns!', have been coded as apostrophe.
61. The same principle almost certainly explains the two outliers on the bottom rung of the table for apostrophe in tragic protagonists (Julius Caesar and Cleopatra).
62. Alex Newell, *The Soliloquies in Hamlet: The Structural Design* (Rutherford: Fairleigh Dickinson University Press, 1991), 61.
63. Joseph Carroll, 'Intentional Meaning in *Hamlet*: An Evolutionary Perspective', *Style* 44 (2010): 230–260, esp. 246–8.
64. Matthew Arnold, 'Preface to the First Edition of *Poems*', in *The Poems of Matthew Arnold*, ed. Kenneth Allot (London: Longman, 1965), 591.
65. Newell, *Soliloquies in Hamlet*, 18–19.
66. Lee, *Shakespeare's Hamlet*, 196.
67. Maynard Mack, *Everybody's Shakespeare* (Lincoln, NB: University of Nebraska Press, 1993), 109.
68. Harmer, 'Hamlet's Introspection', 45.
69. The coding principle for **questions** is spelled out in Appendix 3.
70. If we count the number of codings, the **erotema** count for *Hamlet* (10) is lower than that for *1 Henry IV* (fourteen) and *3 Henry VI* (fifteen). This reflects a stylistic difference between these plays: the history plays contain a large number of brief rhetorical questions, as in Falstaff's catechism on honour, while those in *Hamlet* are far more elaborate.
71. Brian Boyd, 'Literature and Evolution: A Bio-Cultural Approach', *Philosophy and Literature* 29 (2005): 1–23, 16.
72. SID matrix query for **play** and **act**.

Chapter 4

Distribution

It has long been a blanket argument against scientifically informed approaches to literary studies that our proper study should be the literary particulars, nuances, complexities, and ambiguities that cannot be hacked up and measured in positivistic fashion.[1] The idea is usually that humanists should focus on a qualitative concern with the unique and the irreducible, leaving the laws, universals, and generalisations to the scientists. This somewhat dualistic view of humanistic inquiry, where qualitative approaches are seen as simply incommensurate with quantitative approaches, is open to three constructive objections.

The first is that quantitative analysis can be a complement, not an alternative, to traditional forms of literary analysis and interpretation. There is no contradiction between attending to large-scale patterns and subtle literary nuances in the same act of interpretation, provided that we have enough time on our hands, of course. Secondly, the broad generalisations offered by quantitative analysis can sometimes be absolutely necessary if we want our arguments about complex particulars to hold water. It often makes little sense to argue for the special, specific, unusual, particular, or idiosyncratic aspects of a particular work unless one can compare these traits convincingly to a larger totality. This is why a concern with Shakespeare's broader literary habits should ideally go hand in hand with a detailed analysis and interpretation of particular plays, scenes, characters, genres, or modes. The latter point also includes a third objection to the anti-quantitative stance: that coding methods designed specifically for genre-specific research questions can increase the relevance, complexity, and usefulness of quantitative analysis substantially.

The purpose of this fourth and final chapter will be to explore patterns in Shakespeare's general distribution of insides according to variables such as subgenre, phase, play, act, character, gender, and class. Who gets insides, who doesn't, and how does this affect our perception of the characters or the play? Are there significant connections between Shakespeare's choice of subgenre or mode and his distribution of insides and their component parts? Did his dramatic practice change over time? Though I will draw on numerous plays in the Shakespeare canon, my main objective will be to triangulate three plays from the beginning, middle, and end of his career – *The Taming of the Shrew*, *All's Well that Ends Well*, and *The Two Noble Kinsmen* – with a stronger focus on the middle play.

My main point of interest in these readings will be how Shakespeare's distribution of insides affects the distribution of audience sympathy for his characters, with a particular eye to how this process is further inflected by gender and subgenre. I will also explore the closely related trade-off between driving the plot forward and stimulating the audience's empathetic and sympathetic involvement. In order to ground the latter discussion in concrete aspects of the literary text, this chapter places a sustained focus on the dramatic speech acts performed by Shakespeare's characters. (As I suggested in the Introduction, it is very hard to study literary *functions* or *intentions* systematically since these are often very subtle and indirect, but we stand a much better chance of attaining reliable pragmatic knowledge about *actions*.) For the same purpose of maximum clarity, the chapter begins with a philosophical, psychological, and dramatic exploration of the key concept of sympathy, in relation to related phenomena such as empathy and perspective taking.

Fictional Fellow Feeling

The English word 'sympathy' harks back to the Greek words for *feeling* (*-pathos*) *with* (*sym-*) another person. Some learned early modern Englishmen used it to designate various mystical correspondences and affinities in nature, while Shakespeare tended to restrict his usage to different forms of agreement or consonance between persons. In *Othello*, for example, Iago promises the lovesick Roderigo that the lack of 'sympathy in years, manners, and beauties' between Othello and Desdemona is destined to erode their love (2.1.227–8). There are also some signs that the dramatist was gravitating towards a modern association of sympathy with distress. The one word that is associated most frequently with 'sympathy' in his plays is 'woe'.[2]

Today most philosophers and psychologists agree that sympathy has two necessary and sufficient components: the perception of another person's need or distress, and a resulting concern for that person's well-being. As Susan Feagin further explains, experiencing sympathy presupposes that we have singled out someone – whom she calls the 'protagonist' – as our focus of attention. A sympathetic response 'requires having feelings or emotions that are in concert with the interests or desires the sympathizer (justifiably) attributes to the protagonist ... when we are sympathetic, we take on another's interests as our own'.[3] In the words of Amy Coplan, similarly, sympathy involves 'caring about another individual – feeling *for* another'.[4]

Shakespeare invites audience sympathy for his characters by many different means. Most obviously, he places them in situations that most of us would find intolerable, thereby inviting our compassion and concern. Such dramatic sympathy is almost certainly what Aristotle had in mind when he singled out *pathos* and *fear* as central to the tragic experience.[5] Only the most hardened or absent-minded theatregoer can avoid feeling unbearably for Gloucester when his eyes are gouged out sadistically by the Duke of Cornwall. When we watch him lose his eyesight at the hands of his tormentor, our visceral reaction is intensified by the special helplessness that comes with being effectively separated from his play-world.

The most important difference between Shakespeare's usage of the word 'sympathy' and the modern concept is his apparent presupposition that the sympathiser and the object of sympathy must feel the same thing. In this particular case it is analytically useful to avoid replicating Shakespeare's own usage on the verbal level. Sympathy, as I will use it here, can be felt for protagonists without sharing either their own beliefs or emotions.[6] Indeed, sympathisers do not even 'have to be right about the interests or desires they attribute to the protagonist' in order to sympathise in a meaningful sense.[7] This is why sympathy is often a rich source of irony, in real life as in fiction, as when the modern religious conservative feels sorry for gay people. Similar ironies are established routinely when authors cultivate dramatic or attitudinal irony and sympathy by tapping directly into the divide between the character's and the audience's point of view. We cringe helplessly as Othello wanders unwittingly into Iago's arms because we have some insight into the minds of the noble Moor and his deceptive ensign. We cringe because our *sympathy* for Othello is based on a measure of contrastive *emphathetic* insight into the minds of both characters.

'When I empathize with another,' writes Amy Coplan, 'I take up his or her psychological perspective and imaginatively experience, to some degree or other, what he or she experiences.'[8] While audience *sympathy* rarely poses a major problem for literary theorists (because it doesn't require us to feel what characters 'actually' feel), the idea that we *empathise* with them is more controversial because it presupposes a match between first-order and second-order experience. If empathy is essentially a simulation of 'the mental activity and processes' of the protagonist, then 'the extent to which one fails to simulate what is in fact going on in the protagonist is the extent to which one fails to empathize'.[9]

What does it mean to empathise with a literary character that does not really exist as we do? This is not the place to plunge too deeply into this formidable philosophical problem,[10] but suffice it to say that fiction is a narrative convention; that Shakespeare's characters are conventional approximations of real human beings; and, consequently, that we will not realise their conventional nature unless we attribute a considerable amount of cognitive depth to them. It has been argued that the failure or unwillingness to attribute mental depth to dramatic characters amounts to a kind of critical autism,[11] even in those cases where authors deliver stock characters rather than finely chiselled subjectivities. Historical transmutations in the concept of character may be both substantial and deeply interesting, but they are merely epiphenomena compared to this basic point. Since our acts of interpretation are not gratuitous but constrained by concrete evidence and the validity of our theoretical assumptions, it also follows that our attempts to empathise with literary characters can be more or less appropriate, felicitous, and deep.

This is not to say that empathy is an unproblematic term. In the account I have sketched above, it is closely related to sympathy but functionally independent from it. Amy Coplan writes:

> Just as I can sympathize with another without trying to imagine the world from her perspective, I can also empathize with another without experiencing concern for her well-being. As Peter Goldie explains, empathy is consistent with indifference: 'you can imagine the other's suffering, yet simply disregard it, or you might empathize with a person who has committed a terrible crime, yet feel no sympathy for you think he thoroughly deserves his punishment'.[12]

This is a valid point, but the formulation also exemplifies a weak spot in many contemporary accounts of empathy: the incomplete distinction between *feeling* what another person is feeling and *grasping* the same thing intellectually. For some, like the literary scholar Suzanne Keen, empathy is necessarily a question of feeling with others: it is a 'spontaneous, vicarious sharing of affect' where 'we feel what we believe to be the emotions of others'.[13] One of several problems here is that one can readily grasp the feelings of another person without actually sharing them, which raises the question if one is really empathising at all.

Iago's ominous stage presence illustrates the problem lucidly. The classic reading of this character as master empathiser was put forward by Stephen Greenblatt in *Renaissance Self-Fashioning*, where the diabolical ensign's psychic mobility, his capacity to assume the perspective of his unsuspecting victims, was regarded as symbolic of Western colonial power.[14] It can, however, be objected that Iago never really feels what his victims feel, in spite of his sophisticated understanding of human psychology and his sharp eye for personal weaknesses. As A. C. Bradley observed long ago, he is Shakespeare's chilling reminder that

> perfectly sane people exist in whom fellow-feeling of any kind is so weak that an almost absolute egoism becomes possible to them ... [and] that such evil is compatible, and even appears to ally itself easily, with exceptional powers of will and intellect.[15]

Iago's first step is to dissect Othello's individual nature and collapse it into a distinctive type (or 'character' in the early modern sense):

> The Moor is of a free and open nature
> That thinks men honest that but seem to be so,
> And will as tenderly be led by th' nose
> As asses are.

> (1.3.398–401)

This enables him to devise a tailor-made therapy from hell that plays on the weak points of this particular type of person. Seen in this way, Iago's empathy is really a calculation of expected outcomes on the basis of observed behaviour and encyclopaedic knowledge, rather than the sharing of emotional states with his victims. His world is a world of stimulus and response. He does not need to feel what other people feel in order to manipulate them; it is enough for him to understand *what* they are feeling and *why*.

Is it meaningful to call this 'empathy'? Some social scientists have tried to rescue the concept from fluffiness by drawing a subsidiary distinction between *cognitive* and *affective* empathy, which would allow Iago's psychopathic skills to fall neatly into the former category. Cognitive empathy is grasping the feelings of other people (as Iago does so cunningly) and affective empathy is sharing them (which he does not). This distinction seems less than felicitous, however, since 'cognitive empathy' is not really a matter of em-*pathos* at all. One cannot escape the impression that these scholars are squeezing two fairly distinct phenomena, most likely involving distinct neural circuitry, into the same traditional category. It makes more sense, at least from the perspective of the present study, to side with those scholars who replace the awkward term 'cognitive empathy' with 'perspective taking' or 'mentalising' or 'theory of mind' in order to detach the latter terms from the element of *pathos* or fellow feeling.[16]

On the internal level of the dramatic fiction, Shakespeare's characters constantly seek to gauge and predict each other's mental states, and their relative success or failure often influences the direction of the plot. Whenever characters fail to guard their soliloquies from the hearing of other characters and are exposed to eavesdropping, the internal and the external levels of dramatic communication become deeply homologous. A parallel process is constantly churning on the external level of dramatic communication. Shakespeare's soliloquies and solo asides constitute his most important and effective vehicles for audience empathy and perspective taking because they promise fairly direct access to what his characters are 'really' thinking and feeling. Since these thoughts and feelings are often withheld from other characters, the audience experiences a special intimacy with the character whose perspective it has adopted, and this intimacy may easily spill over into a sense of complicity. The sharing of secrets has probably always been a preferred Machiavellian strategy because it promotes social bonding through the formation of an 'in-group' upon which mutual trust and interdependence can be based.

This type of involvement is distinct from sympathy. No reader or audience member in his or her right mind would *sympathise* with Iago, and some may even surprise themselves by rejoicing sadistically at the end when he is dragged off to some grisly form of punishment (5.2.367).[17] Nevertheless, the slippery psychological slope from neutral perspective taking (knowing that Iago is feeling gleeful) to empathetic intimacy and the threat of emotional contagion (sharing some of his glee) is, I believe, one factor that explains his incredible effectiveness on the stage and the written page. In the same way that Iago's rhetoric places Othello in an unbearable no-man's-land of doubt, Shakespeare makes his audience and readership waver between two irreconcilable positions. We recoil in horror from Iago's morally outrageous perspective, but in the best performances we also feel the suggestive pull of empathetic identification with his gloating Vice-like posture. To empathise with evil is not to sympathise with it, but it is a hard act to perform without some moral taint. The second thing that makes Iago such a successful fictional creation is that our gestures towards perspective taking and empathic identification are ultimately frustrated at the level of his basic motivation. We peel away the layers of the onion but never seem to get to the core.

I would now like to sum up the consequences of this discussion for my approach to the Shakespearean inside. These speeches are intensively concerned with the content and quality of private experience, sometimes constituting our only dependable information about the character's point view. Hence it seems natural to expect a positive correlation between insides, on the one hand, and audience empathy and perspective taking, on the other. Plays or roles with many insides will, on the whole, tend to be more deeply concerned with the quality of subjective experience.

This broad claim is, however, in immediate need of qualification since insides have other standard functions than just the expression of individual point of view. Since Shakespeare uses insides habitually as instruments for the advancement of his plots, and since any dramatist can only do so much in a single soliloquy, we can expect a basic tension between their expository and their empathetic function. Furthermore, the analysis of this dramatic trade-off is likely to be enhanced considerably if we ground it in a systematic consideration of the concrete dramatic speech acts performed by Shakespeare's characters. As we shall see in a moment, the earliest phase of his career was marked by a strong preference for expository insides that mainly served to keep the audience abreast of the action. The same tension between exposition and empathetic involvement is, as I shall argue below, particularly central to the audience's perception of *The Taming of the Shrew*.

Given that insides are such central vehicles for audience empathy and perspective taking, they also help promote or reduce the audience's *sympathetic* concern for the soliloquist. They do so through the selective distribution of access to a more private and often more honest view than we typically find in dialogue. A chief difference between the dramatic distribution of empathy and sympathy, however, is that audience sympathy cannot be expected to increase in tandem with the overall distribution of insides. Since soliloquies and solo asides allow characters to speak without direct attention to social considerations, these speeches are particularly effective vehicles for socially unacceptable or even directly antisocial ideas. Iago is a fine example of this inverse correlation between sympathy and insides: the more we learn about him, the less sympathetic concern we feel for him, even if his rhetoric should lock us into an empathetic stranglehold.

Iago also reminds us that insides act as important funnels or proxies for the distribution of audience sympathy towards characters other than the speaker. His malice towards his poor unsuspecting victims – Othello, Desdemona, Cassio, and even Roderigo – has the indirect effect of deepening the audience's concern for their well-being. Although this type of information is often skewed and rendered unreliable by the character's vested interests and characteristics, a soliloquist's surreptitious analysis of another character also constitutes an important proxy for audience empathy on the internal level of the dramatic fiction. It may supply the audience with vital information about what goes on inside both parties (the speaker and the character under scrutiny). Whenever such information constitutes an explicit statement about the nature of a fellow character it has been coded in the SID as an instance of the dramatic speech act **assessing character.** On average, Shakespeare's characters devote around 14 per cent of their insides to this type of social information.

In soliloquies and asides that invite or express a positive social emotion like sympathy, the sympathetic bond between character and audience becomes particularly strong. Soliloquies where one character expresses sympathy for the plight of another character on the internal level of the dramatic fiction typically project audience sympathy in two simultaneous directions: towards the characters for whom the speakers are expressing sympathy, certainly, but also towards the speakers themselves, since these pro-social emotions make them likeable.

Male Planning in *The Taming of the Shrew*

So far we have seen that insides are important conduits for the dramatic distribution of sympathy, and crucial vehicles for empathy and perspective taking. First and foremost, they constitute a means for the dramatist to guide, direct, and constrain the audience's insight into the fictional minds and feelings of his characters. This relative depth of mental insight, in turn, acts as a powerful constraint on, and enabler of, audience sympathy.

Let us now begin to explore Shakespeare's distribution of sympathy and soliloquy at the beginnings of his career, with the comedy *The Taming of the Shrew*. Like *The Merchant of Venice*, this play grates forcefully against modern values and sensibilities in its depiction of Petruchio's successful domestication of his spouse Katherina. As Dana Aspinall notes, this controversy is not entirely new, since the play has 'elicited a panoply of heartily supportive, ethically uneasy, or altogether disgusted responses' ever since its first performance in the late fifteen hundreds.[18] Modern literary scholars have disagreed about what conclusions to draw from Petruchio's successful transformation of Katherina from violent shrew to obedient wife. Is the play a straightforward endorsement of patriarchal values? Is it a chummy farce with some sexist traits that should not be taken so very seriously? Or does the irony run so deep that it even constitutes a subversive critique of patriarchy?[19]

My objective in this section will not be to choose or mediate between these interpretations of Shakespeare's play, or to advance an extravagant alternative, but rather to identify some special characteristics of its private speeches that contribute actively to this controversial status. More specifically, I want to explore how Shakespeare seems to muffle audience empathy and sympathy in *Shrew* by means of dramatic choices that stand out markedly in comparison with his other plays.

A paradoxical aspect of *The Taming of the Shrew* is that its cantankerous woman protagonist is so very often silent at those points when speech would seem to be highly motivated. Frances E. Dolan puts it nicely in her edition of the play:

> Although Katharine is labeled a shrew because she resists attempts to dominate her and asserts herself with fist and tongue, she is characterized more by silence than by speech at important points in the play ... How do we know what Katharine thinks, feels, and wants? ... We see Katharine and Petruchio alone only in 2.1; we never see Katharine by herself; and when she complains, she always has an audience besides or other than Petruchio ... He has soliloquies in which he explains his motives and intentions; Katharine does not.[20]

Katherina is not alone in this fate since no female character gets any insides in *The Taming of the Shrew*. This is not a unique feature in the Shakespeare canon. Eleven Shakespeare plays out of thirty-nine have zero female insides, and male characters deliver no less than 84 per cent of all words spoken as insides. Does this imply that Shakespeare denies his women characters inward language to a greater extent than the men, or does it simply reflect a general paucity of female speech? The corresponding figure for all speech[21] is male dominance by 82 per cent, suggesting that Shakespeare's male and female characters exhibit roughly the same inside/dialogue ratio. The fictional inner lives of Shakespeare's women characters are mapped out in fewer lines because they speak fewer lines overall.

A SID search reveals no obvious pattern among the plays that have zero female insides. They are spread out quite evenly across Shakespeare's subgenres and the different phases of his career. Some of the plays that *minimise* but do not wholly *elide* the inward language of women protagonists are jealousy plays: *Othello* has only 1.4 per cent female insides and *The Winter's Tale* has 0.5 per cent. Like *The Taming of the Shrew*, these plays combine a dominant male protagonist with a marked suppression of the female protagonist's private speech. The free and honest discourse that would normally be offered in soliloquies and asides is instead placed in the mouth of a secondary character (Emilia, Paulina).

A similar absence of female insides also characterises *The Tempest*, where, as we saw in Chapter 2, the omnipotent Prospero even manages to transcend the speech conventions that would normally regulate his own existence as a dramatic character. His stage life is also completely unruffled by female inwardness since his daughter Miranda, the only woman character in the play, never speaks a single inside. It is not a far stretch to say that *The Tempest* has some elements of a jealousy play since Prospero is so focused on preserving his daughter's chastity. The play substitutes a jealous father for a jealous husband.

These general patterns allow us to see *The Taming of the Shrew* in a somewhat broader light, but so far they have merely told us that the play is not so very special. Can we also say something more specific that sets *Shrew* apart from other plays and perhaps even allows us to explain some of its special dramatic effect? In 1966, Robert Heilman published an essay that foregrounded the play's generic dimension:

> The essential procedure of farce is to deal with people as if they lack, largely or totally, the physical, emotional, intellectual, and moral sensitivity that we think of as 'normal' … Farce offers a spectacle that resembles daily actuality but lets us participate without feeling the responsibilities and liabilities that the situation would normally evoke … In farce, the human personality is without depth. Hence action is not slowed down by thought or by the friction of competing motives. Everything goes at high speed, with dash, variety, never a pause for stocktaking, and ever an athlete's quick glance ahead at the action coming up next.[22]

Statements of this kind about the attributes of a particular play are always implicitly comparative: they are meaningful only insofar as they help us clarify the difference of certain plays from certain other plays. (There would be very little point in pointing out that this glass of water is wet or that the pig to the left has a snout.) The SID allows us to reformulate Heilman's analytical description of the play's farcical qualities as a set of predictions about its special nature. If his intuitions about *Shrew* are sound, and if, by extension, they apply to the play's private speeches as well as to the dialogue, then we can expect its soliloquies and solo asides actively to withhold audience sympathy and drive the action forward by at least three concrete means.

First and foremost, we can expect *The Taming of the Shrew* to stand out among Shakespeare's other plays in being demonstrably low on insides, on the assumption that such speeches constitute Shakespeare's most central vehicle for the depth of personality that runs counter to the farcical mode. Secondly, these few insides should be *high* on expository elements, especially 'forward-looking' ones where a character plans a future course of action. Thirdly, they should be *low* on the kind of thematic and moral reflection that might anchor the action in larger ideas about human nature and proper conduct.

The first hypothesis – that the psychologically superficial and farcical *Shrew* ought to have fewer insides than most other Shakespeare plays – holds up fairly well under scrutiny. Its inside count of 3.6 per cent is less than half of the Shakespearean mean. This is even substantially lower than the standard example of Shakespearean farce, *The Comedy of Errors* (5.2 per cent). We come next to Heilman's contention that in farce, 'everything goes at high speed, with dash, variety, never a pause for stocktaking, and ever an athlete's quick glance ahead at the action coming up next'. A crucial aspect of this forward glance is the regular tendency of Shakespeare's characters to commit themselves verbally to a particular course of action in their soliloquies or asides. Even though Shakespeare may not have used the same term, the dramatic speech act **planning** was still a crucial part of his toolkit for the elaboration of plot as well as character. **Planning** can be distinguished clearly from **predicting** (the attempt to foresee other people's actions or other events in situations where the speaker has limited agency), and its definite commitment towards specific actions sets it apart from general deliberation about dilemmas or potential courses of action.

The specific figures for **planning** in *Shrew* stand out starkly in relation to broader patterns in Shakespeare's dramatic practice. A bird's-eye view of the complete insides reveals, unsurprisingly, that **planning** is a central activity for Shakespeare's soliloquists. On average, they spend 17 per cent of their insides announcing to themselves and to the audience what their next step will be. When explored across the length of Shakespeare's career, the distribution of this dramatic speech act looks like an inverted version of the climatographic hockey stick (Figure 4.1).

The plays from the first half of the 1590s are particularly heavy on **planning**: their characters spend almost a fourth (23 per cent) of their insides informing themselves and the audience about what they are about to do.[23] This seems like an interesting corollary of the plot-driven tendencies that some scholars have identified in the early plays.[24] In the next phase, the figures level off quickly to a fairly consistent 14–15 per cent that lasts until the end of Shakespeare's career.

The individual figure for **planning** in *The Taming of the Shrew*, by contrast, is simply *extreme*. Its characters spend no less than 62 per cent of their insides stating what they are about to do. This is extraordinary even by the standards of the early Shakespearean hockey stick, and the chief cause is, unsurprisingly, Petruchio's systematic elaboration of Kate's marital therapy, which peaks at a staggering 86 per cent.[25] A similar focus on individual agency can also be traced in Shakespeare's

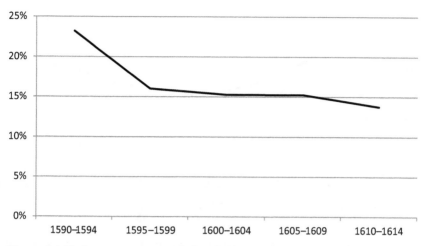

Figure 4.1 Shakespeare's usage of **planning** over time.

Table 4.1 Incidence of 'will' and 'I'll'.[26]

	Complete insides	*Shrew* insides
will	0.61% (4)	0.83% (8)
I'll	0.32% (12)	1.65% (1)
Total	0.93%	2.48%

word usage, since *Shrew* exhibits a corresponding spike in the frequency of words directly associated with individual **planning** ('will', 'I'll'; Table 4.1).

The first-person contraction 'I'll' is the twelfth most frequent lexical item of four letters or more in Shakespeare's complete insides, but in *Shrew* it ranks as number one. It is used no fewer than five times as often as in the complete insides, culminating in a single speech where Petruchio employs it six times in the course of fourteen lines (2.1.169–82). This is strong linguistic evidence for the unusual dominance of **planning** in this play.

Heilman's view of *Shrew* as a 'forward-looking' farce also seems to imply that it is not backward-looking (or as he puts it, not given to 'stocktaking'). In the terminology of this project, the play should be low on the dramatic speech act **reporting**, by which a character relates past actions or events that have happened either offstage (and need to be brought to the audience's attention) or, more rarely, onstage (so that the audience can be reminded of their salience). So how does Heilman's view of *The Taming of the Shrew* as a particularly non-retrospective play survive a systematic SID scrutiny? It does so admirably. Its insides

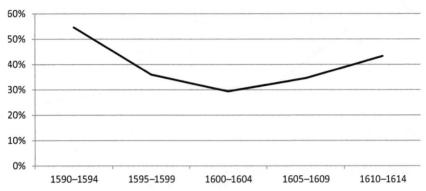

Figure 4.2 Shakespeare's usage of **exposition** over time.

contain only 6 per cent **reporting**, compared to the Shakespearean average of 24 per cent (for the complete insides) or 31 per cent (for insides in plays written between 1590 and 1594).

Though this may be less immediately relevant to the interpretation of *The Taming of the Shrew*, the closely related acts of **planning** and **reporting** can be combined usefully into an aggregated speech act called **exposition** (the sum of the other two). The figures for **exposition** across Shakespeare's career form a curve-like pattern, with highs at the earliest and the last phase (Figure 4.2).

Once again the score is substantially higher for the first phase, suggesting that much more writing space was spent in these early soliloquies and asides on plot-related information that explained past events and prepared the audience for what was to come. Between 1590 and 1594, Shakespeare's soliloquists and speakers of asides spent more than half of these speeches going over past events and informing the audience about their future actions. A plausible explanation for this elevated tendency – at least beside the ever-vexing factor of co-authorship – is that the 'upstart crow' was gradually finding his dramatic bearings and was anxious to keep the audience's eyes on the plot.

After a fifteen-year period of relatively little information of this kind, and with a noticeable slump in the interrogative and disillusioned phase of the early 1600s, the figure goes up again in the last five years of Shakespeare's career. One important reason is that Shakespeare went back to writing long expository soliloquies that expound on the backstory and that often seem unmotivated on the internal level of the fiction. (One thinks immediately of the speeches of Belarius and Autolycus that we examined in Chapter 1.) This is one of several ways in which Shakespeare's dramatic practice seems to come full circle in the final years of his career.[27]

We can now conclude that *The Taming of the Shrew* constitutes an extreme example of the early Shakespeare's tendency to use soliloquies and solo asides as expository devices. The next item on Heilman's list of farcical traits is the tendency to downplay the 'moral sensitivity' and 'responsibilities and liabilities' that a character's plight should normally inspire in the audience. If farce deliberately brackets our sympathetic tendencies in favour of distanced amusement, then we can not only expect a farcical play to reduce its number of insides; we can also predict some reluctance on the part of the dramatist to have his characters engage in explicit moral reflection.

The dramatic speech act **assessing morality** applies whenever a character assesses an action or situation or person with explicit reference to ideas about right and wrong. This is a central activity for Shakespeare's soliloquists and speakers of asides, who spend on average between a fourth and a fifth (22 per cent) of their total insides passing explicit moral judgement on themselves or other characters. *The Taming of the Shrew* is, however, strikingly devoid of such explicit moral commentary, which takes up only around 3 per cent of its insides compared to the substantial Shakespearean mean. This is the second lowest score in the Shakespeare canon. The lowest score – 2 per cent – is found in *A Midsummer Night's Dream*.

To engage in moral reasoning is typically to assess concrete acts (either real or imagined) against impersonal standards that need not be universal but must have some broader validity. **Assessing morality** is, in other words, closely related to another dramatic speech act that extrapolates general truths from particular events: **assessing thematics**. In this study, characters are said to engage in thematic reflection as soon as they rise above their concrete dramatic situation and make statements about broader patterns in human experience. Such thematic reflection is at work in no less than 14 per cent of Shakespeare's complete insides, but there is also considerable variation over time (Figure 4.3).

The graph in Figure 4.3 shows that the thematic impulse was very weak in the strongly plot-oriented beginnings of Shakespeare's career and reached its apex in the first years of the seventeenth century. Although dramatic speech acts are not mutually exclusive in any strict sense – there is, in principle if not in practice, no limit to their potential overlap – it is tempting to picture an inverse relationship between a relatively plot-driven early Shakespeare and the more thematically and morally oriented craftsman in the first years of the seventeenth century. Then, in the final years, the established dramatist seems to reconnect with his earlier practices. He no longer shies away from long expository soliloquies of the kind spoken by Belarius or Autolycus and

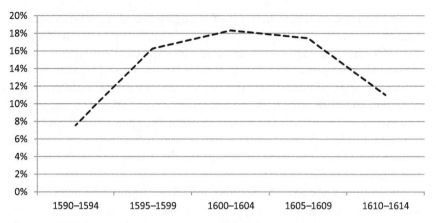

Figure 4.3 Shakespeare's usage of **assessing thematics** over time.

perhaps even courts obscurity on the levels of theme and motivation (Figure 4.4).

Once again the differences between different phases in Shakespeare's career outweigh any minor differences between different subgenres. And once again Heilman's account of *The Taming of the Shrew* is borne out by the SID data, since the play's individual score for **assessing thematics** is only 4 per cent. This is less than a third of the Shakespearean average of 14 per cent, and only half of the modest 8 per cent average for the early phase to which the play belongs (1590–4).

So far we have seen that Heilman's account of the farcical elements in *Taming of the Shrew* captures distinctive, measurable aspects of the play's insides that set it apart from other Shakespeare plays. In these speeches the male speaker maintains a steady instrumental focus on his future actions against the backdrop of several significant silences. Shakespeare has removed most of our standard footholds for empathetic and sympathetic identification with Katherina: we never get to empathise with her private point of view *from inside*, so to speak, nor is Petruchio's scheme anchored in any larger thematic or moral concerns.

These data lend strong support to Heilman's case, but one must be careful not to overextend them by positing too rigid connections between particular dramatic modes or subgenres and particular dramatic speech acts. This is of course particularly important when we extrapolate hypotheses about a particular type of speech from overriding accounts of individual plays. There are, in addition, three other considerations that should give us pause.

The first limitation is that dramatic traits related to Shakespeare's choice of mode or subgenre can hardly be expected to emerge con-

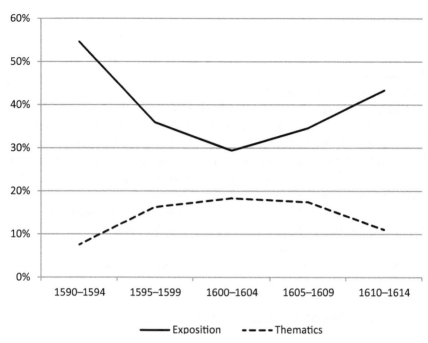

Figure 4.4 Shakespeare's usage of **exposition** and **assessing thematics** over time.

sistently on the level of the individual play. In Chapter 1, we saw that another Shakespeare play with farcical tendencies – *The Two Gentlemen of Verona* – does not minimise its soliloquies and asides for the sake of brisk action but maximises them in order to interrogate their conventional implications and explore their comic potential. This gives *Verona* the second highest internal percentage of insides in the complete plays (16 per cent).

Secondly, we cannot always expect a play's insides to mirror its larger tendencies in microcosmic fashion. If farce should automatically dictate a lawful shift towards excessive **planning** in sparse soliloquies and asides, then we would surely expect another Shakespeare play – *The Comedy of Errors*, the Shakespearean door-swinging farce par excellence – to exhibit a similar pattern. Its insides do exhibit a similar suppression of **assessing thematics** (5 per cent vs. the Shakespearean mean of 14 per cent), but they also come very close to the Shakespearean mean for **reporting** (18 vs. 17 per cent), **planning** (18 per cent vs. 17 per cent), and **assessing morality** (17 vs. 22 per cent). The protagonist's position is crucial here, since, as we saw in Chapter 3, the play's dominant soliloquist, Antipholus of Syracuse, is effectively shorn of agency. His unawareness of being mistaken for his twin brother pushes him into an essentially passive relationship to a world that makes no sense to him. Soliloquy is always an individual response on the part of the character to contextual pressures on the internal level of the dramatic fiction, and it is therefore likely that factors associated with dominant characters will often trump effects related to subgenre or mode on the level of the individual play.

Thirdly, a myopic concern with specific subgenres or modes may easily blind us to other significant but less intuitive patterns that are hard to detect without recourse to descriptive statistics. I believe Heilman's 'farcical' account of *Shrew* has done more than identify a set of local traits that cannot be generalised beyond the confines of the individual play and subgenre, but the really significant connections do not always appear in the expected places. One of the strengths of a systematic, quantitative approach is that it can alert us to such unexpected patterns. An example from the tragic subgenre will be used to illustrate this point before we move on to *Kinsmen* and *All's Well*.

Titus Andronicus: Tragedy and Farce?

The Taming of the Shrew was probably written around the same time as another worrying fixture in the Shakespeare canon, *Titus Andronicus*, but the two plays are seldom if ever discussed together. Interestingly, however, *Titus* comes closer than any other Shakespeare play to the anti-sympathetic and farcical insides of *The Taming of a Shrew*. Like *Shrew*, *Titus* contains few insides by Shakespearean standards (4.1 per cent), and these are squarely focused on **planning**. In fact, *Titus* is the only play in the Shakespeare canon that comes close to *Shrew*'s extreme figures for this dramatic speech act (58 per cent vs. 62 per cent). This elevated score for **planning** is not the co-author George Peele's doing but Shakespeare's. A SID compound query for **planning** and **authorship** shows that Peele's most frequently accepted contributions to *Titus* make up 32 per cent of the play's total word count for insides but only 21 per cent of the passages devoted to **planning**. *Titus* also exhibits elevated word frequencies of the kind that we found in *Shrew* (Table 4.2).

True to this sustained focus on action rather than reflection, the insides of *Titus* have extremely little thematic content (only 1 per cent, compared to the 14 per cent mean for the complete insides, and 3 per cent for the non-thematic *Shrew*).

Admittedly, the play's moral commentary seems much more average on the level of pure numbers; its 20 per cent count for **assessing morality** mirrors the mean for the 1590–4 plays (19 per cent) quite faithfully. But who does most of the moral soliloquising in this play? Quantitatively

Table 4.2 Incidence of 'will' and 'I'll' in *Titus Andronicus* and *The Taming of the Shrew*.

Word	Complete insides	*Titus*	*Shrew*
will	0.61% (4)	1.40% (2)	0.83% (8)
I'll	0.32% (12)	0.54% (8)	1.65% (1)
Total	0.93%	1.94%	2.48%

Note: Weighted frequencies in insides, no stop words, words of four letters or more, ranking in parenthesis.

speaking, the play's dominant moral consciousness is Aaron the Moor, who openly regrets every day that he did not commit some hideous crime against his fellow men (5.1.125–54). He speaks more insides than all the other characters taken together (10 insides vs. 9, or 63 per cent of the total word count). The following passages evince his special fusion of anti-moral commentary and devious stratagems:

Let him that thinks of me so abjectly
Know that this gold must coin a stratagem
Which, cunningly effected, will beget
A very excellent piece of villainy.

(2.2.[2.3.] 4–7)

If that be called deceit, I will be honest
And never whilst I live deceive men so.
But I'll deceive you in another sort,
And that you'll say ere half an hour pass.

(3.1.189–92)

O, how this villainy
Doth fat me with the very thoughts of it.
Let fools do good and fair men call for grace,
Aaron will have his soul black like his face.

(3.1.203–6)

The one area where *Titus* looks fairly normal from a strictly quantitative point of view – moral reflection – is thus dominated by one of the most outrageously one-dimensional evildoers in the complete plays.

How is this relevant to the discussion of farcical traits in *The Taming of the Shrew*? We saw above that a main point of scholarly disagreement about *Shrew* has been whether or not one should take its offensive plot seriously. The central problem for the scholarship on *Titus*, similarly, has always been whether its outrageous horrors are meant to invite sympathetic identification or whether Shakespeare intended it as a farcical send-up of revenge tragedy. Harold Bloom, who dislikes *Titus* intensely, has even called it a 'bloody farce' on more than one occasion,[28] arguing that its insuperable problem is that the 'audience never quite [knows] when to be horrified and when to laugh'. Stanley Wells finds the same problem in *Titus*: 'How do you stage its horrors – murder, rape, mutilation, cannibalism – without driving the audience over the bounds of credulity into giggling hysteria?'[29]

Other scholars have noted the same tonal instability or uncertainty in *Titus Andronicus* without regarding it as an aesthetic flaw or even a problem. M. C. Bradbrook was probably among the first to relate the play to T. S. Eliot's concept of 'savage farce' (in splendid defiance of Eliot's own view that savage farce was 'something which Shakespeare could not do, and which he could not have understood').[30] More recently, Natália Pikli has explored how *Titus* blends farcical comedy and horrific violence to produce grotesque, tragicomic effects that blur the distinction between reality and illusion.[31] In her view, the play exemplifies Philip Thomson's concept of the grotesque, offering a 'problematic juxtaposition of the seemingly incompatible, the laughable and the horrifying or disgusting'.[32]

There is much to be said for Pikli's account of *Titus Andronicus*. It makes sense of its proclivity for stage images and scenes that are at once intensely painful and strangely ludicrous. Titus himself breaks down the barrier between tears and laughter when he collapses under the weight of his grotesque suffering:

> TITUS Ha, ha, ha!
> MARCUS Why dost thou laugh? It fits not with this hour.
> TITUS Why? I have not another tear to shed.
>
> (3.1.265–7)

It would, of course, be ridiculous to single out the insides of *Titus Andronicus* as main contributors to its unnerving impact, which is mostly due to the spectacular savagery on the stage. My point is rather that the play heaps its horrors upon the audience while denying them the emotional, thematic, and moral guidance and the psychological release that would normally be offered by the play's soliloquies and asides. As in *The Taming of the Shrew*, the insides in *Titus* keep the audience's minds uniquely riveted on the action – which is to say, the instrumental machination of its protagonists – without leaving much space for reflection and evaluation.

Given that Heilman has uncovered farcical qualities in *Shrew* that differ widely from all other Shakespeare plays (with the exception of *Titus*), it may be tempting to side with those who argue that its patriarchal shock therapy should not be taken so very seriously. This would be to exaggerate greatly the interpretative scope of this type of analysis. What I have done here is merely to identify some special dramatic qualities that help explain why the play has become so controversial. In order to *settle* the controversy, if this is at all possible, we would have to move to a different analytical level involving larger and more indirect inferences about the motive forces (biographical, sociocultural, and so forth) behind these textual qualities. The interpretative controversy surrounding this curious play can be expected to persist, but we have now come some way towards explaining its underlying mechanisms.

Female Sympathy in *The Two Noble Kinsmen*

We saw above that *The Taming of the Shrew* belongs to a set of eleven Shakespeare plays that fail to generate a single inside spoken by a female character. I would now like to turn to those unusual plays where Shakespeare departs from his habitual practice by giving women the upper hand in soliloquy and solo asides. After a brief consideration of the late collaborative romance *The Two Noble Kinsmen*, which constitutes the most extreme departure from the Shakespearean gender norm in the complete plays, the chapter will gravitate towards its principal object of study, *All's Well that Ends Well*. This is another dissonant comic brew whose distribution of sympathy can be compared very usefully to corresponding elements in both *Kinsmen* and *The Taming of the Shrew*.

The Two Noble Kinsmen is, as we saw in Chapter 3, unusually rich in insides by Shakespearean standards (14 per cent), but this quality looks almost trivial compared to its exceptional gender ratio. The women characters speak no less than 75 per cent of the total insides (Table 4.3).

Since the Jailor's Daughter is a commoner, and since commoners speak only around 14 per cent of all insides and 8 per cent of female insides in the Shakespeare canon,[33] her voice is the voice of the doubly dispossessed. But the one variable that sets the insides of *Kinsmen* far apart from all other Shakespeare plays is gender rather than class. Even if we were to bracket the Daughter's dominant contribution, the remaining 25 per cent spoken by Emilia would still be evenly weighed against the 24 per cent spoken by the male protagonists Palamon (9 per cent) and Arcite (15 per cent).

Since the play was co-authored with John Fletcher one might well suppose that this departure from Shakespeare's habits was Fletcher's doing, but that hypothesis is easily disproven. When we control for

Table 4.3 Insides per protagonist in *The Two Noble Kinsmen*.

Character	Words as insides	% insides
Arcite	506	15.2%
Daughter	1659	50.0%
Emilia	841	25.4%
Palamon	311	9.4%
Total	3317	100%

authorship based on the most commonly accepted scholarly attributions, the male/female ratios for each author turn out to be very similar: Shakespeare wrote 75 per cent female insides in *Kinsmen* and Fletcher 76 per cent. To this extravagant figure we could conceivably add the Epilogue, which was almost certainly spoken by a boy actor in women's clothing, and most likely the Prologue, too. These speeches are not insides in the technical sense, of course, and so they are not included in the figures cited above, but there is a significant parallel between them and the unusual soliloquies delivered by the Jailor's Daughter later in the play.

As we saw in Chapter 3, the Jailor's Daughter is separated from the rest of the action in chorus-like fashion and inspires strong audience sympathy because of her impossible love for Palamon. Fletcher's Prologue and Epilogue express similar worries about being abandoned by men who take what they want and then disappear in a cloud of smoke. When the play begins, the Prologue enters the stage, looks around, and nervously asserts that new stage plays and virginities have one important thing in common: they command a high initial price but then quickly lose their value. This intermingling of the sexual anxiety of the female lover with the artistic and economic performance anxieties of the theatrical company is wedded to an acute sense of inferiority. Unlike the magnificent Chaucer, whose story they are reworking, Fletcher and Shakespeare can only hope to offer a trifle that will be '[w]orth two hours' travel' by keeping 'a little dull time' from its audience.

The play ends the same way it begins, with a fusion of amorous and economic disappointment, this time expressed in the Epilogue's remarkable scripting of the audience's presumed reactions:

> I would now ask ye how ye like the play,
> But, as it is with schoolboys, cannot say.
> I am cruel fearful! Pray yet, stay a while,
> And let me look upon ye. No man smile?
> Then it goes hard, I see. He that has

Loved a young handsome wench, then, show his face –
'Tis strange if none be here – and, if he will,
Against his conscience let him hiss, and kill
Our market.

(Epilogue, 1–8)

This is, of course, false modesty on the part of Fletcher, who seems to have penned this passage. As Lois Potter observes, a speech of this kind would be 'unthinkable unless the authors had confidence both in the play and in the speaker'.[34] From a formal and thematic perspective, however, the Epilogue and Prologue combine into a single framing device whose fear of abandonment parallels the questions explored in the main plot and subplot alike.

In *The Two Noble Kinsmen*, as in *The Taming of the Shrew*, it is ultimately powerful men who call the shots in the mating game. The Jailor's Daughter pays with madness and isolation for her defiance of the Duke's authority when breaking Palamon out of prison. She later undergoes a worrying sexual therapy in the form of a bed-trick, where the Wooer simultaneously cures her and capitalises on her sensory distraction by pretending to be Palamon. In the main plot, Emilia is given a dreadful ultimatum by the very same Duke: she must choose either Palamon or Arcite for her husband and let the other man lose his life. Within the context of this super-strict patriarchal framework, however, the high incidence of female insides results in an unprecedented focus on the inner lives of these women as they seek to reconcile their individual desires with the pressures of a male-dominated society.

The two words in the English language most closely linked to the expression of sympathy are 'pity' and 'compassion'. One simple sign that *Kinsmen* is an unusually 'sympathetic' Shakespeare play is that these words occur more frequently there than anywhere else. 'Pity' is used no fewer than eighteen times, while 'compassion' is even more strikingly over-represented. *Kinsmen* contains five instances of 'compassion', or 45 per cent of the total usage in Shakespeare's plays, though in this particular case they can be traced back to scenes that were probably written by Fletcher (3.6, 4.1, and 4.2).

Is this pronounced emphasis on human sympathy gendered, and thus connected to the play's unusual incidence of female insides? It is a recurrent idea in Shakespeare, a standard assumption in folk psychology, and an established finding in modern psychological research[35] that women tend to be more *tender-minded*, more 'soft, mild, pitiful and flexible' (*3 Henry VI*, 1.4.41) than men.[36] In act 3, scene 6, of *Kinsmen* this difference is actively thematised when Emilia and Hippolyta plead desperately before Theseus for the lives of Palamon and Arcite, and their exhortations gradually awaken feelings of compassion in the men. First they manage to enlist Theseus' friend Pirithous as the former struggles somewhat woodenly to understand their appeal to his feelings:

THESEUS These are strange conjurings.
PIRITHOUS   Nay, then I'll in too. [*Kneels.*]
By all our friendship, sir, by all our dangers,
By all you love most: wars, and this sweet lady –

(201–3)

Theseus vainly tries to stave off their demand by chauvinistically juxta-posing female pity with male reason:

THESEUS You are a right woman, sister: you have pity
    But want the understanding where to use it.

(215–16)

But he is, of course, helpless to prevent the swelling tide of human sympathy:

THESEUS What may be done? For now I feel compassion.

(272)

I hope this is enough to show that these distinctive facets of *The Two Noble Kinsmen* – its many female insides and its intense expressions of sympathy – are intimately connected. In the soliloquies spoken by the Jailor's Daughter and Emilia, the expression of desire for the male protagonists is saturated with compassion and concern. The Daughter's first soliloquy is a case in point:

                    First, I saw him;
I, seeing, thought he was a goodly man;
He has as much to please a woman in him,
If he please to bestow it so, as ever
These eyes yet looked on. Next, I pitied him –
And so would any young wench, o' my conscience,
That ever dreamed, or vowed her maidenhead
To a young handsome man. Then, I loved him,
Extremely loved him, infinitely loved him!
And yet he had a cousin fair as he too,
But in my heart was Palamon and there,
Lord, what a coil he keeps! To hear him
Sing in an evening, what a heaven it is!
And yet his songs are sad ones. Fairer spoken
Was never gentleman. When I come in
To bring him water in a morning, first
He bows his noble body, then salutes me, thus:
'Fair, gentle maid, good morrow; may thy goodness
Get thee a happy husband.' Once, he kissed me.

I loved my lips the better ten days after:
Would he would do so every day! He grieves much –
And me as much to see his misery.

(2.4.7–28)

As the action unfolds, this emphasis on human sympathy and compassion becomes a more or less consistent trait in the play's insides, and it spreads even to the soliloquies and asides spoken by the male characters. Starting with the Daughter's first soliloquy in act 2, scene 4, almost all of the ensuing seventeen insides either invoke the audience's compassion for the speaker and/or contain an explicit expression of sympathy for another character.[37] Once again this sympathetic orientation is reflected in the play's vocabulary. The insides of *Kinsmen* contain more instances than any other Shakespeare play of the word 'poor' used as an attribute in a noun phrase expressing sympathy:[38]

In thy rumination,
That I, poor man, might eftsoons come between
And chop on some cold thought!

(3.1.11–13)

Alas, alas,
Poor cousin Palamon, poor prisoner

(3.1.22–3)

Poor wench, go weep, for whosoever wins
Loses a noble cousin, for thy sins.

(4.2.155–6)

Poor servant, thou hast lost.

(5.3.72)

Alas, poor Palamon!

(5.3. 104)

As I suggested in Chapter 3, the most distinctive thematic aspect of *The Two Noble Kinsmen* is its concern with love's divisiveness. It is this thematic dimension that drives the sympathetic impulse on both levels of dramatic communication. In the main plot, Emelia cannot choose between Palamon and Arcite, and in the subplot, the Daughter goes mad because she cannot have the one she loves. In both cases, Shakespeare and Fletcher arrange their plot so that love becomes a grievous zero-sum game where one person's happiness is inevitably another's loss. Even getting what you want is tinged with frustration (because of what you must give up) and guilt (because you sympathise with the one that pulled the shorter straw).

There can, I think, be little doubt that Shakespeare thought of women as more compassionate creatures than men, for all the individual Gonerils and Regans and Lady Macbeths that populate his plays. It is therefore not surprising to find these sympathetic strands in the one play where the women characters are given the lion's share of the insides. The same interdependency between female dominance of insides and a strong premium on human sympathy is also at work in *All's Well that Ends Well* – that other Shakespeare play where the women characters speak more insides than the men, to which we will now turn.

Sympathy and Exclusion in *All's Well that Ends Well*

In 2007 I published a reading of *All's Well that Ends Well* that defined it as a companion piece to Shakespeare's enfant terrible, *Troilus and Cressida*.[39] These plays were quite probably written in succession. Their plots revolve around the perceived romantic value of a woman called Helena, but they approach this problem from opposing and complementary directions. The central fear that infuses *Troilus* with its profound pessimism and scepticism, I argued, is that the value we place on things as well as other people might be purely relational. If nothing is truly valuable in itself, if human nature is locked into an unending cycle of feverish fetishism and bored satiety, then the act of holding someone or something dear begins to look like a fleeting act of *overvaluation*. Can a single woman, even the beautiful Helen of Troy, really be worth seven years of horrors on the battlefield? Using this classical problem as his point of departure, Shakespeare weaves together an intricate network of interconnected imagery related to value, satiety, and perception.

In *All's Well*, by contrast, Shakespeare uses the figure of Helena to explore the opposing problem of *undervaluation*, as represented by the spectacular failure of one individual (the nobleman Bertram) to perceive the romantic value of another (his social inferior Helena). The central question in this problem comedy is if Bertram will ever come to see Helena in the same sympathetic light in which she is seen by all the other characters, and particularly by an older and more experienced generation that actively supports her quest for Bertram's love. To love wisely, then, is to grasp Helena's irreducible value as an individual – or, as one critic puts it, to perceive her 'intrinsic excellence'.[40]

To this reading I would now like to add that *All's Well* is the only Shakespeare play except *Kinsmen* where the majority of the insides are spoken by the women characters (58 per cent). The play is also of interest because of its special constellation of traits that we found in *Shrew* and *Kinsmen*. As in *Kinsmen*, the soliloquies and asides of *All's Well* become powerful vehicles for fellow feeling, contributing actively to the play's larger thematic vision of sympathy for human flaws and frailty. Since we have already found a strong link between female insides and dramatic sympathy, it is hardly irrelevant that the male protagonist Bertram is effectively excised from this communal spirit through the same treatment that Katherina receives in *Shrew:* he never speaks a single inside. As we shall see, this convergence in *All's Well* of the 'feminine' sympathy and compassion of *Kinsmen* with the forced marriage and the silencing of a marriage partner from *Shrew* contributes importantly to the play's tonal dissonance.

There are important similarities between *Shrew* and *All's Well* on the level of character and plot. The first is that Katherina and Bertram are both married off after declaring that the marriage is entirely against their wishes. In act 2, scene 1, of *Shrew*, Katherina responds to Petruchio's proposal by saying that 'I'll see thee hanged on Sunday first' (2.1.293), but she then remains silent as Petruchio and her father conclude the match. Her response is inscrutable on the written page and must be interpreted in dramatic performance.

In *All's Well*, the forcible nature of the marriage is actively foregrounded by Shakespeare, but Bertram's mental operations remain equally impenetrable. Faced with the King's unexpected demand that he marry Helena as payment for her services as physician, he first asserts boldly that he 'cannot love her nor will strive to do't' (2.3.146). This provokes a naked display of royal power from the King, who realises that his 'honour's at the stake' and that he must therefore 'produce [his] power', threatening to unleash 'all my revenge and hate' upon the young man '[w]ithout all terms of pity' (150–1, 165–7).[41] The result is a rapid volte-face on the part of Bertram, whose subordination of his individual desire to social power smacks of irony: 'Pardon, my gracious lord; for I submit / My fancy to your eyes' (168–9). In both *Shrew* and *All's Well*, therefore, Shakespeare keeps a close lid on the character's rapid trajectory from bold refusal to quiet acceptance of a seemingly unavoidable match. Things will remain that way for the duration of each play since neither character ever delivers a single inside where they might comment privately on their difficult experience.

A second similarity between Katherina and Bertram is that their prospective spouses rein them in by means of a cruel prank. In Bertram's case, this is accomplished by a bed-trick which comes very close to a rape since Helena is substituted for Diana and so consummates their marriage without his consent. This is the same plot device used in *Kinsmen*, but it naturally plays out quite differently for a character whose private speech makes up 50 per cent of the play's insides (the Jailor's Daughter) and a character who never speaks a soliloquy or aside (Bertram). In *Shrew*, Petruchio's 'cure' for Katherina's insubordination consists in systematic disorientation that borders on mental torture. A third significant parallel is that Shakespeare ends both plays by having Katherina and Bertram declare how happy they are to have been brought into the marital fold. The scholarly reception of these scenes has always been characterised by considerable unease.[42]

We saw above that *Shrew*'s problematic nature is reinforced by action-oriented insides that leave little room for evaluation of Petruchio's brutal reformation of his spouse. The tonal instability in *All's Well*, by contrast, results at least partly from the grafting of an elaborate moral and thematic framework onto a farcical plot device. Where *Shrew* systematically empties its insides of sympathy, *All's Well* goes in the opposite direction, in the direction of *Kinsmen*, by enlisting the moral and thematic sensibilities that Shakespeare removes so surgically from *Shrew*. Since Bertram, like Katherina, never gets a single inside, he comes to share only indirectly in the play's soliloquised expressions of sympathy for human imperfection. As a consequence, the play never reconciles its forced marriage and farcical plot device with a private language oriented towards sympathy and forgiveness.

Many feminist critics have questioned *All's Well*'s status as a problem play, arguing that people have a problem with it merely because the woman acts the wooer and wins her mate.[43] This seems both right and wrong. On the one hand, it is not unlikely that a literary history traditionally written by a predominantly male academic readership has been inflected in problematic ways by unquestioned patriarchal assumptions and fears about female empowerment. Such a male bias might go some way towards explaining why Franz Boas originally defined *All's Well* as a 'problem play', when the same generic epithet could just as well be applied to *The Taming of the Shrew*. On the other hand, these critics perform a categorical error when they reduce *All's Well*'s problematic nature to a sexist formula by shifting the focus from the text to its reception. As I have suggested elsewhere, this looks suspiciously like a reversal of the sexist charge, where forced marriages like the ones in *Shrew* and *All's Well* are acceptable so long as they are imposed on men rather than women.[44]

It is a central premise in this study that Shakespeare's literary *intentions* are often inscrutable while his literary *habits* are easier to establish with some measure of objectivity. This is, however, not to say that authorial intentions are either irrelevant or impossible to identify,[45] and I can envisage three potential reasons why Shakespeare gives Bertram no insides in *All's Well*. The first has already been dealt with above: that Shakespeare struggled to reconcile a semi-farcical plot and a sympathetic thematic vision that were pulling him in very different directions. Having Bertram express his inner anguish at having been tied so brutally to the marriage stake would have further undermined a comic resolution that was already threatening to turn sour, and that still frequently fails to convince modern audiences and scholars. When Bertram finally recants, arguing that he did not appreciate Helena enough because he was already in love with another woman, Maudlin (5.3.44–54), he clearly has much to gain from a belated profession of love. The reason we cannot be certain about Bertram's true feelings is that Shakespeare never gives the audience a single moment of undisturbed privacy with him.

A second explanation of Bertram's lack of insides can be derived from the work of Ann Jennalie Cook, who notes that Shakespeare may have needed to make certain concessions to his class-conscious audience when depicting a union between the nobleman Bertram and the commoner Helena.[46] To give a very rounded and noble portrait of Bertram could easily have reinforced the conservative idea that the play seems to call into question, namely, that nobility of *rank* was inseparable from nobility considered as a *personal* or *moral* characteristic. *All's Well* clearly contributes directly to the larger sociocultural redefinition of honour as an internal rather than an external phenomenon,[47] and it therefore makes sense for Shakespeare to paint a highly positive portrait of Helena while restricting Bertram's portrait to *externals* like his social rank and physical appearance. This could explain why he denies this character the rich inner life and noble personality that are revealed in Helena's soliloquies.

A third, largely compatible explanation of Bertram's silencing can be derived from my aforementioned reading of the play from 2007. My argument there was that Shakespeare did not simply fail to strike a harmonious chord *All's Well*, but actively pursued tonal dissonance as part of a thematic concern with the tension between the individual and the group. It is not amiss to regard *All's Well* as an early forerunner of the distinctively bittersweet sentiments of the romances, especially *The Two Noble Kinsmen*. All the characters in *All's Well* except Bertram perceive what a wonderful woman Helena really is, and on a superficial level, the plot simply records his path towards acceptance of the consensus view put forward primarily by the older generation. He must learn to love Helena as everyone else loves her. Seen from this perspec-

Table 4.4 Words as insides per character in *All's Well that Ends Well*.

Character	Words as insides	% insides
Countess	117	8.6%
Diana	87	6.4%
Helena	583	43.1%
Lafew	149	11%
Parolles	416	30.8%
Total	1352	100%

tive, the insistent commentary of the older generation and the muffling of Bertram further underscore the ironic tension between social and individual appraisal.

However we may explain Shakespeare's motives, the result of his dramatic choice is that Bertram comes across as a fairly shallow character. He seems flat partly because he has no insides in a literal sense, and partly because he concerns himself so much with the disparity in social rank between himself and his suggested spouse. Helena, by contrast, has been described poignantly by Barbara Everett as 'a radically new comic heroine. For [she] is *inward* ... She is much given to secrecies and reticences.'[48] A SID query for **character** reveals that Helena speaks almost half of the play's insides, with Parolles as the runner-up (Table 4.4).

There are two ways in which Helena's role corresponds directly to Petruchio's in *Shrew*. Like Petruchio, she appeals to a patriarchal figure for marriage to an unwilling spouse, and like Petruchio she speaks more lines and more insides than any other character. But while Petruchio remains something of a farcical stick figure, Shakespeare's portrait of Helena is subtle, nuanced, and characterised by great moral and psychological complexity.

Some fairly objective aspects of this difference can be gleaned from Shakespeare's distribution of speech types and dramatic speech acts. The hardnosed Petruchio may speak 23 per cent more *lines* than Helena overall (589 lines vs. 478),[49] but she speaks many more insides than he does (587 words vs. 329). Petruchio's insides are, as we have seen, extraordinarily instrumental and empty of moral and thematic content, while Helena follows Shakespeare's habitual norms almost to the letter (Table 4.5).

These overriding patterns form an instructive background to the special way in which Helena's soliloquies – beside their standard functions of **exposition** and **assessing character** – guide audience sympathy, for herself as well as for other characters.

The main effect of Helena's first soliloquy, apart from its expository

Table 4.5 **Assessing morality, assessing thematics,** *and* **planning** per character in *The Taming of the Shrew* and *All's Well that Ends Well*.

Character	Words	Assessing morality		Assessing thematics		Planning	
Helena	583	132	22.4%	102	17.3%	101	17.2%
Petruchio	329	0	0%	17	5.1%	284	86.3%
Complete insides	65225	14057	21.6%	8724	13.3%	11182	17.1%

function, is to attract considerable audience sympathy for her plight at the hands of cruel Cupid:

> HELENA O, were that all! I think not on my father,
> And these great tears grace his remembrance more
> Than those I shed for him. What was he like?
> I have forgot him; my imagination
> Carries no favour in't but Bertram's.
> I am undone; there is no living, none,
> If Bertram be away; 'twere all one
> That I should love a bright particular star
> And think to wed it, he is so above me.
> In his bright radiance and collateral light
> Must I be comforted, not in his sphere.
> Th'ambition in my love thus plagues itself:
> The hind that would be mated by the lion
> Must die for love. 'Twas pretty, though a plague,
> To see him every hour; to sit and draw
> His arched brows, his hawking eye, his curls,
> In our heart's table – heart too capable
> Of every line and trick of his sweet favour.
> But now he's gone, and my idolatrous fancy
> Must sanctify his relics.

> (1.1.80–99)

Even at this early point in the play, Shakespeare begins to blend intense audience sympathy for his female protagonist with more problematic considerations. The key phrase is Helena's concluding remark that her 'idolatrous fancy' must make up for Bertram's absence by 'sanctify[ing] his relics'. The notion that love is, or at least might become, a form of idolatry is a frequent idea in Shakespeare. Like the religious worshipper, the lover may become too deeply invested in sensory experience, confuse appearances with essences, and end up attributing too much value to the object of veneration. The central risk, in other words, is the tendency that Shakespeare had just dissected so systematically in *Troilus and Cressida*: is Achilles worth the admiration showered upon him by the Greek camp? Thersites thinks not:

THERSITES Why, thou picture of what thou seemest, and idol of idiot-worshippers, here's a letter for thee.

(5.1.6–7)

Is the hand of Helen of Troy worth seven years of bloodshed? Hector thinks not:

TROILUS What is aught, but as 'tis valued?
HECTOR But value dwells not in particular will:
It holds his estimate and dignity
As well wherein 'tis precious of itself
As in the prizer. 'Tis mad idolatry
To make the service greater than the god;
And the will dotes that is attributive
To what infectiously itself affects,
Without some image of th'affected merit.

(2.2.53–61)

The notion that the infatuated Helena might be similarly over-invested in Bertram is borne out by her first soliloquy. The initial reference to her dead father shows that her romantic passion has become a form of tunnel vision that blocks out even the most central relationships in her life. Where Cordelia in *Lear* suggests that her future husband will carry away half her love, Helena's love for Bertram has simply erased the memory of her previously beloved father. Nothing else is. This idea of youthful excessiveness is echoed by the Duchess a little later when she learns of Helena's love for her son. She may be deeply sympathetic to Helena's desires and fully supportive of her plans to win him, but that does not prevent her from regarding the young woman's passion as a moral weakness:

Even so it was with me when I was young;
If ever we are nature's these are ours; this thorn
Doth to our rose of youth rightly belong;
Our blood to us, this to our blood is born:
It is the show and seal of nature's truth,
Where love's strong passion is impress'd in youth.
By our remembrances of days foregone,
Such were our faults, or then we thought them none.
Her eye is sick on't; I observe her now.

(1.3.125–33)

How is Helena's passion for Bertram a 'fault'? Shakespeare is almost certainly treating us to a distinctively early modern emotional regimen here, where the passions are not inherently sinful but must be culti-vated, domesticated, and directed by reason and experience.

Helena's love for Bertram runs the risk of becoming idolatrous because it is focused on externals: his social rank and his handsome appearance. When she dwells lovingly and sympathetically on his 'arched brows, his hawking eye, his curls', her concern with his physical appearance is notable as much for what it leaves out as what it leaves in: it contributes indirectly to our 'shallow' perception of Bertram as a man composed mainly of outward show.

This brings us to yet another facet of Helena's idolatrous tunnel vision which was foregrounded in my original reading from 2007: that strong passion may render us insensitive to other people's point of view (including, ironically, that of the ones we love). It is significant that Helena never once asks herself if her feelings for Bertram are requited; she remains entirely focused on the question of her own merit and the means by which he might be won. Her second soliloquy continues to invite audience sympathy for her daring project, but it is also Petruchio-like in its single-minded concern with how to win the object of her affections:

> Our remedies oft in ourselves do lie,
> Which we ascribe to heaven; the fated sky
> Gives us free scope; only doth backward pull
> Our slow designs when we ourselves are dull.
> What power is it which mounts my love so high,
> That makes me see, and cannot feed mine eye?
> The mightiest space in fortune nature brings
> To join like likes, and kiss like native things.
> Impossible be strange attempts to those
> That weigh their pains in sense, and do suppose
> What hath been cannot be. Who ever strove
> To show her merit that did miss her love?
> The king's disease – my project may deceive me,
> But my intents are fix'd, and will not leave me.

(1.1.216–29)

In act 3, when Bertram has responded to the forced marriage by jumping ship and escaping to Florence, Helena undergoes a distinctive moral awakening. This is evidenced by the soliloquy that follows hard upon his elopement (3.2.100–29), where her previous tunnel vision gives way to selfless concern for his safety and happiness:

>   Poor lord, is't I
> That chase thee from thy country, and expose
> Those tender limbs of thine to the event
> Of the none-sparing war? And is it I
> That drive thee from the sportive court, where thou
> Wast shot at with fair eyes, to be the mark
> Of smoky muskets? O you leaden messengers,
> That ride upon the violent speed of fire,

Fly with false aim; move the still-piecing air
That sings with piercing; do not touch my lord.
Whoever shoots at him, I set him there;
Whoever charges on his forward breast,
I am the caitiff that do hold him to't;
And though I kill him not, I am the cause
His death was so effected. Better 'twere
That all the miseries which nature owes
Were mine at once.

(3.2.103–19)

This tender-minded speech is reminiscent of Emilia's anguished soliloquy in *Kinsmen*, another instance of female inwardness that mingles sympathy and desire:

Yet may I bind those wounds up, that must open
And bleed to death for my sake else; I'll choose,
And end their strife. Two such young, handsome men
Shall never fall for me; their weeping mothers,
Following the dead cold ashes of their sons,
Shall never curse my cruelty.

(4.2.1–6)

Like Emilia's speech, Helena's third soliloquy illustrates how characters expressing concern for other characters become proxies for audience sympathy, projecting it in two simultaneous directions: towards their object of sympathy and towards themselves.

What may be less apparent, however, is that Helena's sympathy for Bertram in this soliloquy masks a continued failure of empathy and perspective taking. Her concern for him is partly rooted in her own fear that he will come to harm, and partly in her guilty recognition that she has driven him into harm's way. But Shakespeare has already given Bertram a speech in act 2, scene 1, that prevents the audience from accepting this version of events at face value. When his comrades prepare to depart for the war against Italy, Bertram reflects bitterly on the fact that the King has commanded him to stay at court:

2 LORD   O, 'tis brave wars!
PAROLLES Most admirable! I have seen those wars.
BERTRAM I am commanded here, and kept a coil with
    'Too young', and 'The next year' and ''Tis too early'.
PAROLLES
    And thy mind stand to't boy, steal away bravely.
BERTRAM I shall stay here the forehorse to a smock,
    Creaking my shoes on the plain masonry,
    'Till honour be brought up, and no sword worn
    But one to dance with. By heaven, I'll steal away!

(2.1.25–33)

There is certainly a sense in which Bertram goes to war because his options at court have been curtailed, but his forced marriage to Helena has really only been the catalyst for a plan that was hatched (and then abandoned) much earlier. The shotgun wedding has, ironically and paradoxically, enabled him to take the step that could only be thought and never acted: to pursue his own desires in defiance of the King's express command. He does not simply run away from Helena; he also runs towards a highly desired goal.

This is the last inside spoken by Helena in the play. We have seen how her soliloquies generate strong audience sympathy for her own person; how they spread some of this sympathy to Bertram, even as they contribute further to his 'hollow' characterisation through their strict focus on his externals (rank, physical appearance) and her own agency; and, finally, how even Helena's most profound expression of sympathy in the third soliloquy seems to lack genuine empathetic engagement. I would now like to explore how the speeches of other characters in the play contribute further to its deeply sympathetic tone.

Although *All's Well* closely resembles *Kinsmen* in its combination of sympathetic concern and emotional dissonance, its tonal qualities are quite different, as evidenced by the central thematic statements in each play. The sympathetic dissonance in *Kinsmen* results from the collision between incompatible desires whose lack of resolution generates pity for mankind:

> O, cousin!
> That we should things desire, which do cost us
> The loss of our desire! That nought could buy
> Dear love, but loss of dear love!
>
> (*Kinsmen*, 5.4.109–12)

The dominant note struck in *All's Well* is of a mellower kind, projecting sympathy for the moral mediocrity of mankind. It is one of those Shakespeare plays where it seems meaningful to speak of a fairly coherent moral vision that can be pieced together from the speeches of several different characters. The first building block is the King's recognition that our individual differences form part of a shared human nature:

> Strange is it that our bloods,
> Of colour, weight, and heat, pour'd all together,
> Would quite confound distinction, yet stands off
> In differences so mighty.
>
> (*All's Well*, 2.3.119–22)

The second is a functional view of moral ambiguity:

> The web of our life is of a mingled yarn, good and ill together; our
> virtues would be proud if our faults whipp'd them not, and our crimes
> would despair if they were not cherish'd by our virtues.
>
> (4.3.68–71)

I have argued elsewhere[50] for the Montaignesque quality of this view of human imperfections:

> Both in public and in private we are built full of imperfection. But there is
> nothing useless in Nature – not even uselessness. Nothing has got into this
> universe of ours which does not occupy its appropriate place. Our being
> is cemented together by qualities which are diseased. Ambition, jealousy,
> envy, vengeance, superstition and despair lodge in us with such a natural
> right of possession that we recognize the likeness of them even in the
> animals too ... If anyone were to remove the seeds of such qualities in Man
> he would destroy the basic properties of our lives.[51]

Taken together, these thematic statements in *All's Well* suggest strongly that the play's tonal dissonance is not attributable to a failed dramatic experiment. It forms part of a coherent dramatic purpose. They also help explain the frequent tendency of the soliloquists in *All's Well* to use their private speeches as bridges between individual faults and common humanity, absorbing the one into the other. As we have already seen, the Countess censors herself and others in the act of censoring Helena, and Diana, for her part, censors all men in the act of censoring Bertram: 'My mother told me just how he would woo / As if she sat in's heart. She says all men / Have the like oaths' (4.2.69–71).

This tendency in *All's Well* to turn individual flaws into general flaws becomes particularly pronounced when Shakespeare employs a specific speech convention: the overheard soliloquy. James Hirsh explains the conventional rules for such speeches on Shakespeare's stage: '*whenever a character is unaware of the presence of a second character, the second character overhears the first character's soliloquy unless the second character is asleep or there is some other obvious impediment*'.[52] Shakespeare uses such scenes for many different purposes in his plays, from the merciless exposure of evil and hypocrisy in *Macbeth* or the elicitation of deep sympathy in *Romeo and Juliet* to biting satire in *Love's Labour's Lost*. The special thing about the overheard soliloquies of *All's Well* is that they consistently allow other characters to bathe the shortcomings of the unwitting and exposed soliloquist in a forgiving light – even when these flaws are so serious that they result in the total destruction of individual honour.

The first overheard inside in *All's Well* takes place offstage. We learn about it in act 1 when the steward Reynaldo gives a lengthy account to the Countess of how he has eavesdropped on Helena's profession of love for Bertram (1.3.104–18). When Reynaldo leaves, the Countess launches her aforementioned meditation on the nature of youthful passion. At first sight, its combination of strong sympathy and moral qualms may seem vastly different from the most famous scene involving an overheard inside in this play: the brutal, merciless exposure of Parolles as a self-serving coward in act 4, scene 1. As we shall see, however, Shakespeare's treatment of Parolles is a choice example of his firm control of audience sympathy through the medium of soliloquy.

As his name suggests, Parolles is a man made up entirely of words. His role is the third largest in *All's Well that Ends Well* if we count the total number of lines; he is barely beaten by the King and distanced quite comfortably by Helena. If we count the number of words delivered as insides, Parolles becomes the undisputed runner-up to Helena's dominance – she speaks 43 per cent of the play's insides, he 31 per cent – since the King never speaks a single inside. In a count of individual insides rather than the number of words delivered as insides, finally, Parolles easily outstrips all the other characters including Helena. This is because the women characters only deliver soliloquies, while Lafew[53] and Parolles also comment surreptitiously on their experience by means of numerous brief asides (Table 4.6).

In act 4, Parolles is subjected to a nasty practical joke by Bertram and the French lords where he is made to think that he has been captured by the enemy and is being interrogated for information about the French army. His overly accommodating offer of detailed intelligence about his friends and fellow soldiers in order to save his own life is the sort of revelation from which a person cannot expect to recover fully; not in any social environment, and certainly not in the martial honour culture of early modern Europe. It is therefore all the more interesting that Shakespeare vindicates Parolles so very systematically by means of carefully orchestrated soliloquies and additional dialogical commentary.

We will not appreciate how expertly Shakespeare modifies the audience's response to Parolles unless we consider the exact sequencing of the first three scenes of act 4. Shakespeare structures these events in such a way that the plot line focused on Parolles's capture

Table 4.6 Number of insides per character in *All's Well that Ends Well*.

	Countess	Diana	Helena	Lafew	Parolles
Insides in *All's Well*	2	1	3	6	12

(4.1) and interrogation (second half of 4.3) is interrupted by Bertram's opportunistic attempt to seduce Diana (4.2) and Bertram's moral censure by the two Lords for having slighted Helena (first half of 4.3). The structural effect is that our moral assessment of Parolles in 4.3 will be filtered through Bertram's immoral pursuit of Diana and his failure to appreciate Helena. The two Lords play a pivotal role throughout this process as they imaginatively absorb the individual failings of both Parolles and Bertram into their forgiving vision of a half-baked humanity.

Just before he is captured (4.1) Parolles speaks a soliloquy where he bitterly regrets the reckless boastfulness that led him to undertake the impossible recovery of the enemy's drum. The frustration he expresses at his own blabbermouth becomes an effective empathetic foothold on both levels of dramatic communication, since the audience's direct perception of his qualms is punctuated by a series of interjections from the eavesdropping Captain Dumesne (who is waiting to ambush him). Dumesne's initial comments on Parolles's tortured attempts to wriggle his way out of his moral quagmire are not exactly sympathetic. They are very much in line with Parolles's previous alteration with Lafew (2.3.185–265):

> 1 LORD This is the first truth that e'er thine own tongue was guilty of.
>   ...
> 1 LORD Is it possible he should know what he is, and be that he is?
>
> (4.1.31–2, 43–4)

There can, however, be little doubt that Shakespeare ultimately intended the moral commentary by Captain Dumesne and the other, unnamed French lord to guide the audience's response away from initial repugnance towards a more sympathetic view. When act 4, scene 3, begins, we find the two Lords involved in a discussion of Bertram's failings which begins with a simple negative assessment:

> 1 LORD He has much worthy blame laid upon him for shaking off so good a wife and so sweet a lady.
>
> (4.3.5–6)

As they continue the discussion for about seventy lines, however, their response to Bertram's shortcomings switches from the detached and individualised third person singular to the inclusive first person plural:

> 1 LORD Now, God delay our rebellion! As we are ourselves, what things are we!
> 2 LORD Merely our own traitors.
>   ...

1 LORD Is it not damnable in us to be trumpeters of our unlawful intents?

...

1 LORD How mightily sometimes we make us comforts of our losses!
2 LORD And how mightily some other times we drown our gain in tears!

(4.3. 18–20, 25–6, 62–5)

This systematic absorption of individual flaws into the collective failings of mankind culminates in the Montaignesque statement I cited above, where Dumesne notes that the 'web of our life is of a mingled yarn' and that our 'virtues' and our 'faults' are mutually supportive (68–71).

When Bertram enters the stage and the mock interrogation of Parolles begins, the audience has, in other words, just been treated to the play's most powerful vindication of human fallibility. The process of sympathetic rehabilitation does not end there. As Parolles slanders his fellow soldiers with great gusto and imagination, Dumesne continues to meet his offensive remarks with human sympathy and affection:

1 LORD I begin to love him for this.

...

1 LORD He hath out-villain'd villainy so far that the rarity redeems him.

(256, 267–8)

The view that Parolles's faults are vindicated or redeemed by their special integrity is not a new idea at this point in the play. Shakespeare has introduced it at the precise moment when Parolles entered the stage for the first time and received the following characterisation at the end of Helena's first soliloquy:

> Who comes here?
> Enter PAROLLES.
> One that goes with him; I love him for his sake,
> And yet I know him a notorious liar,
> Think him a great way fool, solely a coward;
> Yet these fix'd evils sit so fit in him
> That they take place when virtue's steely bones
> Looks bleak i'th' cold wind; withal, full oft we see
> Cold wisdom waiting on superfluous folly.

(1.1.99–106)

Once again we find a soliloquy put in the service of human sympathy – and also prophecy, since the 'cold wisdom' that Helena prognosticates is precisely what Parolles discovers after his painful exposure.[54]

His instinctive response after the revelation of his cowardice and lack of loyalty in act 4 is to thematise his own disastrous situation as follows:

PAROLLES Who cannot be crush'd with a plot?

He then embraces a wondrously life-affirming acceptance of human frailty where even his personal weakness becomes a strength:

> Yet am I thankful. If my heart were great
> 'Twould burst at this. Captain I'll be no more,
> But I will eat and drink and sleep as soft
> As captain shall. Simply the thing I am
> Shall make me live.
>
> (4.3.324–8)

Parolles's exposure as a coward and a braggart would have been simply merciless and catastrophic if it were not for Shakespeare's tight control of the distribution of audience sympathy from the very first pages of the play-text. Helena's initial characterisation, the running commentary by the Lords, and his own life-affirming speech all contribute to bathe his considerable faults in a forgiving light, and most of it happens in the context of soliloquy. As a result, we come to share Helena's view of Parolles as deeply flawed and highly likeable, an attractive grey thread in the mingled yarn that constitutes humanity.

In *All's Well*, Shakespeare thus uses soliloquy mainly (if not exclusively) as a source of sympathy. It paints a strangely inspiring portrait of the boastful and cowardly Parolles, and it also gives us rich psychological insight into the quality of Helena's character and affection. The same can hardly be said about Bertram. We learn the following things about him from the speeches of other characters: that he is young and handsome, that he is wrong to disobey the King, and that he is subject to the same moral flaws as other men, and, more generally, those of mankind. Throughout the play his mind remains a black box, with the result that the audience never quite knows what to make of his timely asseverations and recantations in the fifth act, where he courts two different marriage partners in the course of 250 lines.

Closing Remarks

I would like to end this discussion of *All's Well*, this chapter on distribution, and this entire book by zooming out and comparing the fifth act of this problem comedy to broader patterns in Shakespeare's dramatic practice. The last scenes of a comedy typically patch up the social

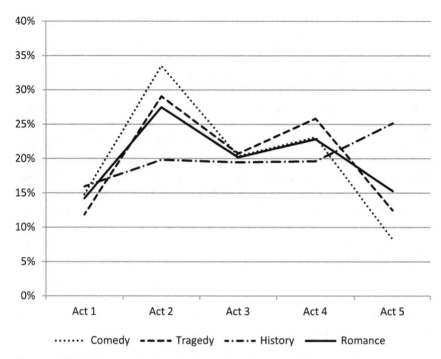

Figure 4.5 Shakespeare's distribution of insides according to subgenre.

conflict that has driven the action and restore a sense of community where previously antagonistic social roles have been redefined and reintegrated. Since insides typically complicate the relationship between the individual and the group by supplying the audience with inside information about what characters *actually think* or *intend to do*, they are largely antithetical to the joyous social harmony of the comic ending. It is therefore to be expected that comedies will have fewer insides in the fifth act than Shakespeare's other subgenres. How do they compare in this respect?

As I suggested in the Introduction, the fact that the printed versions of Shakespeare's plays were not always divided into acts should not prevent us from using the act as a pragmatic tool for studying the narrative distribution of insides. Figure 4.5 tracks the overriding distribution of insides per act across thirty-nine plays according to subgenre.

Three interesting things become apparent here. The first is that Shakespeare's distribution of insides follows an M-shaped pattern in three subgenres out of four, with particularly frequent insides in act 2 and a slightly less pronounced hump in act 4. It is almost as if there were a normal rhythm to the interplay of dialogue and soliloquy across time. Why this happens seems like an exciting topic for future research.

One promising hypothesis is that the distribution of insides is inversely correlated with the rising and falling action in the classic Freytag pyramid: the moments of falling and rising action are also those when Shakespeare's characters begin to soliloquise more frequently.

A second finding in Figure 4.5 is that the fourth subgenre – the history play – departs from the general pattern and packs *more* insides into the fifth act. The pattern does become a little less striking if we remove the statistical outliers *Edward III* and *Richard II* (with 0 per cent and 92 per cent of their insides in the fifth act), but the remaining plays still exhibit a rise in the number of insides from act 4 to act 5 that is contrary to the M-shaped pattern. Why should this be?

Some of the histories differ from Shakespeare's other plays by means of their sequential division into parts of a larger historical narrative, and they are all part of a larger narrative known as the history of England. Although most Shakespeare scholars agree today that the order of composition of these plays did not match the linear progression of the history they describe, we can still assume that most were written with at least a vague sense of this larger story in mind. Shakespeare and his co-authors would naturally have wanted to ensure that each part paved the way for the next. More specifically, it would have made sense to complement the classic dénouement of the fifth act with the kind of social subterfuge and unresolved tensions that insides are uniquely equipped to create, thus setting the scene for the next part in the series.

Table 4.7 shows that both Henriads exhibit a falling ratio of insides for the fifth act as we move from the first part to the last, presumably because of a dwindling need for social cliff-hangers as the story draws to a close. In fact, the first instalment in each Henriad packs no less than three times as many of its insides into the fifth act as the average Shakespeare play (15 per cent).

We must not forget, however, that even the final part of a Henriad forms part of a larger historical sequence where another Shakespeare play may follow hard upon it. The first part of *Henry VI* ends with a

Table 4.7 Distribution of insides according to act in the Henriads (%).

	Act 1	Act 2	Act 3	Act 4	Act 5
Henry IV, part 1	11	22	0	22	45
Henry IV, part 2	5	0	38	40	16
1 Henry VI	10	12	20	16	43
2 Henry VI	27	0	25	25	23
3 Henry VI	7	41	33	2	17

forward-looking soliloquy where Suffolk gives a sneak preview of the next play in the series:

> Thus Suffolk hath prevail'd; and thus he goes,
> As did the youthful Paris once to Greece;
> With hope to find the like event in love,
> But prosper better than the Trojan did.
> Margaret shall now be Queen, and rule the King;
> But I will rule both her, the King, and realm.
>
> (*1 Henry VI*, 5.5.103–8)

The last part of the same Henriad may have fewer insides in the fifth act than the previous two, but it too builds up systematically towards the continued story of Gloucester's misdeeds. The last eighty lines of this play are distributed entirely evenly between, on the one hand, the conventional restoration of social order as Edward looks forward to a rosy future as King of England (*3 Henry VI*, 5.7.1–20, 26–32, 35–46), and, on the other, a series of soliloquies and solo asides where Richard of Gloucester hatches the plots that will unravel in the play bearing his own name (5.6.61–93, 5.7.21–5, 33–4).

My third point about Figure 4.5 – which leads us back to *All's Well* one final time – is that the final acts of Shakespeare's comedies tend to be just as soliloquy-thin as one might expect. On average, his comedies pack only 8 per cent of their soliloquies into the fifth act, compared to the average of 18 per cent for the other genres, and five comedies out of thirteen have less than 1 per cent of their insides in act 5. There are six plays in the Shakespeare canon that have zero insides in the fifth act. There is one apocryphal history where Shakespeare almost certainly did not write act 5 (*Edward III*); three 'normal' comedies (*As You Like It, Love's Labour's Lost, Twelfth Night*); and two problem comedies (*Measure for Measure* and – you guessed it – *All's Well that Ends Well*).[55]

In other words, the comic restoration of social cohesion does seem to leave a noticeable dent in the distribution of the Shakespearean inside. From a structural point of view, *All's Well* is an ultra-comic play because there are no soliloquies whatsoever in the fifth act. This does not mean, however, that there is a shortage of tension between the inward and the outward person in its final scenes. Quite the contrary: the fifth act feels full of tension because we sense that some very important things are not being disclosed. By the time that the central characters are gathered together once again at the French court, Bertram has been doubly deceived: he has unwittingly consummated his marriage to Helena thinking she was Diana, and he has been led to believe that his wife is dead. When Maudlin's hand is offered to him he immediately accepts it, protesting that she was really the one he loved all along. This somewhat unexpected declaration of love cannot perhaps be written off as a studied attempt to regain the King's favour, but the audience is hardly given any reason to deem it sincere. Bertram's mind continues to be a black box for audience members and fictional characters alike. This uncertainty naturally spills over on to his later profession of love for Helena some 250 lines later, when he discovers that she is still among the living.

One important reason why *All's Well* becomes such a problem comedy is that the restoration of social order in the fifth act does not fulfil its thematic vision of profound sympathy for human failings. Instead, the comic resolution is pasted over an unresolved tension that results substantially from Bertram's lack of insides, the farcical plot device known as the bed-trick, and the forced marriage. A bed-trick need not ordinarily pose a major problem in comedy, and it is even used without much bitter aftertaste when Angelo gets his money's worth in another problem comedy, *Measure for Measure*. Even the silenced Katherina in *The Taming of the Shrew* can always be written off by some (but certainly not all) readers as a farcical stick figure in a primarily action-oriented play. In *All's Well*, however, very similar components chafe considerably against the larger sympathetic vision that Shakespeare holds up to view.

It is hoped that this reading of *All's Well* will have woven some of its formal and thematic attributes into a partial explanation of its dissonant literary effect. First and foremost, I hope to have shown that the play's selective deployment of insides is essential to how it will be experienced by the audience or reader. Since the play's insides function primarily (if not entirely exclusively) as vehicles for sympathy, Shakespeare's decision to place a principal character outside the sphere of private language produces a marked tension that remains unresolved even in the fifth act.

Secondly, this uneven distribution is distinctively gendered. *All's Well* is hardly a female-dominated play given the King's unquestioned dominance, but it is one of only two plays in the Shakespeare canon where the women get the upper hand in soliloquy. It is hardly a coincidence that Shakespeare suppresses the private language of the male protagonist in a play that so firmly embodies a perceived feminine principle of human sympathy. As a result, the play is best described as a tonally dissonant crossbreed between the heartless male plotting of *The Taming of the Shrew* and the sympathetic female qualms that dominate *The Two Noble Kinsmen*.

Thirdly, this reading is offered as a final example of the methodological principle that has guided my exploration of the Shakespearean inside. The central idea expressed in these pages has been that our interpretations of individual Shakespeare plays can be enriched considerably, and sometimes even validated, by systematic attention to overriding habits or tendencies in his dramatic practice.

Notes

1. Stephen Marché, 'Literature is not Data: Against Digital Humanities', *Los Angeles Review of Books*, 28 October 2012, web.
2. Keyword search for 'sympathy' in the *Literature Online* full-text database, including variant spellings and with the search parameters set to 'Shakespeare' and 'Publication Year = 1580–1640'. It would, however, be rash to posit a simple linear progression in the evolution of this concept from general *fellow feeling* to modern *pity and concern*. As David Marshall notes in his study of the eighteenth-century discourse of sympathy, Adam Smith actually proposed an obverse historical development in the *Theory of Moral Sentiments*. Sympathy, Smith argued, might previously have denoted things like pity or compassion, but now it seemed to be of more general application, denoting 'our fellow feeling with any passion whatsoever'. David Marshall, *The Surprising Effects of Sympathy: Marivaux, Diderot, Rousseau, and Mary Shelley* (Chicago and London: University of Chicago Press, 1988), 3.
3. Susan Feagin, *Reading with Feeling: The Aesthetics of Appreciation* (Ithaca: Cornell University Press, 1996), 114.
4. Amy Coplan, 'Empathic Engagement with Narrative Fictions', *The Journal of Aesthetics and Art Criticism* 62:3 (2004): 141–52, 145.
5. Strictly speaking, Aristotle's *pathos* should probably not be translated into English as 'pity' since it denotes an *action* that brings pain or destruction and thereby produces a fearful response on the part of the audience. See B. R. Rees, 'Pathos in the Poetics of Aristotle', *Greece and Rome* 19 (1972): 1–11.
6. My usage of this modern concept of sympathy can be contrasted usefully with David Marshall's explicit adoption of an eighteenth-century discourse where sympathy denotes 'not just feeling or the capacity for feeling but more specifically the capacity to feel the sentiments of someone else' (*Surprising Effects of Sympathy*, 3.) Today this capacity to 'feel what others feel' is usually filed under 'empathy', but Marshall rejects this concept on the grounds of its 'vaguely psychologistic connotations' (3).
7. Feagin, *Reading with Feeling*, 115.
8. Coplan, 'Empathic Engagement', 143.
9. Feagin, *Reading with Feeling*, 115–16.
10. Those who want to take the plunge might want to begin with Richard Palmer, *Fictional Minds* (Lincoln, NB: University of Nebraska Press, 2004) and James Phelan, *Living to Tell about It: A Rhetoric and Ethics of Character Narration* (Ithaca: Cornell University Press, 2004).

11. The comparison with autism as a cognitive failure to read minds is made explicitly, if cautiously, by Lisa Zunshine in *Why We Read Fiction: Theory of Mind and the Novel* (Columbus: Ohio State University Press, 2006).
12. Coplan, 'Empathic Engagement', 145.
13. Suzanne Keen, *Empathy and the Novel* (Oxford: Oxford University Press, 2010), 4.
14. Stephen Greenblatt, *Renaissance Self-Fashioning: From More to Shakespeare* (Chicago: University of Chicago Press, 1980). The rest of Greenblatt's argument about Othello's supposed sexual anxiety is based on an obvious misreading of the text. When Iago vows to 'abuse Othello's ear that he hath been too familiar with his wife', Greenblatt argues that the first personal pronoun ('he') may refer back to Othello himself rather than to Cassio. This may seem like a possible reading on the level of the individual sentence, but the wider literary context shows clearly that Cassio's potential adultery with Desdemona is the focal point of the entire passage. Othello's problem is not, as Greenblatt submits unconvincingly, that he himself has enjoyed sex too much with Desdemona, but rather that Cassio may have crept underneath her sheets.
15. Bradley, *Shakespearean Tragedy*, 190.
16. 'The human cognitive capacity to draw inferences about other people's beliefs, intentions and thoughts has been termed mentalizing, theory of mind or cognitive perspective taking. This capacity makes it possible, for instance, to understand that people may have views that differ from our own. Conversely, the capacity to share the feelings of others is called empathy. Empathy makes it possible to resonate with others' positive and negative feelings alike – we can thus feel happy when we vicariously share the joy of others and we can share the experience of suffering when we empathize with someone in pain.' Tania Singer and Olga Klimecki, 'Empathy and Compassion', *Current Biology* 24:18 (2014): 875–8, 875.
17. On the central role of altruistic punishment in literature, see William Flesch, *Comeuppance: Costly Signaling, Altruistic Punishment, and other Biological Components of Fiction* (Cambridge, MA: Harvard University Press, 2009).
18. Dana E. Aspinall, 'The Play and the Critics', in *The Taming of the Shrew: Critical Essays*, ed. Dana E. Espinall (London: Routledge, 2002), 3–40, 3.
19. These perspectives and many more are covered in Dana Aspinall's excellent collection of criticism on *The Taming of the Shrew*.
20. Frances E. Dolan, 'Introduction', in William Shakespeare, *The Taming of the Shrew: Texts and Contexts*, ed. Frances E. Dolan (Boston: Bedford, 1996), 1–38, 24–6.
21. This calculation is based on the number of lines rather than words, using the web-based statistical resource *Shakespeare's Words*, accessed 15 October 2014.
22. Robert B. Heilman, 'The *Taming* Untamed, or, The Return of the Shrew', 1966, reprinted in Aspinall, *Shrew: Critical Essays*, 45–57, 49.
23. This elevated score is not produced by extreme values of the kind that we find in *Shrew*. If we remove the outliers for 1590–4 (*Shrew* and *Verona*), the average actually increases to 24.6 per cent.
24. See, for example, Cynthia Marshall, 'Shakespeare, Crossing the Rubicon',

Shakespeare Survey 53 (2000): 73–88, where Shakespeare's departure from the plot-driven tendencies of the early plays is explained with reference to his renewed concern with Plutarch. Marshall's reading postdates this development somewhat compared to my own figures since she sees the plays written throughout the 1590s, and not just the early 1590s, as plot-driven.

25. Petruchio's dominance is not reflected in the play's total distribution of insides: he speaks only 45 per cent of the play's soliloquies and solo asides, a fairly normal figure for a Shakespearean protagonist.

26. Weighted frequencies in insides, no stop words, words of four letters or more, ranking in parenthesis. This word frequency list (like the one given later in this chapter) is based on all text in the SID source files, including brief stage directions ('aside') and character prefixes ('Hamlet'). The top-ten ranking for individual plays is therefore impure and somewhat conservative, given that individual character names can be expected to have an powerful impact on the level of individual plays but not on the level of the complete corpus. (In the results for Shrew, the word 'Hortensio' comes second and 'aside' comes fourth in the list.)

27 There are larger differences between these different phases in Shakespeare's career than between different subgenres, in spite of the perfectly reasonable expectation that history plays should require an unusual amount of expository information. Compare Wolfgang Clemen on the histories: 'Shakespeare takes over too many events and episodes from his chronicles and tries to transform them into drama. Consequently the messenger's report has to replace the acted scene and has to fill the gaps in the sequence of events.' *Shakespeare's Dramatic Art: Collected Essays* (London: Methuen, 1972), 100.

28. Harold Bloom, *How to Read and Why* (New York: Touchstone, 2001), 199. He uses the same formulation in *Shakespeare: The Invention of the Human* (New York: Riverhead, 1998), 80.

29. Cited in Dessen, *Titus Andronicus*, 70.

30. M. C. Bradbrook, *Shakespeare: The Poet in His World*, 1978 (London: Routledge, 2005), 42; T. S. Eliot, 'Notes on the Blank Verse of Christopher Marlowe', in *The Sacred Wood*, 1921, Bartleby edition, web.

31. Natália Pikli, 'The Crossing Point of Tears and Laughter: A Tragic Farce: Shakespeare's Titus Andronicus', *The AnaChronisT* 6 (2000): 51–69, accessed 15 October 2014.

32. Pikli, 'The Crossing Point', web, no page number.

33. SID matrix query for **gender** and **class**.

34. In John Fletcher and William Shakespeare, *The Two Noble Kinsmen*, Arden 3, ed. Lois Potter (London: Methuen, 1997), 328n.

35. As Richard Lippa notes in *Gender, Nature, and Nurture* (London: Lawrence Erlbaum, 2002), Alan Feingold's classic meta-analysis of gender difference in personality (1994) found the largest effect sizes in agreeableness and extraversion: 'The agreeableness component that showed the largest sex difference was tender-mindedness ($d = 0.97$, with women more tender-minded than men)' (*Gender, Nature, and Nurture*, 13). Feingold's result was acknowledged even in Janet Shibley Hyde's much-publicised meta-analysis in support of the Gender Similarities Hypotheses, but rendered as ($d = 0.91$). See Janet Shibley Hyde, 'The Gender Similarities Hypothesis', *American Psychologist* 60:6 (2005): 581–92, 585.

36. There are of course many exceptions to this general rule, from Lady Macbeth to York's description of Queen Margaret's as a 'tiger's heart wrapp'd in a woman's hide' (*3 Henry VI*, 1.4.137).

37. The exceptions are Palamon's soliloquy in act 3, scene 6, and perhaps also Emilia's third soliloquy in act 5, scene 3.

38. On a more general note, the play's insides contain more instances of the word 'poor' – seven of them – than we find in any other Shakespeare play. Only *King Lear* has the same word count, and not surprisingly so, given its thematic concern with questions about poverty and wealth and the grounds of human sympathy. The same word search for 'poor' in the complete plays (and not just insides) puts *Lear* alone in the driver's seat with a remarkable score of forty-seven instances of 'poor', while *Kinsmen* scrapes together 'only' eighteen (*Shakespeare's Words*, accessed 27 October 2014). Since *Lear* has fewer insides than *Kinsmen*, the same word count for 'poor' in its insides generates a higher percentage, 0.23 per cent compared to *Kinsmen*'s 0.15 per cent.

39. See Marcus Nordlund, *Shakespeare and the Nature of Love: Literature, Culture, Evolution* (Evanston: Northwestern University Press, 2007), ch. 4.

40. Carl Dennis, '*All's Well that Ends Well* and the Meaning of Agape', *Philological Quarterly* 50: 1 (1971): 75–84, 75.

41. As Vivian Thomas notes, this is a significant departure by Shakespeare from Painter's version of Boccaccio, where Beltramo 'quickly acquiesces to marriage'. See *The Moral Universe of Shakespeare's Problem Plays* (London: Croom Helm, 1987), 63. Thomas continues elsewhere: 'What in the source material was a private transaction behind closed doors is in Shakespeare's play a public occasion which is embarrassing and humiliating to all three participants [i.e. Helena, Bertram, and the King]'(148).

42. Few, if any, readings of *Shrew* fail to address or at least mention the problem of how to interpret Katherina's final defence of patriarchal marriage. The 'passionate critical debate over this speech' is summed up usefully and then related to the historical context of household manuals by Margaret Misekell in ''Love wrought these miracles': Marriage and Genre in *The Taming of the Shrew*', in Aspinall, *Taming of the Shrew*, 106–29, esp. 119. The problems with Bertram's speech in *All's Well* are summed up nicely by David Scott Kastan in '*All's Well that Ends Well* and the Limits of Comedy', *ELH* 52:3 (1985): 575–89.

43. Dianne Dreher, *Domination and Defiance: Fathers and Daughters in Shakespeare* (Lexington: University of Kentucky Press, 1986), 136, 138–9; Kay Stanton, 'All's Well in Love and War', in *Ideological Approaches to Shakespeare: The Practice of Theory*, ed. Robert P. Merrix and Nicholas Ranson (Lewiston, NY: Edwin Mellen, 1992),155–63; Carol Thomas Neely, *Broken Nuptials in Shakespeare's Plays* (New Haven: Yale University Press, 1985), 65, 70, 71; Alison Findlay, *A Feminist Perspective on Renaissance Drama* (Oxford: Blackwell, 1999), 96. A similar point is made in Marliss C. Desens, *The Bed-Trick in English Renaissance Drama: Explorations in Gender, Sexuality, and Power* (Newark: University of Delaware Press, 1994), 141. In the introduction to the Oxford edition, Susan Snyder argues convincingly for a more balanced view, but she still contends that the 'key' to the critical division regarding Helena's moral stature 'is the upsetting of the

gender role system created by having the woman rather than the man take the sexual initiative' (William Shakespeare, *All's Well that Ends Well*, ed. Susan Snyder (Oxford: Oxford University Press, 1993), 31). This approach reduces the play's moral problem to a gender problem, and thus fails to consider the more basic question of whether it is right to treat *any* human being as a commodity that can be bought and sold against his or her will.

44. Nordlund, *Shakespeare and the Nature of Love*, 149–50.
45. Paisley Livingston gives an excellent defence of moderate intentionalism in 'Intentionalism in Aesthetics', *New Literary History* 29:4 (1998): 831–46.
46. Ann Jennalie Cook, *Making a Match: Courtship in Shakespeare and His Society* (Princeton: Princeton University Press, 1991), 65.
47. See Charles L. Barber, *The Theme of Honour's Tongue: A Study of Social Attitudes in the English Drama from Shakespeare to Dryden*, Gothenburg Studies in English 58 (Göteborg: Acta Universitatis Gothoburgensis, 1985).
48. Barbara Everitt's edition of *All's Well*, 1970, p. 16, cited in William Shakespeare, *All's Well that Ends Well*, RSC edition, ed. Jonathan Bate and Eric Rasmussen (Basingstoke: Macmillan, 2011), 10.
49. <http://www.shakespeareswords.com/Special-Features-All-Characters>, accessed 26 September 2014.
50. Marcus Nordlund, 'Pride and Self-Love in Shakespeare and Montaigne', in *Shakespearean International Yearbook* 6, ed. Graham Bradshaw et al. (Aldershot: Ashgate, 2006), 77–98.
51. Michel de Montaigne, *The Complete Essays*, trans. and intro. M. A. Screech (London: Penguin, 2003), vol. 3, ch. 1, 892.
52. Hirsh, *History of Soliloquies*, 125–6; italics in original.
53. My editorial principle for distinguishing insides from dialogue in uncertain cases is explained in Appendix 3, in the 'Choice of Editions' section. Since the Complete Arden's treatment of Lafew in act 2, scene 3, seems slightly inconsistent I have instead followed the Norton Shakespeare and the RSC edition in treating all four lines as asides. These differences between the different editions do not impinge on my findings in this chapter except that an Arden-based interpretation would raise the female share of insides slightly from 58 per cent to 62 per cent.
54. Shakespeare's use of the word 'fit' may even betray direct influence from John Florio's translation of the *Essays*, which was published around the same time that Shakespeare probably wrote *All's Well*. In Florio's version, Montaigne contends that nothing 'hath beene insinuated in this huge universe but holdeth some *fit* place therein.' *The Essays of Montaigne*, vol. 3, ch. 1, 6.
55. Interestingly, Shakespeare's third problem comedy, *Troilus and Cressida*, goes in the other direction and packs more than half of its insides (56.5 per cent) into the fifth act, building up considerable tension before it peters out so very strangely. See the section 'Subgenre' in Appendix 3 for a brief discussion of this generically unstable play, which, it might be argued, should really be treated as a species apart from the other plays.

Appendix 1 General Coding Principles

The overriding purpose behind the construction of the *Shakespearean Inside Database* (SID) has been to uncover general patterns, and exceptions from these patterns, in Shakespeare's dramatic practice. In the pages that follow I will account for the theoretical and methodological principles behind the coding. As we shall see, the main challenge has been to find the right level of complexity; the codes (or 'nodes' in 'NVivo speak') must be sufficiently complex to generate interesting data, but not so complex that the coding becomes controversial.

A project of this kind is bound to meet with two basic objections, the first of which has language-philosophical roots. If – as so many postmodern theorists have kept reminding us over the years – interpretation 'goes all the way down', then surely any quantitative approach to literary interpretation is just a scientistic dream of objectivity? How can it possibly escape the slippery nature of language? The same complaint comes in a specifically historical and dramatic version. How can we hope to quantify anything of real literary interest in Shakespeare – except perhaps the most rudimentary linguistic elements – when even basic categories like act and scene divisions, types of speech, genres, and even the scholarly texts themselves turn out to be pragmatic compromises or modern impositions upon fluid early modern practices?

Yes, in a fundamental sense we are all toiling in the shadow of the Tower of Babel. But the most appropriate response to this insight is neither to formulate an escape plan from the prison-house of language nor to iterate how trapped we all are. More than a decade ago, Susan Haack noted how fully scholars in the humanities had succumbed to a stance that Anthony Gottlieb dubbed the Higher Dismissiveness:

> again and again true, fallibilist premises are transmuted into false, cynical conclusions: what is accepted as known fact is often enough no such thing, *therefore* the concept of known fact is ideological humbug; one's judgment of the worth of evidence depends on one's background beliefs, *therefore*

there are no objective standards of evidential quality; science isn't sacred, *therefore* it must be a kind of confidence trick; etc., etc.[1]

The fallibilistic alternative put forward by Haack is simple enough: that 'the less than perfect is a lot better than nothing at all'.[2] It seems more meaningful to try and gauge the seriousness of the problem by exploring how far our language and methodology can take us; to try and distinguish between different kinds of research questions that can be answered with different degrees of objectivity and handled with different tools; and, last but not least, to render our critical procedures as transparent as possible, opening them up to intersubjective scrutiny. This is not a dream of the positivist beyond. It is an attempt to work constructively with the imperfect tools we have at our disposal, on the assumption that the 'less than perfect' can also get a little better.

In this particular project, interpretation 'goes all the way down' in an overt sense because the computational procedure is not based on raw text files but on manual markup. Coding around 7 per cent of thirty-nine Shakespeare plays is a time-consuming and fallibilistic endeavour, obviously, but the notable payoff is that one can quantify much more intellectually stimulating phenomena than any computer software could handle on its own. It is also unlikely that minor coding errors or uncertainties will have catastrophic consequences for large-scale searches conducted across almost forty plays. A second bulwark against coder unreliability is the social nature of research. The plan is to publish the research files on the web so that complex propositions can be traced back to simpler ones; indeed, each individual coded passage can be scrutinised and even corrected by others (who can also run their own searches on the material if they so desire). A third principle of quality control is that statistical outliers – that is, the kind of unusual or extreme results that often prove interesting to the interpreter – have always been double-checked carefully before they were employed in the literary analysis.

Another frequent objection to quantitative analysis of literary texts is that all the really interesting questions require sensitive attention to fine nuances and shades of meaning that simply cannot be captured by a finite set of codes. This emphasis on fine points, particulars, and complex inferences has long been a standard complaint against any attempt to make literary studies more scientific. Unfortunately, it has too often been wedded to the simple-minded notion that humanities scholars should only deal with cultural or aesthetic particulars and leave the general laws or patterns to the scientists.[3] This is a shame since the problem itself is both real and challenging. As David Hoover opined in 2008, quantitative studies have too often 'fail[ed] to address problems of real literary significance, ignore[d] the subject-specific background, or concentrate[d] too heavily on technology or software'.[4] A related practical point was made a few years earlier by Claire Warwick:

> Even if [literary scholars] could define the sort of literary nuances that they are looking for, or translate them into an encoding system, would this really be a good use of time? The text would have to be so heavily marked up that the critic might as well just read it anyway.[5]

The second part of Warwick's meditation has already been dealt with above: that the payoff offered by a computational approach must be very different from the insights derived from just reading the plays. Few people can browse through the complete plays of Shakespeare and make detailed calculations in their heads about, say, the relative distribution of different figures of speech in different genres. If we can do this effectively by computational means then we can generate new kinds of data, and, indirectly, new interpretations. The key to the first part of Warwick's query – the problem of capturing fine nuances – lies partly in the division of labour between the human interpreter and the software, and partly in the distinction between the different interpretative tasks performed by the human. From a fallibilistic viewpoint there will never be a *perfect* solution to these problems, but they do admit of a *robust* solution.

'Going digital' in Shakespeare studies need not mean that we renounce traditional modes of analysis such as close reading in favour of chi square or ANOVA tests. Instead we can use the computer as a powerful prosthetic device or workhorse that extends the processing power of the interpreter's brain for closely defined purposes while reserving the high-inference literary work for ourselves. In order for this to work in a project based on manual coding, it is necessary to distinguish clearly between simple interpretative tasks with a high degree of objectivity (so that texts can be coded manually and then computed and quantified) and more complex, controversial, and potentially pluralistic inferential processes (such as interpretations of the quantitative patterns or close readings of individual passages). The quantitative patterns unearthed in this study will rarely lend themselves to, say, computations of statistical probability, and the results will frequently admit more than one causal explanation; if interpretation goes all the way down, then it naturally goes all the way up, too. It can also be expected that a project that generates a new kind of data about Shakespeare's works will also produce any number of new interpretative problems.

Here is a rhapsodic, schematic, and somewhat idealised account of the research methodology employed in this project:

1. *Preparation of the text.* Creation of text files containing all insides in the complete plays.
2. *Coding.* Low-inference tagging of all insides in the complete plays using predefined codes.
3. *Computation.* Computer-assisted exploration of the coded data (testing hypotheses, doing guesswork, running random searches).
4. *Interpretation.* High-inference interpretation of overriding patterns across the complete plays ('distant reading') and of particular plays, scenes, characters, or speeches ('close reading') in the light of the overriding patterns.

In phase three the software acts as the middle man, doing all the tedious counting and correlating of various codes. But handing over the dirty work to the software does more than just allow us to process large piles of data at lightning speed; the methodological distinction between textual nuts and bolts (phase 2) and more complex interpretative inferences (phase 4) also makes it possible to formulate testable hypotheses in the form of search strings that are processed independently by the computer. This helps restore something valuable that was seriously threatened in the age of Grand Theory: namely, the capacity to be thwarted, disappointed, and sometimes pleasantly surprised by one's data. It can even be expected that the quantitative exploration of a set of predefined textual attributes carries with it a substantial reduction of observer bias.

The first step was to prepare a text file for each individual play, which was then imported into the software NVivo 9 (and later NVivo 10) for coding. The text files were based on the conflated Complete Arden Shakespeare edition, but other editions were consulted whenever the nature of a speech was deemed ambiguous (a problem that the recent RSC edition recognises actively by means of question marks). Potential codes were proposed and tested in hypothetico-deductive fashion until they were deemed sufficiently robust to enable effective and dependable coding. The codes (referred to as 'nodes' in nVivo) were grouped according to three basic categories: *locus* (the location of the speech), *genus* (the nature of the speaker), and *modus* (the nature of the speech) and formalised by means of a coding sheet (appendix 2).

Coding for some aspects of *locus* and *genus* – such as character, social class, and gender – was typically a walk in the park, except in those situation where a character's class journey made the coding a little more convoluted.[6] True to the fallibilistic credo that 'the less than perfect is better than nothing at all', I also coded for such notoriously problematic aspects as *subgenre*, *approximate year of composition*, and *act*. The coding by *year* employed averages based on the dating proposed in three different Shakespeare editions: Arden, Oxford/Norton, RSC. Here I was less interested in the exact year of composition for each play – which is often impossible to determine – than in slightly broader patterns distinguishing different phases in Shakespeare's career. For *subgenre* I used a standard division into comedy, tragedy, history, and romance, on the assumption that these distinctions were not so much natural kinds as convenient labels.

A similar pragmatism ruled when I coded the insides according to *act*, with full awareness that act divisions were not used in published plays until a few years into the seventeenth century. Coding the plays in this way, in the manner of the First Folio and most modern editions, was deemed a convenient and productive way to study the distribution of insides across Shakespeare's plays. As seen in Chapter 4, Shakespeare distributes his insides according to a distinctive pattern in three subgenres out of four, while the fourth genre – the history play – departs from the standard graph for identifiable reasons.

Most of the codes described above define different textual attributes that can be combined into highly intricate textual queries. NVivo can be instructed to search for, say, all **solo asides** spoken by **female commoners** addressing **apostrophes** to **deities** in the **fifth acts** of **history plays** written **before 1600**. (The bold words in the previous sentence all represent individual nodes that can be combined at will.) Or one can study the broad distribution of soliloquies and asides across time, across genres, or across the complete plays. Of course, such simple attributes may not always capture specifically *dramatic* questions of their own accord. As A. C. Sprague pointed out many decades ago, soliloquies and asides 'form a valuable part of Shakespeare's technique of exposition. In them, character and motive are unfolded, plot and counterplot set going, events narrated, and the issues of the play made clear.'[7] What is needed, therefore, is an additional set of robust categories that might capture something of the dramatic import of a given passage.

The problem is that neither a purely formal nor a purely functional approach will do the trick: the former is tied too closely, and the latter too loosely, to the form of the utterance. Attention to the *formal* aspects of Shakespeare's language (e.g. his grammar) is inadequate since the same literary effect can be accomplished by means of a bewildering diversity of syntactic and semantic structures.[8] It might seem like a good alternative to study the dramatic *function* of an utterance, but functions are almost impossible for the opposite reason: they tend to be indirect and indefinite in number, and they operate both on the internal and on the external level of dramatic communication. When Ansgar Nünning and Roy Sommer studied how Shakespearean narrations 'exceed the dramaturgic function of moving the action forward', they pointed to the conveyance of offstage information, explanations of 'motives, aims, and intentions', characterisation, 'sense-making and identity construction', and even the illumination of the 'social dynamics' and the 'cultural significance of storytelling' in early modern culture.[9] Such a broadly conceived functionalism illustrates the problem quite clearly: if these are all potential 'functions' of any given passage then we must surely despair of ever using them systematically for coding purposes.

My pragmatic solution to this problem was to identify a Searle-inspired[10] set of *dramatic speech acts* that capture what Shakespeare's characters are actually *doing* when they speak. A character may, for example, be reporting past events, assessing another character, asking for something, drawing thematic conclusions, passing moral judgement, predicting future events, or planning an action. Some readers may note a parallel here with my discussion of authorial intention: that it is extremely hard to determine what Shakespeare is trying to do, but much easier to determine what he is actually doing. Unlike some of the functions described by Nünning and Sommer, these dramatic speech acts tend to be so distinctive that they can be coded with a high degree of objectivity. Unlike textual attributes like gender, genre, or type of speech they are also additive: that is, an indefinite number of distinctive speech acts can be realised simultaneously, allowing for the systematic study of any overlaps between them.

Even when speakers actively eschew dialogue with others, their speech is still likely to retain a strong dialogical quality for both 'internal' and 'external' reasons. One 'internal' reason, expanded upon in chapter 3, is that real humans are deeply dialogical beings, and this is likely to be reflected somehow in their fictional counterparts. Another, 'external' reason is that speeches become more dynamic or dramatic if the characters speak figuratively as if they were addressing an absent person, or indeed address *themselves* as if they were a different person. Some formal aspects of this dialogue, such as figures of speech with a strong dialogical component can be subjected to quantitative analysis with interesting results. I therefore coded systematically for selected figures of speech that somehow mimicked ordinary dialogue (such as **apostrophe, prosopopoeia, illeism,** and **erotema**). Given the special centrality of apostrophe to Shakespeare's dramatic practice this particular trope was divided into subcategories based on their object (an absent character, abstraction, dead person, etc.).

Finally, I appended a less structured grab-bag of promising codes to my coding sheet. Is the character reading a **letter** or, more generally, repeating what someone else has said (**reported speech**)? Is it commonly accepted that this particular passage was written by a **co-author**, which would mean that we can either investigate it as part of the 'Shakespeare canon' or separate it from passages almost certainly by Shakespeare himself? Is the speech problematic from a **textual** aspect? Or is there any evidence that this might be an instance of **audience address**? A systematic account of the coding and the principles behind it can be found in Appendices 2 ('Coding Sheet') and 3 ('Definitions and Explanations of Nodes').

Notes

1. Susan Haack, 'Staying for an Answer: The Untidy Process of Groping for Truth', in *Theory's Empire: An Anthology of Dissent*, ed. Daphne Patai and Will H. Corral (New York: Columbia University Press, 2005), 552–61, 553.
2. Haack, 'Staying for an Answer', 553.
3. A strong argument against this residual Two Cultures logic is offered by Edward Slingerland in *What Science Offers the Humanities* (Cambridge: Cambridge University Press, 2008).
4. David L. Hoover, 'Quantitative Analysis and Literary Studies: History, Goals, and Theoretical Foundation', in *A Companion to Digital Literary Studies*, ed. Susan Schreibman and Ray Siemens (Oxford: Blackwell, 2008), part 4, ch. 28. <http://www.digitalhumanities.org/companionDLS/>
5. Claire Warwick, 'English Literature, Electronic Text and Computer Analysis: An Impossible Combination?' Conference paper, *ACH-ALLC International Humanities Computing Conference*, 12 June 1999 (abstract). <http://www2.iath.virginia.edu/ach-allc.99/proceedings/warwick.html>
6. Since NVivo allows the user to specify an indefinite number of 'nodes' with different 'attributes', individual characters were defined as nodes with their gender and class as attributes. When, for instance, an individual character changed his social rank in the course of a play this was solved by means of nested coding: a superordinate node called 'Macbeth' was combined with two subordinate nodes with different class attributes, 'Macbeth aristocrat' and 'Macbeth king', with the option of aggregating the two levels depending on the specific research question.
7. Sprague, *Shakespeare and the Audience*, 72.
8. For a digital approach that explores potential links between Shakespeare's subgenres and particular grammatical features, see Jonathan Hope and Michael Witmore, 'The Hundredth Psalm to the Tune of "Green Sleeves": Digital Approaches to Shakespeare's Language of Genre', *Shakespeare Quarterly* 61:3 (2010): 357–90.

9. Ansgar Nünning and Roy Sommer, 'The Performative Power of Narrative in Drama: On the Forms and Functions of Dramatic Storytelling in Shakespeare's Plays', in *Current Trends in Narratology*, ed. Greta Olson (Berlin: de Gruyter, 2011), 200–31, 219–20.
10. John Searle, *Speech Acts: An Essay in the Philosophy of Language*, 1969 (Cambridge: Cambridge University Press, 1999).

Appendix 2 Coding Sheet

This is a complete list of the nodes employed in the *Shakespearean Inside Database* (SID). Nodes in *italics* have not been used in this book project but may be released in a future version of SID.

ASPECT	VARIABLE	NODES AND ATTRIBUTES		COMMENT
LOCUS	PLAY	SUBGENRE		
		YEAR		
	ACT	1–5		
	LOCATION	ENTRANCE SPEECH		
		EXIT SPEECH		
		SCENE BEGINS		
		SCENE ENDS		
GENUS	CHARACTER	SEX (M/F)		
		CLASS		
MODUS	TYPE	SOLILOQUY		
		SOLO ASIDE		
		OVERHEARD		
		AMBIGUOUS		
	DRAMATIC SPEECH ACTS	ASSESSING	CHARACTER	
			COUNTERFACTUALS	
			MORALITY	
			DILEMMA	
			MOTIVATION	
			REALITY CHECK	
			THEMATICS	
			OTHER	
		PREDICTING		
		REPORTING		
		REQUESTING		
		PLANNING (incl. RENOUNCING)		
	FIGURES OF SPEECH	APOSTROPHE (various types)		
		ASTEISMUS		
		EROTEMA		
		ILLEISM		
		TUISM		
		PROSOPOPOEIA		
	DIRECT ADDRESS	RELATIONAL MARKER		
		REDUNDANCY		
		METALEPSIS		
	MISCELLANEOUS	SONG		
		QUESTION		
		REPORTED WORDS		
		LETTER		
		SPELL		
		CO-AUTHOR		
		TEXTUAL		
		REFERENCES		

Appendix 3 Definitions and Explanations of Nodes

Choice of Editions

This project applied a conservative principle to the attribution of plays to Shakespeare. The text used in the *Shakespearean Inside Database* (SID) is based almost entirely on the Arden Shakespeare, *Complete Works*, which contains the accreted efforts of many scholars over time, conflates selections from Quarto and Folio versions, and only includes plays that can be safely attributed to Shakespeare (in part or as a whole). One notable addition to this Arden-based roster is *Edward III*, which contains a number of insides that were almost certainly written by Shakespeare. This text had not yet been published by Arden when the database was compiled, and it was therefore collected from the New Cambridge Shakespeare edition.

It is likely that the list of thirty-nine plays is still incomplete and that a future version of the database will need to include other texts. One potential contender, especially if we are to trust the most recent stylometric tests indicating minimal adjustments by the eighteenth-century editor Theobald, is *Double Falsehood*, which was published in the Arden Shakespeare series in 2010 (when this project had already begun). Since the distinction between dialogue and asides can some-times be tenuous I have also double-checked ambiguous examples against two other editions (the Norton Shakespeare and the RSC edition). Whenever a passage was handled differently by the editors of these three editions, e.g. when two editors rendered a speech as an aside, while the third editor defined it as dialogue, I applied a simple majority rule.

A. LOCUS: where do we find the speech?

The word 'locus' covers both the place of the individual play in the Shakespeare canon (entries 1 and 2 below) and the location of the individual speech inside the individual play (3–4). All plays were defined as individual nodes and given two attributes: subgenre and year of composition. The internal position of the speech inside the play was coded directly in the text according to act (entry 3) and its relative location in the scene (entry 4).

1. Subgenre

Shakespeare's plays can be grouped or categorised in many different ways based on widely differing criteria. The most historically stringent approach might be to restrict oneself to the categories in the First Folio (comedies, tragedies, and histories), endowing the editors of this particular volume with considerable authority and stretching the comic subgenre to the point of bursting. Modern scholars have introduced their own subdivisions based on criteria such as geographical location ('Roman plays'), tonal qualities ('problem play', 'problem comedy'), or taste ('great tragedies').

The SID groups Shakespeare's plays into the four most commonly accepted subgenres: **comedy, tragedy, history, and romance.** Individual plays were also organised into larger 'sets' in order to generate data for specific research questions. For example, the question of whether Shakespeare considered the rhetorical figure of speech called **'illeism'** to be a Roman phenomenon could be answered in Chapter 3 thanks to the formation of a set called 'Roman plays'.

The most problematic of the generic attributions below is that of *Troilus and Cressida*, which appears sandwiched between the histories and tragedies in the *First Folio* (perhaps as an afterthought, since it is not listed in the table of contents). Since *Troilus* is clearly neither a tragedy nor a history, the play was defined as a *comedy* in keeping with the prefatory letter affixed to the 1609 Quarto, which defines it very clearly as a comedy. This is not a satisfying solution but the one that most closely approximates the nature of this highly unusual, not to say idiosyncratic, play.

Tragedy

ANTONY AND CLEOPATRA	*MACBETH*
CORIOLANUS	*OTHELLO*

HAMLET	*ROMEO AND JULIET*
JULIUS CAESAR	*TIMON OF ATHENS*
KING LEAR	*TITUS ANDRONICUS*

History

KING EDWARD III	*2 KING HENRY VI*
KING HENRY IV, part 1	*3 KING HENRY VI*
KING HENRY IV, part 2	*KING HENRY VIII*
KING HENRY V	*KING JOHN*
1 KING HENRY VI	*KING RICHARD II*
KING RICHARD III	

Comedy

ALL'S WELL THAT ENDS WELL	*THE MERRY WIVES OF WINDSOR*
AS YOU LIKE IT	*A MIDSUMMER NIGHT'S DREAM*
THE COMEDY OF ERRORS	*MUCH ADO ABOUT NOTHING*
LOVE'S LABOUR'S LOST	*THE TAMING OF THE SHREW*
MEASURE FOR MEASURE	*TROILUS AND CRESSIDA*
THE MERCHANT OF VENICE	*TWELFTH NIGHT*
THE TWO GENTLEMEN OF	
VERONA	

Romance

CYMBELINE	*THE TWO NOBLE KINSMEN*
PERICLES	*THE WINTER'S TALE*
THE TEMPEST	

2. Year of composition

The time of composition for some Shakespeare plays is highly uncertain and it is not impossible that future evidence will overthrow even commonly accepted datings. In some cases, their genesis is so uncertain that it is impossible to pin them down to an individual year. These substantial problems must, however, be weighed against the considerable benefits of exploring patterns in Shakespeare's dramatic practice across time.

One way to solve this problem – in the fallibilistic sense of a robust, but far from infallible solution – is to group the plays into five-year phases. These phases were arrived at by first generating a mean for each play of the years of composition proposed in three different editions – Arden, Oxford/Norton, and RSC – and then assigning these amalgamated years of composition to five-year phases: **1590–4, 1595–9, 1600–4, 1605–9, 1610–14.** The date for one play – *Edward III*, which was not included in the Complete Arden Shakespeare and was therefore taken from the New Cambridge edition – was calculated slightly differently, as the average of the years proposed in the New Cambridge, Oxford, and Norton editions. This method explains the use of fractioned dates for some individual editions in the list below, where a suggested dating of '1596–7' has been recalculated as 1596.5.

Needless to say, this method is not sufficiently fine-grained to take a range of complicating factors into account, such as continual revision by Shakespeare or the combination of Folio and Quarto passages from different periods in the conflated text, but it can still be expected to generate meaningful results.

PLAY	ARDEN	NORTON	RSC	AVERAGE
ALL'S WELL THAT ENDS WELL	1603.5	1604	1604.5	**1604**
ANTONY AND CLEOPATRA	1606	1606.5	1606.5	**1606**
AS YOU LIKE IT	1599	1599.5	1599.5	**1599**
THE COMEDY OF ERRORS	1592	1593	1593.5	**1593**
CORIOLANUS	1608	1608	1608	**1608**
CYMBELINE	1610	1610.5	1610	**1610**
HAMLET	1600	1600.5	1600	**1600**
JULIUS CAESAR	1599	1599	1599	**1599**
KING EDWARD III		1592		**1592**
1 KING HENRY IV	1597	1596.5	1596.5	**1597**
2 KING HENRY IV	1598	1597.5	1597.5	**1598**
KING HENRY V	1599	1599	1599	**1599**
1 KING HENRY VI	1590.5	1591.5	1592	**1591**
2 KING HENRY VI	1594	1590.5	1591	**1592**
3 KING HENRY VI	1590	1591	1591	**1591**
KING HENRY VIII	1613	1613	1613	**1613**
KING JOHN	1592.5	1595	1596	**1595**
KING LEAR	1604.5	1606.5	1605.5	**1606**
KING RICHARD II	1595	1595	1595.5	**1595**
KING RICHARD III	1597	1592.5	1593	**1594**
LOVE'S LABOUR'S LOST	1594.5	1594	1595.5	**1595**
MACBETH	1606	1606	1606	**1606**
MEASURE FOR MEASURE	1604	1604	1604	**1604**
THE MERCHANT OF VENICE	1596.5	1596.5	1596.5	**1597**
THE MERRY WIVES OF WINDSOR	1598	1597	1599	**1598**
A MIDSUMMER NIGHTS DREAM	1594.5	1594.5	1595.5	**1595**
MUCH ADO ABOUT NOTHING	1598.5	1598.5	1598	**1598**
OTHELLO	1602.5	1603.5	1604	**1603**
PERICLES	1609	1608.5	1608	**1609**
ROMEO AND JULIET	1594	1594.5	1595.5	**1595**
THE TAMING OF THE SHREW	1592	1591.5	1592	**1592**

PLAY	ARDEN	NORTON	RSC	AVERAGE
THE TEMPEST	1610.5	1610.5	1611	**1611**
TIMON OF ATHENS	1608.5	1605.5	1605	**1606**
TITUS ANDRONICUS	1593.5	1590.5	1592.5	**1592**
TROILUS AND CRESSIDA	1601.5	1602.5	1601.5	**1602**
TWELFTH NIGHT	1601	1601.5	1601	**1601**
THE TWO GENTLEMEN OF VERONA	1590	1591	1592	**1591**
THE TWO NOBLE KINSMEN	1613.5	1614	1613.5	**1614**
THE WINTER'S TALE	1609.5	1609.5	1611	**1610**

This approach generated the following five-year phases that were then assigned as attributes for each play:

1590–1594

THE COMEDY OF ERRORS
KING EDWARD III
1 KING HENRY VI
2 KING HENRY VI
3 KING HENRY VI
KING RICHARD III
THE TAMING OF THE SHREW
TITUS ANDRONICUS
THE TWO GENTLEMEN OF VERONA

1595–1599

AS YOU LIKE IT
JULIUS CAESAR
KING HENRY IV, part 1
KING HENRY IV, part 2
KING HENRY V
KING JOHN
KING RICHARD II
LOVE'S LABOUR'S LOST
THE MERCHANT OF VENICE
THE MERRY WIVES OF WINDSOR
A MIDSUMMER NIGHT'S DREAM
MUCH ADO ABOUT NOTHING
ROMEO AND JULIET

1600–1604

ALL'S WELL THAT ENDS WELL
HAMLET
MEASURE FOR MEASURE
OTHELLO
TROILUS AND CRESSIDA
TWELFTH NIGHT

1605–1609

ANTONY AND CLEOPATRA
CORIOLANUS
KING LEAR
MACBETH
PERICLES
TIMON OF ATHENS

1610–1614

CYMBELINE
KING HENRY VIII
THE WINTER'S TALE
THE TEMPEST
THE TWO NOBLE KINSMEN

3. Act

Acts and scenes are treacherous units in Shakespeare's works. The former may seem particularly problematic for a study of the complete plays since published plays were not divided into acts until a few years into the seventeenth century. This explains why many Quarto publications of Shakespeare's plays are only divided into scenes while the First Folio has act divisions. The SID still codes individual Shakespeare plays according to **acts 1–5** for a simple reason. Unlike scenes, which can vary enormously in terms of number and length, the act division used in the First Folio and in most modern editions of Shakespeare is a uniform and reliable pragmatic tool for studying the overriding distribution of insides across the individual play. Once all plays have been coded in this way it possible to chart larger patterns of distribution according to, for example, genre or phase. From this point of view, it does not matter greatly whether a particular act division was made in the original publication(s) of a Shakespeare play or is a modern editorial imposition.

4. Location

The location of the individual speech identifies its position within the larger scene, as follows.

4.1. Entrance speech
Insides are coded as entrance speeches whenever they coincide with a character's entrance. The criterion was applied very strictly so that speeches preceded by even one word of dialogue were excluded.

4.2. Exit speech
Insides are coded as exit speeches whenever they coincide with a character's exit. The criterion was applied very strictly so that speeches followed by even one word of dialogue have been excluded.

4.3. Scene begins
Insides are deemed to begin a scene when they constitute its first spoken words.

4.4. Scene ends
Insides are deemed to end a scene when they constitute its last spoken words.

B. GENUS: what is the nature of the speaker?

1. Character

All characters that speak at least one inside in the corpus of Shakespeare plays were assigned to a separate node that bears their name together with a suffix based on the name of the play. Each individual character node was then coded according to two attributes: sex and class.

1.1. Sex

The coding for sex is relatively straightforward: all characters are coded as either **male** or **female**, with the option of defining ambiguous characters as **unclear**.

1.2. Class

Coding for **class** is more complicated. The basic categories were derived from the social hierarchy of early modern England (and sometimes translated from comparable hierarchies in other cultures):

1.2.1. Royalty (includes Emperors or any other characters at the utmost top of a social hierarchy, including the triumvirs of *Antony and Cleopatra*).

1.2.2. Nobilitas major (includes Dukes, Archbishops, Earls, Barons, Bishops, etc. Cardinals were deemed most closely comparable to Archbishops and so were coded as nobilitas major.)

1.2.3. Nobilitas minor (includes Baronets, Knights, Esquires, Gentlemen, Clergymen, etc.)

1.2.4. Commoner.

1.2.5. Unclear.

Class attributes were derived primarily from the lists of dramatis personae, which usually contained detailed information of this kind. This information sometimes had to be complemented by scouring the text for terms of address (such as 'My Lord/My Lady', 'Sir', 'Gentlemen', 'Master') or similar information of a more indirect nature.

Children and spouses were seen as belonging to the same social class as their parents/spouses. One necessary exception was that illegitimate children like Edmund or Philip Faulconbridge were defined as commoners (though Faulconbridge is officially promoted to gentry before he speaks his first soliloquy). Fools were deemed to have ambiguous social status and were coded as unclear when more detailed information was lacking; so were any other characters that could not be safely categorised on the basis of textual information.

One complicated problem was posed by characters who changed their class in the course of the action. This was solved by constructing two separate characters with separate class attributes that were subordinate to an overriding character node. This meant that information about the same character could be either aggregated or separated in relation to specific questions about class. The character of Macbeth, for example, was coded as an aggregate character node composed of two subordinate character nodes: Macbeth as Thane (nobilitas major) and Macbeth as King (royalty).

C. MODUS: how is the speech constructed?

1. Type

1.1. Soliloquy
Insides are deemed soliloquies where speakers do not intend to be heard by another character on the stage and believe themselves to be alone.

1.2. Solo aside
Insides are deemed solo asides where speakers engage in guarded speech that is kept from the hearing of all other characters who are present on the stage.

1.3. Overheard
Soliloquies or solo asides are categorised as overheard where the speaker's intention not to be heard by another character is thwarted (usually because the speaker is unaware of the other character's presence).

1.4. Ambiguous
Passages are deemed ambiguous when they are unclear from the point of view of delivery because the distinction between dialogue and inside cannot be made easily.

2. Dramatic speech acts

These nodes are loosely inspired by John Searle's speech act theory but are perhaps better described as deeply pragmatic amalgams of speech acts and dramatic cues. They typically have functions on the internal level of the fiction (as dramatisations of how characters engage with their fictional play-world) as well as the external level (supplying the audience with various types of information, as refracted through the subjectivity of the individual character). There is, in principle, no limit to the potential overlap between certain speech acts (e.g. the assessment of character and morality), while others are more or less mutually exclusive (e.g. reporting and predicting).

2.1. Assessing

This category covers a number of actions by which the speaker assesses an action, a person, or a situation. Such dramatic speech acts need not take the form of straightforward *assertives* that commit the speaker to the truth of a proposition, since the assessment is often tentative and uncertain.

2.1.1. Character. The speaker gives information about what another character is like. This focus on constant traits (personality, personal attributes, biographical information, and so forth) distinguishes this speech act from **2.4.3. Motivation**, but there may be considerable overlap with **2.4.2. Morality**.

2.1.2. Morality. The speaker assesses a person or situation in relation to ideas about right and wrong, good or bad.

2.1.3. Motivation. The speaker assesses another character's reasons for a specific action or inaction.

2.1.4. Thematics. The speaker derives generalised ideas or truths from a concrete situation. This act typically functions as an *assertive* in the Searlean sense.

2.2. Predicting

Predicting occurs when the speaker predicts future events or outcomes over which he or she has limited control (thus distinguishing this speech act clearly from **2.3. Reporting**). This is one of two speech acts that perform the narratological function of *prolepsis*, albeit through the limited and potentially erroneous perspective of an individual character who cannot see the future.

2.3. Reporting

Reporting is held to occur when the speaker gives an account of events that have already transpired. These may be offstage events or other things that are not visible to the physical eyes of the audience. Functionally speaking, this speech act typically performs the narratological act of *analepsis* and typically constitutes an *assertion* in Searle's sense.

2.4. Requesting

In requesting, the speaker *asks for* or *demands* something in the manner of a Searlean *directive*.

2.5. Planning

Planning occurs when the speaker announces a future course of action on his or her part. This is the other speech act that frequently functions *proleptically* (but again, always from the individual character's limited perspective). It corresponds to the *commissive* in Searle's speech act theory.

3. Rhetorical Figures of Speech

3.1. Apostrophe

Apostrophe is defined as speech directed to an addressee that is not physically present on the stage and/or cannot be expected to hear what is said. Apostrophe was subdivided further into different types depending on the object of address: *absent character, abstraction, the dead, deity, nature, own body, own soul or mind, uncategorised.*

3.2. Asteismus

Asteismus is defined as a quick retort where the speaker bounces back the previous speaker's words in modified form.

3.3. Erotema

In erotema, the speaker poses a question that is clearly rhetorical in nature.

3.4. Illeism

Illeism is third-person reference to one's own person.

3.5. Tuism

Tuism is second-person address to one's own person.

3.6. Prosopopoeia

Also known as *personation*, prosopopoeia is the adoption of a speaking role that is different from one's own person.

4. Signals of direct address

4.1. Relational marker

A relational marker is a formulation that seems to address the audience explicitly, focus their attention, and/or include them as participants in the discursive act.

4.2. Redundancy

A speech that seems to lack any motivation for the character on the internal level of the dramatic fiction is coded as redundant.

4.3. Metalepsis

Metalepsis is transgression of the conventional boundary between the internal and the external level of communication.

5. Miscellaneous

5.1. Song

The speaker sings a song.

5.2. Question

Since questions constitute directives in Searle's speech act theory it might seem natural to include them among the dramatic speech acts above. In this case it was, however, deemed more precise to use a grammatical definition. The node covers only direct questions of the following kinds. (1) Questions that make up a complete sentence or an independent phrase have been coded in their entirety ('The King?'). (2) Sentences where the question forms the main clause have also been coded in their entirety. (3) In sentences where the question is a coordinated or subordinate clause, only the interrogative clause has been coded. (In the line 'To be i'the field, and ask "what news?" of me!' – only the exact question 'what news?' has been coded.)

5.3. Reported words

Reported words are a subset of *reporting* where the speaker incorporates the offstage or onstage speech of another character into his or her own words. This can be done either directly in the form of a quotation or indirectly in the form of a paraphrase.

5.3.1. Letter. A subset of reported words where the speaker reads a letter written by another character.

5.4. Spell

The speaker casts a magic spell.

5.5. Co-author

This code is used when there is strong evidence that the passage in question was written by one of Shakespeare's co-authors. Some of the attributions below must be regarded as tentative while others have very strong validity. They are based primarily upon the work of Brian Vickers and Gary Taylor, and the collaborative work of Hugh Craig and Arthur Kinney. It must also be stressed emphatically that the list is almost certainly incomplete, especially as regards the second and (probably also) third parts of *Henry VI*.

Play	Co-author	Attributions
TIMON OF ATHENS	Middleton	1.2, 3.1–6, 4.3.458–536
PERICLES	Wilkins	1, 2.
TITUS ANDRONICUS	Peele	1, 2.1, 2.2,4.1
TWO NOBLE KINSMEN	Fletcher	Prologue, 1.5, 2.2–6, 3.3–4.2, 5.2, Epilogue.
KING HENRY VIII	Fletcher	Prologue, 1.3–2.2, 3.1, 4.1–2, 5.2–4, Epilogue.
KING HENRY VI-1	Unclear	1, 2.1–3, 2.5, 3, 4.1, 4.7.33–, 5 (Craig and Kinney) 2.2, 2.4, 4.5 (Vickers)
KING EDWARD III	Unclear	Shakespeare wrote 1.2, 2.1, 2.2. and probably 4.4
MACBETH	Middleton	3.5, plus five lines and two songs in 4.1

5.6. Textual

This code is used when a particular passage is especially problematic from a textual point of view: it may, for example, be missing from, or unique to, a Quarto publication.

5.7. References

This version of the SID includes stage references, character prefixes, and references to act, scene, and line(s) in **boldface** in order to ensure maximum legibility. This node enables the investigator to *exclude* these materials (for example, when they might affect the word count in a particular query).

Works Cited

Adamson, Sylvia. 'The Grand Style.' In *Reading Shakespeare's Dramatic Language: A Guide*. Ed. Sylvia Adamson et al. London: Arden Shakespeare, 2001. 31–50.

Adler, Patricia A., and Peter Adler. Abstract. 'The Glorified Self: The Aggrandizement and the Constriction of Self.' *Social Psychology Quarterly* 52, no. 4 (1989): 299–310.

Alexander, Gavin. '*Prosopopoeia*: The Speaking Figure.' In *Renaissance Figures of Speech*. Ed. Sylvia Adamson, Gavin Alexander, and Karrin Ettenhuber. Cambridge: Cambridge University Press, 2007. 97–112.

Almond, Philip C. *England's First Demonologist: Reginald Scot and the 'Discoverie of Witchcraft.'* London and New York: I. B. Tauris, 2011.

Arnold, Morris LeRoy. *The Soliloquies of Shakespeare: A Study in Technic*. New York: Columbia University Press, 1911.

Arnold, Matthew. *The Poems of Matthew Arnold*. Ed. Kenneth Allot. London: Longman, 1965.

Aspinall, Dana E. 'The Play and the Critics.' In *The Taming of the Shrew: Critical Essays*. Ed. Dana E. Espinall. London: Routledge, 2002. 3–40.

Barber, Charles L. *The Theme of Honour's Tongue: A Study of Social Attitudes in the English Drama from Shakespeare to Dryden*. Gothenburg Studies in English 58. Göteborg: Acta Universitatis Gothoburgensis, 1985.

Bate, Jonathan. 'Introduction.' In William Shakespeare, *A Midsummer Night's Dream*. RSC edition. Ed. Jonathan Bate and Eric Rasmussen. Houndmills: Macmillan, 2008. 1–18.

——. 'Introduction.' In William Shakespeare, *Richard II*. RSC edition. Ed. Jonathan Bate and Eric Rasmussen. Basingstoke: Macmillan, 2010. 1–22.

——. 'Introduction.' In William Shakespeare, *The Tempest*. RSC edition. Ed. Jonathan Bate and Eric Rasmussen. Houndmills: Macmillan, 2008. 1–19.

Baynes, Kenneth. 'Self, Narrative and Self-Constitution: Revisiting Taylor's "Self-Interpreting Animals."' *Philosophical Forum* 41, no. 4 (2010): 441–57.

Beckerman, Bernard. *Shakespeare at the Globe, 1599–1609*. London: Macmillan, 1962.

Bethell, S. L. *Shakespeare and the Popular Dramatic Tradition*. Durham, NC: Duke University Press, 1944.

Bloom, Harold. *How to Read and Why*. New York: Touchstone, 2001.

——. *Shakespeare: The Invention of the Human*. New York: Riverhead, 1998.

Blum, Deborah. *Love at Goon Park: Harry Harlow and the Science of Affection*. Chichester: Wiley, 2003.

Boyd, Brian. 'Literature and Evolution: A Bio-Cultural Approach.' *Philosophy and Literature* 29 (2005): 1–23.

Bradbrook, M. C. *Shakespeare: The Poet in His World*. 1978. London: Routledge, 2005.

——. *Themes and Conventions of Elizabethan Tragedy*. 2nd edn. Cambridge: Cambridge University Press, 1980.

Bradley, A. C. *Shakespearean Tragedy: Lectures on Hamlet, Othello, King Lear, Macbeth*. 1904. London: Macmillan, 1957.

Bristol, Michael. 'Introduction: Is Shakespeare a Moral Philosopher?' In *Shakespeare and Moral Agency*. Ed. Michael Bristol. London and New York: Continuum, 2010. 1–12.

Brooks, Harold F. 'Two Clowns in a Comedy (To Say Nothing of the Dog): Speed, Launce (and Crab) in *The Two Gentlemen of Verona*.' Reprinted in *Two Gentlemen of Verona: Critical Essays*. Ed. June Schlueter. New York: Garland, 1996. 71–8.

Burns, Edward. *Character: Acting and Being on the Pre-Modern Stage*. New York: St. Martin's Press, 1990.

Burrow, Colin. *Shakespeare and Classical Antiquity*. Oxford Shakespeare Topics. Oxford: Oxford University Press, 2013.

Butler, Michelle Markey. '"All hayll, all hayll, both blithe and glad": Direct Address in Early English Drama, 1400–1585.' PhD dissertation, Duquesne University, 2003.

Campbell, Kathleen. 'Shakespeare's Actors as Collaborators: Will Kempe and *The Two Gentlemen of Verona*.' In *Two Gentlemen of Verona: Critical Essays*. Ed. June Schlueter. New York: Garland, 1996. 179–87.

Carroll, Joseph. 'Intentional Meaning in *Hamlet*: An Evolutionary Perspective.' *Style* 44 (2010): 230–60.

Champion, Larry S. *The Evolution of Shakespeare's Comedy: A Study in Dramatic Perspective*. Cambridge, MA: Harvard University Press, 1970.

Charney, Maurice. 'Asides, Soliloquies, and Offstage Speech in *Hamlet*: Implications for Staging.' In *Shakespeare and the Sense of Performance*. Ed. Marvin and Ruth Thompson. Newark and London: University of Delaware Press, 1989. 116–31.

Chatman, Seymour. *Story and Discourse: Narrative Structure in Fiction and Film*. Ithaca: Cornell University Press, 1978.

Clemen, Wolfgang. *Shakespeare's Dramatic Art: Collected Essays*. London: Methuen, 1972.

——. *Shakespeare's Soliloquies*. Trans. Charity Scott Stokes. London: Methuen, 1987.

Coghill, Nevill. *Shakespeare's Professional Skills*. Cambridge: Cambridge University Press, 1965.

Coleridge, Samuel Taylor. *Shakespearean Criticism*. Ed. Thomas Middleton Raysor. London: J. M. Dent, 1961.

Collington, Philip D. 'Self-Discovery in Montaigne's "Of Solitarinesse" and *King Lear*.' *Comparative Drama* 35 (2002): 247–69.

Cook, Ann Jennalie. *Making a Match: Courtship in Shakespeare and His Society*. Princeton: Princeton University Press, 1991.

Coplan, Amy. 'Empathic Engagement with Narrative Fictions.' *The Journal of Aesthetics and Art Criticism* 62, no. 3 (2004): 141–52.

Corfield, Cosmo. 'Why Does Prospero Abjure His Rough Magic?' *Shakespeare Quarterly* 36, no. 1 (1985): 31–48.

Craig, Hugh. 'Shakespeare's Vocabulary: Myth and Reality.' *Shakespeare Quarterly* 62, no. 1 (2011): 53–74.

Davies, Oliver Ford. *Playing Lear*. London: Nick Hern, 2003.

Dawson, Anthony B., and Paul Yachnin. 'Introduction.' In William Shakespeare, *Richard II*. Oxford Shakespeare. Oxford: Oxford University Press, 2011. 7–46.

Deaton, John E., et al. 'Coping Activities in Solitary Confinement of U.S. Navy POWs in Vietnam.' *Journal of Applied Social Psychology* 7, no. 3 (1977): 239–57.

Delany, Paul. *British Autobiography in the Seventeenth Century*. London: Routledge and Kegan Paul, 1969.

Dennis, Carl. '*All's Well that Ends Well* and the Meaning of Agape.' *Philological Quarterly* 50, no. 1 (1971): 75–84.

DePape, Anne-Marie, et al. 'Self-Talk and Emotional Intelligence in University Students.' *Canadian Journal of Behavioural Science* 38, no. 3 (2006): 250–60.

Desens, Marliss C. *The Bed-Trick in English Renaissance Drama: Explorations in Gender, Sexuality, and Power*. Newark: University of Delaware Press, 1994.

Dessen, Alan C. *Elizabethan Stage Conventions and Modern Interpreters*. Cambridge: Cambridge University Press, 1984.

——. *Recovering Shakespeare's Theatrical Vocabulary*. Cambridge: Cambridge University Press, 1995.

——. *Titus Andronicus*. Shakespeare in Performance. Manchester: Manchester University Press, 1989.

Dillon, Janette. 'Elizabethan Comedy.' In *The Cambridge Companion to Shakespearean Comedy*. Ed. Alexander Leggatt. Cambridge: Cambridge University Press, 2001. 47–63.

Dissanayake, Ellen. *Art and Intimacy: How the Arts Began*. Seattle: University of Washington Press, 2000.

Dolan, Frances E. 'Introduction.' In William Shakespeare, *The Taming of the Shrew: Texts and Contexts*. Ed. Frances E. Dolan. Boston: Bedford, 1996. 1–38.

Donaldson, E. Talbot. *The Swan at the Well: Shakespeare Reading Chaucer*. New Haven and London: Yale University Press, 1985.

Dowden, Edward. *Shakespeare: A Critical Study of His Mind and Art*. 1875. London: Routledge & Kegan Paul, 1967.

Dreher, Dianne. *Domination and Defiance: Fathers and Daughters in Shakespeare*. Lexington: University of Kentucky Press, 1986.

Duncan, Robert M., and J. Allan Cheyne. 'Incidence and Functions of Self-Reported Private Speech in Young Adults: A Self-Verbalization Questionnaire.' *Canadian Journal of Behavioural Science* 31, no. 2 (1999): 133–6.

Duncan-Jones, Katherine. *Ungentle Shakespeare: Scenes from his Life*. London: Arden Shakespeare, 2001.

Eliot, T. S. *The Sacred Wood.* 1921. Bartleby edition. Web.

Enterline, Lynn. *The Tears of Narcissus: Melancholia and Masculinity in Early Modern Writing.* Stanford: Stanford University Press, 1995.

Escolme, Bridget. *Talking to the Audience: Shakespeare, Performance, Self.* Abingdon: Routledge, 2005.

Estill, Laura. '*Richard II* and the Book of Life.' *SEL* 51, no. 2 (2011): 283–303.

Evans, Bertram. *Shakespeare's Comedies.* Oxford: Clarendon Press, 1960.

Fahmi, Mustapha. 'Quoting the Enemy: Character, Self-Interpretation, and the Question of Perspective in Shakespeare.' In *Shakespeare and Moral Agency.* Ed. Michael Bristol. London and New York: Continuum, 2010. 129–41.

Feagin, Susan. *Reading with Feeling: The Aesthetics of Appreciation.* Ithaca: Cornell University Press, 1996.

Ferry, Ann. *The Inward Language.* Chicago: University of Chicago Press, 1983.

Findlay, Alison. *A Feminist Perspective on Renaissance Drama.* Oxford: Blackwell, 1999.

Fiske, Alan Page. *Structures of Social Life: The Four Elementary Forms of Human Relations.* New York: Free Press, 1991.

Flesch, William. *Comeuppance: Costly Signaling, Altruistic Punishment, and other Biological Components of Fiction.* Cambridge, MA: Harvard University Press, 2009.

Fletcher, John, and William Shakespeare. *The Two Noble Kinsmen.* Arden 3. Ed. Lois Potter. London: Methuen, 1997.

Forker, Charles. 'Introduction.' In William Shakespeare, *King Richard II.* Arden 3. London: Methuen, 2002. 1–169.

Freeman, John C. 'Interrogating the Soliloquist: Does it Really Go without Saying?' *symplokē* 18, nos. 1–2 (2010): 131–54.

Gawande, Atul. 'Hellhole.' *The New Yorker.* 30 March 2009. Web.

Goffman, Irving. *The Presentation of Self in Everyday Life.* 1959. London: Penguin, 1990.

Grant, Patrick. 'The Magic of Charity: A Background to Prospero.' *Review of English Studies*, n.s. 27, no. 105 (1976): 1–16.

Greenblatt, Stephen. *Renaissance Self-Fashioning: From More to Shakespeare.* Chicago: University of Chicago Press, 1980.

Gurr, Andrew. *The Shakespearean Stage, 1574–1642.* 2nd edn. Cambridge: Cambridge University Press, 1980.

Haack, Susan. 'Staying for an Answer: The Untidy Process of Groping for Truth.' In *Theory's Empire: An Anthology of Dissent.* Ed. Daphne Patai and Will H. Corral. New York: Columbia University Press, 2005. 552–61.

Harmer, J. K. 'Hamlet's Introspection.' *Essays in Criticism* 61, no. 1 (2011): 31–53.

Hazlitt, William. *The Collected Works of William Hazlitt.* Ed. W. E. Henley, London: J. M. Dent, 1903. Vol. 8.

Heilman, Robert B. 'The *Taming* Untamed, or, The Return of the Shrew.' 1966. Reprinted in *The Taming of the Shrew: Critical Essays.* Ed. Dana E. Espinall. London: Routledge, 2002. 45–57.

Hillman, Richard. *Self-Speaking in Medieval and Early Modern English Drama: Subjectivity, Discourse and the Stage.* Basingstoke: Macmillan; New York: St. Martin's Press, 1997.

Hirschfield, Heather. Review of Eric Langley, *Narcissism and Suicide in Shakespeare and His Contemporaries. Shakespeare Quarterly* 63, no. 2 (2012): 265–70.

Hirsh, James. 'Dialogic Self-Address in Shakespeare's Plays.' *Shakespeare* 8, no. 3 (2012): 312–27.

——. *Shakespeare and the History of Soliloquies.* Cranbury, NJ: Fairleigh Dickinson University Press, 2003.

——. 'The Origin of the Late Renaissance Dramatic Convention of Self-Addressed Speech.' *Shakespeare Survey* 68 (2015): 131–45.

——. 'The "To be, or not to be" Speech: Evidence, Conventional Wisdom, and the Editing of *Hamlet*.' *Medieval and Renaissance Drama in England* 23 (2010): 34–62.

Hogan, Patrick Colm. 'Narrative Universals, Heroic Tragi-Comedy, and Shakespeare's Political Ambivalence.' *College Literature* 33, no. 1 (2006): 34–67.

Holbrook, Peter. *Shakespeare's Individualism.* Cambridge: Cambridge University Press, 2010.

Honigmann, E. A. J. 'Re-Enter the Stage Direction: Shakespeare and Some Contemporaries.' *Shakespeare Survey* 29 (1976): 117–25.

Hoover, David L. 'Quantitative Analysis and Literary Studies: History, Goals, and Theoretical Foundation.' In *A Companion to Digital Literary Studies.* Ed. Susan Schreibman and Ray Siemens. Oxford: Blackwell, 2008, part 4, ch. 28. Web.

Hope, Jonathan, and Michael Witmore. 'The Hundredth Psalm to the Tune of "Green Sleeves": Digital Approaches to Shakespeare's Language of Genre.' *Shakespeare Quarterly* 61, no. 3 (2010): 357–90.

Hoskins, John. *Directions for Speech and Style.* Ed. and intro. Hoyt H. Hudson. Princeton Studies in English 12. Princeton: Princeton University Press, 1935.

Hussey, S. S. *The Literary Language of Shakespeare.* 2nd edn. London: Longman, 1992.

Hyde, Janet Shibley. 'The Gender Similarities Hypothesis.' *American Psychologist* 60, no. 6 (2005): 581–92.

Hyland, Ken. 'Persuasion and Context: The Pragmatics of Academic Discourse.' *Journal of Pragmatics* 30 (1998): 437–55.

Jockers, Matthew L. *Macroanalysis: Digital Methods and Literary History.* Champaign: University of Illinois Press, 2013.

Johnson, Nora. *The Actor as Playwright in Early Modern Drama.* Cambridge: Cambridge University Press, 2003.

Kantorowicz, Ernst H. *The King's Two Bodies: A Study in Medieval Political Theology.* Princeton: Princeton University Press, 1957.

Kastan, David Scott. '*All's Well that Ends Well* and the Limits of Comedy.' *ELH* 52, no. 3 (1985): 575–89.

Keen, Suzanne. *Empathy and the Novel.* Oxford: Oxford University Press, 2010.

Keller, Stefan Daniel. *The Development of Shakespeare's Rhetoric: A Study of Nine Plays.* Swiss Studies in English. Tübingen: Franke, 2009.

Kermode, Frank. *Shakespeare's Language.* London: Penguin, 2000.

Kernan, Alvin B. *Shakespeare, the King's Playwright: Theater in the Stuart Court 1603–1613.* New Haven: Yale University Press, 1995.

Kronk, Carol Marie. 'Private Speech in Adolescents.' *Adolescence* 29, no. 116 (1994). EBSCOHOST. Web.

Langley, Eric. *Narcissism and Suicide in Shakespeare and His Contemporaries.* Oxford: Oxford University Press, 2009.

Lee, John. *Shakespeare's Hamlet and the Controversies of Self.* Oxford: Oxford University Press, 2000.

Lin, Erika T. 'Performance Practice and Theatrical Privilege: Rethinking Weimann's Concepts of Locus and Platea.' *NTQ* 22, no. 3 (2006): 283–98.

Lippa, Richard. *Gender, Nature, and Nurture.* London: Lawrence Erlbaum, 2002.

Literature Online. Web. ProQuest LLC. Accessed via Gothenburg University Library.

Livingston, Paisley. 'Intentionalism in Aesthetics.' *New Literary History* 29, no. 4 (1998): 831–46.

Mack, Maynard. *Everybody's Shakespeare.* Lincoln, NB: University of Nebraska Press, 1993.

Marché, Stephen. 'Literature is Not Data: Against Digital Humanities.' *Los Angeles Review of Books*, 28 October 2012. Web.

Marcus, Leah S. *Unediting the Renaissance: Shakespeare, Marlowe, Milton.* London: Routledge, 1996.

Marshall, Cynthia. 'Shakespeare, Crossing the Rubicon.' *Shakespeare Survey* 53 (2000): 73–88.

Marshall, David. *The Surprising Effects of Sympathy: Marivaux, Diderot, Rousseau, and Mary Shelley.* Chicago and London: University of Chicago Press, 1988.

Maus, Katherine Eisaman. *Inwardness and Theater in the English Renaissance.* Chicago: University of Chicago Press, 1995.

McConachie, Bruce. *Engaging Audiences: A Cognitive Approach to Spectating in the Theatre.* New York: Palgrave Macmillan, 2008.

McEwan, Ian. *Atonement.* London: Vintage, 2001.

MacFaul, Tom. *Male Friendship in Shakespeare and His Contemporaries.* Cambridge: Cambridge University Press, 2007.

McKay, Margaret Rachael. 'Shakespeare's Use of the Apostrophe, Popular Rhetorical Device of the Renaissance.' PhD dissertation, University of Colorado, 1969.

Misekell, Margaret. '"Love wrought these miracles": Marriage and Genre in *The Taming of the Shrew*.' In *The Taming of the Shrew: Critical Essays.* Ed. Dana E. Espinall. London: Routledge, 2002. 106–29.

Montaigne, Michel de. *The Complete Essays.* Trans. and intro. M. A. Screech. London: Penguin, 2003.

——. *The Essays of Montaigne, Done into English by John Florio.* 3 Vols. Ed. W. E. Henley. Intro. George Saintsbury. New York: AMS Press, 1967.

Myhill, Nova. '"Hark, a word in your ear": Whispers, Asides, and Interpretation in *Troilus and Cressida*.' In *Who Hears in Shakespeare? Shakespeare's Auditory World, Stage, and Screen.* Ed. Laury Magnus and Walter W. Cannon. Lanham, MD: Fairleigh Dickinson University Press, 2012. 163–80.

Neely, Carol Thomas. *Broken Nuptials in Shakespeare's Plays.* New Haven: Yale University Press, 1985.

Newell, Alex. *The Soliloquies in Hamlet: The Structural Design*. Rutherford: Fairleigh Dickinson University Press, 1991.

Norbrook, David. 'The Emperor's New Body? *Richard II*, Ernst Kantorowicz, and the Politics of Shakespeare Criticism.' *Textual Practice* 10, no. 2 (1996): 329–57.

Nordlund, Marcus. 'Divisive Desires in *The Two Noble Kinsmen*.' In *Pangs of Love and Longing: Configurations of Desire in Premodern Literature*. Ed. Anders Cullhed, Carin Franzén, Anders Hallengren, and Mats Malm. Newcastle: Cambridge Scholars, 2013. 130–43.

——. 'Pride and Self-Love in Shakespeare and Montaigne.' In *Shakespearean International Yearbook* 6. Ed. Graham Bradshaw, Tom Bishop, and Peter Holbrook. Aldershot: Ashgate, 2006. 77–98.

——. *Shakespeare and the Nature of Love: Literature, Culture, Evolution*. Evanston: Northwestern University Press, 2007.

Nünning, Ansgar, and Roy Sommer. 'The Performative Power of Narrative in Drama: On the Forms and Functions of Dramatic Storytelling in Shakespeare's Plays.' In *Current Trends in Narratology*. Ed. Greta Olson. Berlin: de Gruyter, 2011. 200–31

Nuttall, A. D. *The New Mimesis: Shakespeare and the Representation of Reality*. London: Methuen, 1983.

Orgel, Stephen. 'Introduction.' In William Shakespeare, *The Tempest*. Oxford Shakespeare edition. Oxford: Oxford University Press, 1987. 1–89.

Oxford English Dictionary Online. Oxford: Oxford University Press, 2010–15. Web.

Palfrey, Simon, and Tiffany Stern. *Shakespeare in Parts*. Oxford: Oxford University Press, 2007.

Palmer, Richard. *Fictional Minds*. Lincoln, NB: University of Nebraska Press, 2004.

Panksepp, Jaak, et al. 'The Philosophical Implications of Affective Neuroscience.' *Journal of Consciousness Studies* 19, nos. 3–4 (2012): 6–48.

Pater, Walter. *Appreciations: With an Essay on Style*. London: Macmillan, 1910.

Pfister, Manfred. *The Theory and Analysis of Drama*. Trans. John Halliday. Cambridge: Cambridge University Press, 1991.

Phelan, James. *Living to Tell about It: A Rhetoric and Ethics of Character Narration*. Ithaca: Cornell University Press, 2004.

Philips, James. 'Practicalities of the Absolute: Justice and Kingship in *Richard II*.' *ELH* 79, no. 1 (2012): 161–77.

Pikli, Natália. 'The Crossing Point of Tears and Laughter: A Tragic Farce: Shakespeare's Titus Andronicus.' *The AnaChronisT* 6 (2000): 51–69.

Plowden, Edward. *The Commentaries, or Reports*. London: S. Brooke, 1816.

Proudfoot, G.R. 'Introduction.' In John Fletcher and William Shakespeare, *The Two Noble Kinsmen*. Ed. G. R. Proudfoot. Regents Renaissance Drama. London: Edward Arnold, 1970. xi–xxvi.

Puttenham, George. *The Art of English Poesy: A Critical Edition*. Ed. Frank Whigham and Wayne A. Rebhorn. Ithaca: Cornell University Press, 2007.

Rees, B. R. 'Pathos in the Poetics of Aristotle.' *Greece and Rome* 19 (1972): 1–11.

Richardson, Alan. 'Point of View in Drama.' *Comparative Drama* 22, no. 3 (1988): 193–214.

Riehle, Wolfgang. *Das Beiseitesprechen bei Shakespeare: ein Beitrag zur Dramaturgie des elisabethanischen Dramas.* Munich: Ludwig-Maximilians-Universität, 1964.

——. 'Shakespeare's Reception of Plautus Reconsidered. ' In *Shakespeare and the Classics.* Ed. Charles Martindale. Cambridge: Cambridge University Press, 2004. 109–21.

Rose, Mary Beth. *The Expense of Spirit: Love and Sexuality in English Renaissance Drama.* Ithaca: Cornell University Press, 1998.

Rowley, William. *A Shoo-maker a Gentleman* (London, 1638). *Literature Online.*

Schwartz, Peter Hammond. '"His majesty the baby": Narcissism and Royal Authority.' *Political Theory* 17, no. 2 (1989): 266–90.

Searle, John. *Speech Acts: An Essay in the Philosophy of Language.* 1969. Cambridge: Cambridge University Press, 1999.

Selleck, Nancy. *The Interpersonal Idiom in Shakespeare, Donne, and Early Modern Culture.* Basingstoke: Palgrave Macmillan, 2008.

Shakespeare, William. *A Midsummer Night's Dream.* RSC edition. Ed. Jonathan Bate and Eric Rasmussen. Basingstoke: Macmillan, 2008.

——. *All's Well that Ends Well.* RSC edition. Ed. Jonathan Bate and Eric Rasmussen. Basingstoke: Macmillan, 2011.

——. *All's Well that Ends Well.* Oxford Shakespeare edition. Ed. Susan Snyder. Oxford: Oxford University Press, 1993.

——. *Complete Works.* Arden 2. Ed. Richard Proudfoot, Ann Thompson, and David Scott Kastan. Walton-on-Thames: Thomas Nelson and Sons, 1998.

——. *Complete Works.* RSC edition. Ed. Jonathan Bate and Eric Rasmussen. New York: Modern Library/Random House, 2007.

——. *Hamlet.* Arden 3. Ed. Ann Thompson and Neil Taylor. London: Methuen, 2006.

——. *King Edward III.* New Cambridge Shakespeare. Ed. Giorgio Melchiori. Cambridge: Cambridge University Press, 1998.

——. *King Lear.* Arden 3. Ed. R. A. Foakes. Walton-on-Thames: Thomas Nelson and Sons, 2007.

——. *King Richard II.* Arden 3. Ed. Charles R. Forker. London: Methuen, 2002.

——. *Othello.* Arden 3. Ed. E. A. J. Honigmann. London: Methuen, 1997.

——. *Richard II.* RSC edition. Ed. Jonathan Bate and Eric Rasmussen. Basingstoke: Macmillan, 2010.

——. *The Norton Shakespeare.* 2nd edn. Based on the Oxford edition. Ed. Stephen Greenblatt et al. New York: W. W. Norton, 2008.

——. *The Tempest.* RSC edition. Ed. Jonathan Bate and Eric Rasmussen. London: Macmillan, 2008.

——. *The Two Gentlemen of Verona.* Arden 3. Ed. William C. Carroll. London: Methuen, 2004.

Shakespeare's Words. <shakespeareswords.com> Web.

Shannon, Laurie J. 'Emilia's Argument: Friendship and Human Title in *The Two Noble Kinsmen.*' *ELH* 64, no. 3 (1997): 657–82.

——. *Sovereign Amity: Figures of Friendship in Shakespearean Contexts.* Chicago: Chicago University Press, 2002.

Shin, Hiewon. 'Single Parenting, Homeschooling: Prospero, Caliban, Miranda.' *SEL* 48, no. 2 (2008): 373–93.

Singer, Tania, and Olga Klimecki. 'Empathy and Compassion.' *Current Biology* 24, no. 18 (2014): 875–8.

Skura, Meredith Anne. *Shakespeare the Actor and the Purpose of Playing.* Chicago: University of Chicago Press, 1993.

Slingerland, Edward. *What Science Offers the Humanities.* Cambridge: Cambridge University Press, 2008.

Smith, Peter Scharff. 'The Effects of Solitary Confinement on Prison Inmates: A Brief History and Review of the Literature.' *Crime and Justice* 34, no. 1 (2006): 441–528.

Smith, Warren. 'The Third Type of Aside in Shakespeare.' *Modern Language Notes* 64, no. 8 (1949): 510–13.

Soellner, Rolf. *Shakespeare's Patterns of Self-Knowledge.* Columbus: Ohio State University Press, 1972.

Sprague, A. C. *Shakespeare and the Audience: A Study in the Technique of Exposition.* Cambridge, MA: Harvard University Press, 1935.

Springborg, Patricia. '"His majesty is a baby?": A Critical Response to Peter Hammond Schwartz.' *Political Theory* 18, no. 4 (1990): 673–85.

Stanton, Kay. 'All's Well in Love and War.' In *Ideological Approaches to Shakespeare: The Practice of Theory.* Ed. Robert P. Merrix and Nicholas Ranson. Lewiston, NY: Edwin Mellen, 1992. 155–63.

Stephenson, Jenn. 'Spatial Ambiguity and the Early Modern/Postmodern in *King Lear*.' In *Drama and the Postmodern: Assessing the Limits of Metatheatre.* Ed. Daniel K. Jernigan. Amherst, NY: Cambria, 2008. 23–44.

Stewart, Alan. *Shakespeare's Letters.* Oxford: Oxford University Press, 2008.

Sutton, Brian. '"Virtue rather than vengeance": Genesis and Shakespeare's *The Tempest*.' *Explicator* 66, no. 4 (2008): 224–9.

Taylor, Charles. *Sources of the Self: The Making of the Modern Identity.* Cambridge: Cambridge University Press, 1989.

Thomas, Vivian. *The Moral Universe of Shakespeare's Problem Plays.* London: Croom Helm, 1987.

Timpane, John. '"I am but a foole, looke you": Launce and the Social Functions of Humor.' In *Two Gentlemen of Verona: Critical Essays.* Ed. June Schlueter. New York: Garland, 1996. 189–211.

Triandis, Harry C. *Individualism and Collectivism: New Directions in Social Psychology.* Boulder: Westview Press, 1995.

Tribble, Evelyn. 'Distributing Cognition in the Globe.' *Shakespeare Quarterly* 56, no.2 (2005): 135–55.

Tsang, Jo-Ann. 'Moral Rationalization and the Integration of Situational Factors and Psychological Processes in Immoral Behavior.' *Review of General Psychology* 6, no. 1 (2002): 25–50.

Understanding Shakespeare. <labs.jstor.org/shakespeare> Web.

Velz, John W. 'The Ancient World in Shakespeare: Authenticity or Anachronism? A Retrospect.' *Shakespeare Studies* 31 (1979): 1–12.

Vickers, Brian. *Shakespeare, Co-Author: A Historical Study of Five Collaborative Plays.* Oxford: Oxford University Press, 2002.

Viswanatham, S. '"Illeism with a Difference" in Certain Middle Plays of Shakespeare.' *Shakespeare Quarterly* 20, no. 4 (1969): 407–15.

Waith, Eugene M. 'Shakespeare and Fletcher on Love and Friendship.' *Shakespeare Studies* 18 (1986): 235–50.

Warwick, Claire. 'English Literature, Electronic Text and Computer Analysis: An Impossible Combination?' Abstract, conference paper. *ACH-ALLC International Humanities Computing Conference*. 12 June 1999. Web.

Weimann, Robert. *Author's Pen and Actor's Voice: Playing and Writing in Shakespeare's Theatre*. Cambridge: Cambridge University Press, 2000.

——. *Shakespeare and the Popular Tradition in the Theater: Studies in the Social Dimension of Dramatic Form and Function*. Ed. Robert Schwartz. 1978. Baltimore: Johns Hopkins University Press, 1987.

—— and Douglas Bruster. *Shakespeare and the Power of Performance: Stage and Page in the Elizabethan Theatre*. Cambridge: Cambridge University Press, 2008.

Weller, Barry. 'The Two Noble Kinsmen, the Friendship Tradition, and the Flight from Eros.' In *Shakespeare, Fletcher, and The Two Noble Kinsmen*. Ed. Charles H. Frey. Columbia: University of Missouri Press, 1989. 93–108.

Wiles, David. *Shakespeare's Clown: Actor and Text in the Elizabethan Playhouse*. Cambridge: Cambridge University Press, 2005.

Williams, Raymond. *Writing in Society*. London: Verso, 1983.

Winsler, Adam, Charles Fernyhough, and Ignacio Montero. *Private Speech, Executive Functioning, and the Development of Verbal Self-Regulation*. Cambridge: Cambridge University Press, 2009.

Young, S. Mark, and Drew Pinsky. 'Narcissism and Celebrity.' *Journal of Research in Personality* 40, no. 5 (2006): 463–71.

Zimbardo, Rose Abdelnour. 'Form and Disorder in *The Tempest*.' *Shakespeare Quarterly* 14, no. 1 (1963): 49–56.

Zunshine, Lisa. *Why We Read Fiction: Theory of Mind and the Novel*. Columbus: Ohio State University Press, 2006.

Index

act, distribution according to, 148, 192–6
Adler, Patricia, 88
Adler, Peter, 88
Alexander, Gavin, 127
ambiguous insides, 64–71
Arnold, Matthew, 141
Aspinall, Dana, 161

Bakhtin, Mikhail, 109
Baltimore Shakespeare Factory, 19
Bate, Jonathan, 74, 122
Baynes, Kenneth, 110
behaviourism, 61–2
blend, cognitive, 43–6, 51, 56
Bloom, Harold, 171–2
Boyd, Brian, 145
Bradbrook, M. C., 61, 172
Bradley, A. C., 27–8, 158
Bruster, Douglas, 51
Burns, Edward, 45

Carroll, Joseph, 140
Champion, Larry S., 36–7
character class, 2, 11, 52, 69, 85, 131, 154, 173, 181
character detachment
  conventional, 16, 46, 56
  mental, 16, 33–8, 46, 56
  structural, 16, 28–33, 46, 56
  in *The Two Gentlemen of Verona*, 46–57
character sex, 2, 11, 161, 173–8
Chaucer, Geoffrey, 118, 174
chorus, Shakespearean, 5–6
Clemen, Wolfgang, 96
Coghill, Nevill, 4
Coleridge, Samuel Taylor, 86, 96

Collington, Philip, 86
Cook, Ann Jennalie, 181
Coplan, Amy, 156–7

Davies, Oliver Ford, 84
Dessen, Alan, 4
dialogical figures of speech
  apostrophe, 10–11, 23, 34, 75, 109, 113–22, 125–6, 129, 136–41, 147
  asteismus, 125
  erotema (rhetorical question), 10, 113, 142–8
  illeism, 10, 113, 129–35
  prosopopoeia (personation), 10, 101, 113, 126–9
  tuism, 10, 24, 113, 129–35
dialogical self, the, 109–13
Dolan, Francis E., 162
dramatic speech acts
  assessing character, 161, 182
  assessing morality, 167, 169
  assessing thematics, 167–9, 183
  exposition, 160, 166, 169, 182
  planning, 12, 161–70, 182
  predicting, 164
  reporting, 2, 5, 117–18, 122, 165–6, 169
  requesting, 137–8
Duncan-Jones, Katherine, 73–4

Eliot, T. S., 53, 172
empathy, theoretical account of, 156–60
entrance inside, 29–33
Escolme, Bridget, 19–20
Estill, Laura, 88
exit inside, 29–33